Dr. Jacqueline Zaleski Mackenzie is, in my opinion, a truly courageous person. By having communicated with her I found a philanthropic, almost saint-like quality of her unselfishness, coupled with deep understanding and the desire to share her research. This book is recommended as an addition to all school libraries, and for course studies designed around this information for use as a text book. Anyone and everyone with an interest or curiosity in the Mexican culture, and wishing to become aware of the emerging Spanish speaking majority, should seize the opportunity to buy this book and read it cover to cover. Real change will only occur through understanding, education, and having "our eyes wide open."

—GARY SORKIN,
Pacific Book Review

Dr. Mackenzie's study of Spanish/Mexican children and the culture that affects their lives and their ability to learn is a compelling and informative work that allows greater understanding of the difficulties facing educators, not just those who teach Spanish/Mexican children; but also those who work with any child from a multicultural background. *Empowering Spanish Speakers*, is definitely recommended by award-winning author and Allbooks reviewer,

—EMILY-JANE HILLS ORFORD,
Allbooks Reviews, www.allbooksreviewint.com.

Empowering Spanish Speakers is the first book of its kind to identify the problems facing rural Mexican families. It's a book that could change the lives of the millions of our Mexican neighbors who are living 18th century lives while the rest of the world rapidly advances through the 21st century.

—CAROLE SCHOR,
Reviewer for the San Miguel Literary Sala

This kind of proximity allows her to reach conclusions not readily afforded to other researchers...*Empowering Spanish Speakers* covers all aspects the Mexican culture from childrearing to gender roles in the extended family and workplace. It includes a Q&A section, appendices of nutrition and developmental challenges for educators and caregivers, and a thorough works cited list.

Although this book should be read straight through, Mackenzie adopts a standard how-to format. By using a series of symbols highlighting key areas regarding differences in learning styles, educators and business trainers will find this book invaluable for both detailed study and as a quick reference guide. And casual readers will discover new depths when savoring the literary traditions that gave the world Ignacio Padilla and Octavio Paz.

—JOSEPH THOMPSON,
Foreword Book Reviews

This is the best book I have ever read on the Mexican culture and I've read a lot of them.

—JON SEVERT,
Humble Press, San Miquel de Allende, Mexico

A guide to dealing with Spanish speaking individuals in many aspects of life, education, and business: Not everyone speaks English or can easily learn it, and it's best to understand that. *Empowering Spanish Speakers: Answers for Educators, Business People, and Friends of Latinos* is a guide to dealing with Spanish speaking individuals in many aspects of life, education, and business. From cultural differences that aren't entirely obvious and how this applies to teaching, reaching Spanish speaking marketing, and working with Spanish speakers in the business world. *Empowering Spanish Speakers* realizes there is more to communication than language and does well in filling readers into a more complete understanding across culture.

—MIDWEST BOOK REVIEW,
Oregon, WI

This is a singular book. Well-researched data coupled with poignant personal experiences in the research field makes for a read that is captivating as well as informative. Written especially for teachers by a an educator motivated to make this critical information easily accessible, the format is engaging and utilitarian and therefore available for a wide ranging interest group. Most of all it is extremely timely given President Obama's recent speech regarding this very issue. Highly recommended.

—DESERT TEACHER

Tribute to a deeply researched and lived experience—Dr. Jacqueline Z. Mackenzie takes us into a live project that includes real kids in a rural setting and allows us to explore educational realities. We are brought face to face with the challenges that students face when placed in an environment where languages other than their own are used, not because the learner chose this situation. Unlike other places in the world where multilingualism is honored and respected the US tends to consider this a tolerable problem and inconvenience. This book helps those who are and will be involved in the teaching process to recognize the connection between culture and language and its importance in the learning process. Maybe this book will help us turn this teaching process into a pleasurable exploration child's family and background...

—MIKE ROHRBACH,
SE Arizona based Information Literacy group
implementing Digital Libraries in rural Mexico

Mackenzie's program, "Speak with your heart" is her reply to teachers of Spanish speakers who say, "What should I do? I don't speak a word of Spanish." Sales of her book will be used to build libraries in rural Mexico.

Sacrificing the comforts of western civilization to live in rural Mexico, Mackenzie's book is a guide to working with Spanish speaking persons from all walks of life. Her work combines scientific research, statistical analysis, and personal exploits in an easy-to-read textbook format.

—MIRIAM RODRÍGUEZ,
Assistant Director of Public Services, Dallas Public Library

Opposite: Ramon Ascencio, undersecretary of economic stability for Irapuato, Guanjuato, Mexico, endorses Dr. Jacqueline Mackenzie's speech about the need for more rural libraries in Central Mexico, at the United States-Mexico Chamber of Commerce Conference in Dallas, Texas, July 2010.

Empowering
Spanish
Speakers

Answers for Educators,
Business People, and
Friends of Latinos

Dr. Jacqueline Zaleski Mackenzie

SUMMERLAND CORPORATION

Photos were used by permission
Edited by Carole Schor, Julia Kantor, Don Mackenzie, Emilie Vardaman, & Judy Westerman
Proofreading by Jolene Gailey
Photos by Jacqueline Mackenzie. Artwork by Jolene Gailey. Cover and interior design by John Reinhardt Book Design. Symbols by Rob Oates

NOTE: Our publications reflect our opinions of what we have observed over a lifetime of living with Mexican- American immigrants and/or while living as residents in an impoverished, rural community in Central Mexico. We have recorded what we have learned with an academic's attention to detail in order to tell the whole story and improve comprehension by the reader. We may have made some incorrect assumptions about Mexican culture due to our own cultural biases; if so, we apologize to any people of Mexican background whom we may have offended. Our nonprofit organization has published this information to help non-Mexicans to better comprehend Mexican culture.

Volunteers wrote and/or researched this book as an extension of the mission of our nonprofit 501©3 corporation, not as a public trade or business. Our publications are directly related to our exempt purpose: the education of disadvantaged Mexicans to reduce emigration from Mexico to the U.S. and the education of disadvantaged Mexican immigrants living in the U.S. We are offering these books for public viewing. Unquestionably, we have specifically directed our voices to the uninformed public teachers and corporate trainers of Spanish speakers who are Mexican nationals or Mexican immigrants. We would also like to welcome others, such as federal and state government officials, academic administrators, CEOs of corporations, foundation leaders, and school administrators, to read this book as well. We hope that what we have learned will help those working with any Mexican students anywhere. We hope, too, that this information will enable students to have an opportunity to earn an education that will facilitate self-sustainability.

We have priced the book for financial accessibility because we want to distribute it without undue hardship to the reader. We choose for the information to be widely and conveniently distributed to those we aim to serve; sales price covers the distribution expenses. Materials, computers, Internet access, and fees paid to print this book were donated to our nonprofit. Many people also donated their labor. All proceeds from the sale of this book will be used directly to allow our religious order to maintain our mission: the education of disadvantaged (predominately indigenous) Mexicans.

ISBN 978-1-936425-02-0

Published by: Summerland Corp. ATC
              aka Summerland Monastery, Inc. ATC
              2343 West Old Ajo Hwy Tucson, Arizona 85746-9113

Visit www.summerlandmonastery.org or www.spanishimmersioneducation.org for more information.

Printed in the United States of America

This book is dedicated to teaching volunteers who traveled to Mexico to ignite a change. Those unselfish individuals donated countless hours, experience, wisdom, and money to help marginalized Mexican children to acquire a dual literacy and other priceless skills.

May all volunteers travel safely, be enlightened from their experiences in Mexico, and share acquired knowledge with peers, family members, nonprofit organizations, politicians, school administrators, business leaders, and others.

With understanding comes tolerance.

ACKNOWLEDGMENTS

Many thanks to the University of Arizona professors and staff who supported this research.

Many thanks to those who made certain this document met the highest standards of quality, including editors Carole Schor, Julie Kantor, Emilie Vardman, and Judy Westerman, cover and interior text designer John Reinhardt, and original symbol designer Rob Oates.

I would like to thank my husband, Donald James Mackenzie, and my soul sister Jolene Gailey for always overlooking my personal struggle for perfection.

Contents

PART THREE: Techniques, Solutions, Options, and Considerations

PART FOUR: Research, References, and Other Information

Symbols

The hand symbol stands for the traits of the student: What they ask, how they act, what interests them, etc. In Latin American countries, the student's school experience is typically confined to an indoor environment. The young person is usually shown abstract ideas that are taught using rote memory. He or she is given the answers to specific questions, and after memorizing the questions and the correct answers, the student is expected to answer assessments exactly as memorized. This process is completed without individual analysis and can even be completed without the understanding of the concepts. The training in youth establishes lifelong patterns.

The heart symbol stands for the instructor: What actions the teacher might take, or what types of lessons, modifications to the classroom environment, or other empowerment techniques he or she might implement to increase learning.

The plant symbol relates to the acquired knowledge of the student. He or she adds new information to the already acquired information, thereby building on the established foundation. This is the childhood pattern of learning in the outdoors, which results in enriched understanding and accelerated processing of information. This learning pattern is the result of being raised in outlying areas of Latin America. Outdoors, around family members of all ages, is where the rural Spanish speaking child actually learns and applies critical thinking skills. The child watches the elders and peers work, rarely speaking with them, and then he or she imitates the observed activities. The child applies individual analysis through trial and error, gaining understanding from personal failures and successes, and retaining what is learned.

Inspiration

Latina mothers have been a central part of my life since 1949, the year my only sibling died. They taught me that I, even as a female child, had value. I cannot imagine I would have accomplished much in life if it hadn't been for Latina mothers who nurtured me at a time when my parents were incapable of doing so. My parents had no immediate family to either help them care for me or to take me in.

My parents dreamed of having six tall sons. There was an obvious attraction between them due to their strong physical differences. At 20, my mother, Rosaline, was a striking, cameo-perfect, olive-skinned beauty of Scottish heritage and Lutheran faith. She was 6'1" tall. My father, Joseph, 24 at the time, appeared to be of Mexican heritage. He was barely 5'6" tall, dark-skinned, handsome, charming, uniformed (in U.S. Air Force) and sporting a handlebar mustache. He was mistaken for a Mexican his entire life. Joseph was the first-born son of a Polish immigrant and raised in the Roman Catholic faith. His first language was Polish, his second was English, and he spoke excellent Spanish and a fair amount of Russian and Italian as well.

People always remarked on my parents' physical differences. My mother and father always told the same story of their attraction, and their short 28-day courtship led to their matrimonial goal of becoming parents to six tall sons. Nevertheless, after six years of trying, they had only one girl. They lacked joint heritages, rituals, family ties, and geographic stability to strengthen their marriage. Joseph was totally rejected by his family for marrying outside the Roman Catholic faith. They told the couple that the lack of children was God's punishment for marrying outside their faiths.

Eighteen months after I was born, Rudolph David Zaleski entered the world. My parents' overwhelming joy was very short lived, however. Rosaline had RH-negative blood and Joseph had RH-positive blood. Rosaline had become sensitized, and her antibodies had crossed the placenta and attacked the baby's blood like he was an enemy to her body. She developed hemolytic disease. The infant was large and appeared perfectly healthy, but died in only four days. My parents were devastated, and neither ever totally recovered. Joseph loved his work, which included frequent travel; he spent his life as a workaholic (in U.S. Air Force and at NASA). Rosaline branded herself a failure; she sank into a deep depression and became an alcoholic—a state from which she never emerged.

Every day I thank God for my many Latina mother role models. They inspired my life's work—to help those who are marginalized or disabled.

Had I not felt so deeply indebted to Latina women, I could have never written this book. My own social marginalization is being a Polish immigrant's granddaughter and my author's disability is dyslexia. Nevertheless, with my hands on the keyboard and a great deal of fear of failure, I listened to the words of Eleanor Roosevelt:

We gain strength, and courage, and confidence by each experience in
which we really stop to look fear in the face . . .
we must do that which we think we cannot.

Preface

A sensible man will remember that the eyes may be confused in two ways—by a change from light to darkness or from darkness to light; and he will recognize that the same thing happens to the soul.

—PLATO

Every teacher possesses the power to bring a student out of the darkness of ignorance and into the light of knowledge. Conversely, that power can also transform a lighthearted, eager student into a broken child wallowing in despair with permeating fear of anything associated with school.

Wise educators handle their responsibilities with care. They approach each child (note: in this book, the word "child or children" refers to "infants, children, and youth") with anticipation of positive miracles.

This book was written because all children deserve access to a quality education, and all educators deserve to have both *the authority* and *the responsibility* to give them that education.

Instructors should be using culturally appropriate methods of teaching and interacting with students from diverse backgrounds.

Educators have *the responsibility* for ensuring their students' retention of learned material, but often lack *the authority* to use evidence-based or scientifically researched teaching methods in their own classrooms.

Currently, thousands of students of all ages and backgrounds lack access to quality education for too many reasons to discuss here; the focus of this book is only on Spanish speakers. This book was written to explain to educators or instructors how to help students learn their material in a culturally appropriate way and how to make them want to learn even more.

Students love being appreciated, receiving respect, doing activities that build on what they know, and working as equals with other peers.

Educators or instructors who are well informed and sensitive can accomplish miracles. In the words of Dr. Wayne Dyer, "Be a caregiver, not a controller."

Professional development classes frequently profess to be helping teachers to obtain better student assessment results. The material the instructors are told to follow, however, is often flawed, inaccurate, misleading, and biased against the teachers' best academic efforts.

The same is sometimes true for business training classes for *diverse populations*: The material is frequently flawed, inaccurate, misleading, and biased, thereby working against the corporate mission statement.

Business partners, employees, peers, and even volunteers often find that although they follow published advice, they do not reap the promised rewards due to the inherent flaws within the advice.

From my own research, I have concluded the same consideration should be applied to all students in all aspects of classroom learning that which is allocated for children with learning disabilities. My area of expertise is exceptional education. I have experience growing up with a chronic illness that caused deafness in both of my ears. I also have a learning disability. Throughout my childhood, I cared for my mother who wore a full body brace. I was the mother of three children with special educational needs, a foster mother of six children with exceptionalities, and a special-education teacher of Mexican immigrants. Nonetheless, when I moved to Mexico in 2005, I suddenly realized I, too, had exceptional needs and needed "exceptional" education. I was terribly challenged when I attempted to interact with residents in Central Mexico because I lacked fluency in Spanish. I needed to improve my Spanish to better communicate with them, because to them I appeared cognitively challenged. I felt very stupid and needed all the help

I could get. Fortunately for me, I was able to buy food from helpful, respectful, friendly people who touched my soul; I felt this connection because they wanted to communicate with and assist me. These Spanish-speaking merchants were patient enough to teach me the language, and I soon increased my self-reliance and once again appeared mentally capable in my interactions within the community.

After that experience, I could not help but ask, "Do Spanish-speaking students deserve anything less from their educators or instructors?"

The answer is, "No!" This book was conceived to help educators and others to communicate clearly with Spanish speakers. All students deserve equal consideration from their educators or instructors; all of them deserve the same level of patient care I received in Mexico from the local shopkeepers. It is unfortunate marginalized Mexican students are often not given the same considerations. When one lacks proper nutrition, access to knowledge, informed educators or instructors, economic security, a common language or dialect, and/or cultural awareness, communication is difficult. Any of those factors can put a person at a disadvantage in a classroom or in business—in Mexico, the U.S., or anywhere else. Without appropriate teaching or communication methods, students may be kept behind and/or even labeled as developmentally delayed or disabled.

The book *Subtractive Schooling*, written by Angelica Valenzuela, gives an excellent example of the harm that can be done to students as a result of classroom or curriculum mismanagement. Instead of adding to their knowledge base in the classroom, students slip behind when the language of the instruction is not understood. The same situation can occur when a person is *improperly labeled*.

If I had been "labeled" by the Mexican store owners as another *loco Gringa* or a *stupid Polack*, the outcome would have been very different. I would have remained hungry, disoriented, and unable to gain knowledge. I came to Mexico without the ability to speak Spanish. I was bright and educated, but, like a student with a learning disability, I had to work hard to make my needs known and to understand others. I was, in fact, viewed as a learning-disabled person only because I lacked the language. The local people were patient and informative, however—they offered feedback in a respectful manner and encouraged me to speak up and mimic them. As a result, I could soon manage with less one-on-one help. Do your students, patrons, clients, or friends deserve any less?

Summary

Consider the following advice: Treat all children with Response to Intervention (RTI)[1] techniques or with the same consideration that the U.S. law provides to the disabled student. All students will benefit.

The tool for applying culturally appropriate techniques to enact this principle—this book—now lies in your hands.

NOTE: Throughout this book, as in the example above, I, the author, was a participant in qualitative research projects. Therefore, in this book I have reported what I observed, how I felt, and what understanding I gained throughout the processes. Like me, other qualitative researchers have learned insightful information about themselves in the process of learning about others. My wish is primarily that educators or business people, who read this book, will learn what techniques assist Latinos when learning. Secondly, I anticipate instructors will learn more about themselves in the process of learning about the culture of Latinos.

This revised edition is the result of feedback from people raised in all parts of Latin America. Those who contacted me said I was doing a disservice to other Spanish speakers if the title and the book did not address all Latinos instead of only Mexicans.

PART ONE

Defining
Challenging Areas

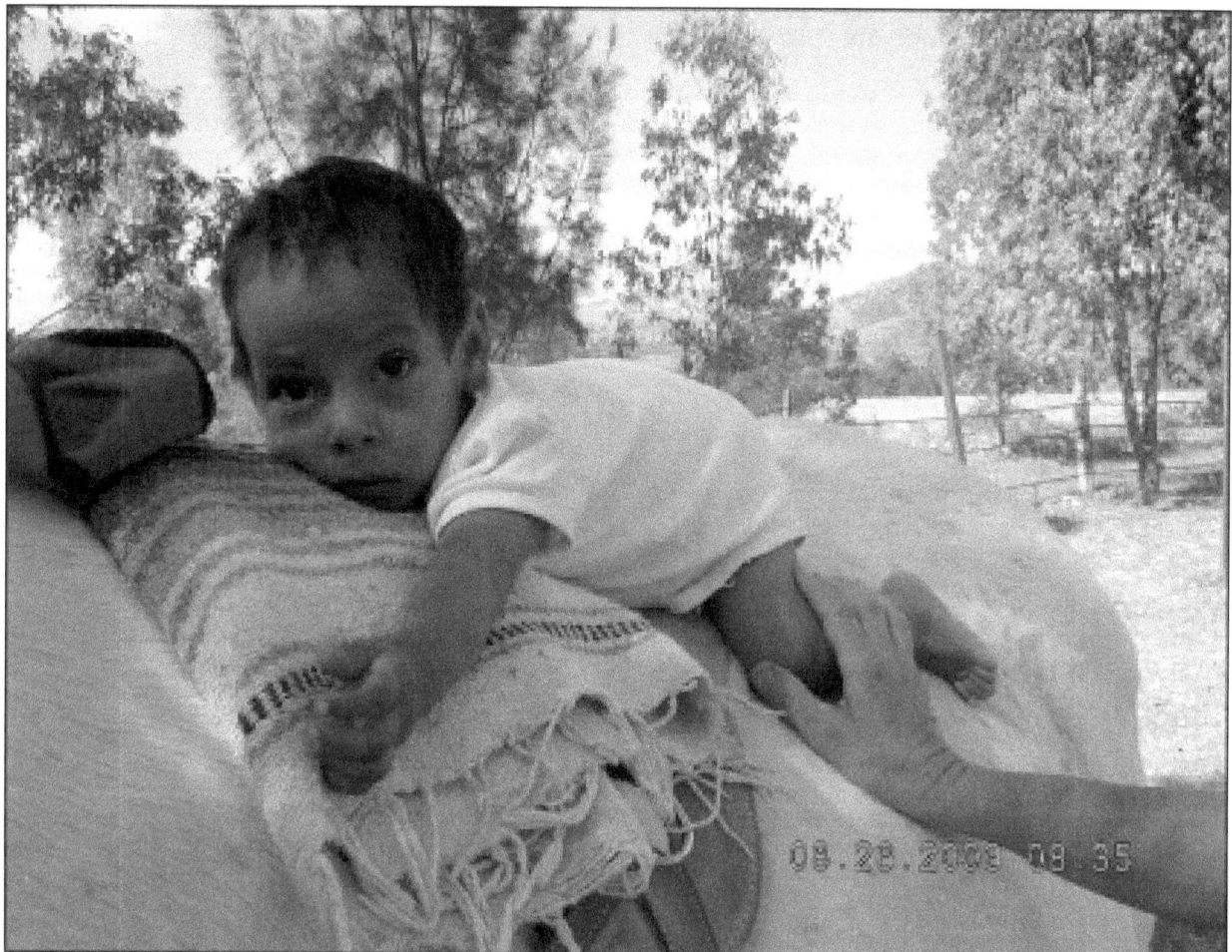

This 2-year-old boy is the victim of several physical and mental challenges. His mother accepts her role as his parent without complaints. She does all that she is capable of in order to help him and his younger brother. She has few options for medical or financial assistance, and has to largely rely on her own and her husband's personal resources. She has no options for finding information about how to better help her son, because she has no access to medical textbooks; there is no library and no Internet for her to use.

1 The Pathway to Learning

"The difficulties experienced by immigrant students indicate that cross-cultural differences in cognition are most probably related to learning practices characteristics of different cultures.... These differences can be observed not only between cultures but also within a given culture."

—Alex Kozulen (1998)

Attitude Determines Outcome

I am appalled that:

In the U.S.:
- About 49% of Latino students do not graduate from high school.
- Those Latino students who should graduate from high school instead qualify for welfare lines, social discrimination, and lifelong underemployment.

In Mexico:
- About 90% of rural Mexican students do not attend school after sixth grade.
- Undereducated rural children grow up in absolute poverty, feeling lifelong hopelessness, lacking access to knowledge, and being socially oppressed.

The problems with education of marginalized students have come to light under the Obama administration, but solutions are elusive. According to the New York Times on February 14, 2011, Rep. John Kline,

3

R-Minn., the chairman of the House Education and the Workforce Committee, stated the following:

> *"Over the last 45 years we have increased our investment in education, but the return on that investment has failed to improve student achievement,"* Mr. Kline said. *"Throwing more money at our nation's broken education system ignores reality and does a disservice to students and taxpayers."*

This book explains that helping someone overcome challenges will begin not with political disagreements or learning how to speak Spanish, but with learning how to speak with your heart. Teachers whose students come from diverse cultures have never been fluent in the native language of each child in the room—that is not as necessary as understanding the key aspects of every culture in the room. Understanding the culture of Spanish speakers is especially valuable in education, because theirs is a culture of relationships. *Speaking with your heart* is what I call this activity. Relate to the Spanish-speaking student, trainee, co-worker, peer, neighbor, and/or friend with the goal of empowering them, and a positive outcome is likely. The rest of this book explains why.

Understanding the Motivation to Migrate

My stomach knots when my gate bell fails to ring a few seconds after the 3:45 P.M. bus passes. I replay a familiar assumption: "Kirt's mother must not have had four pesos this week."

When I last saw 3-year-old Kirt, his spine behaved as though it was as flaccid as cooked spaghetti. He was unable to hold himself upright, and he was tiny and thin. He had never walked. He smiled at me between gurgles that sounded like the symptoms of cystic fibrosis. Both of his legs and both of his arms exhibited the characteristics of cerebral palsy. I had observed his abnormalities many times before, because for the last two years his mother had trusted me enough to offer her helpless son into my care for therapy. She brought him to therapy when she had 4 pesos for the hour-long bus ride.

Each time I took him into my arms, he immediately curled his lower lip in an expression of sadness; he often cried. He was totally helpless, and therefore, terrified to be out of his mother's arms. His mother was not yet 30 years old, yet her own spine was bent like a question mark from years of malnourishment. Nevertheless, she was his protector. "Who protects her?" I often thought. However, she did not appear to ever ask that question herself. She performed her parental role with natural movements like one who had years of training as a caretaker of her siblings. She always climbed up on the tall white therapy horse to receive her son back into her arms—and he usually quieted down right away in her hold.

Most parents get a break during equine therapy, but the only break this mother got was when someone else watched her other son, an 18-month-old who traveled with her and Kirt to therapy. They rode for an hour each way on a public bus for 25 minutes of equine therapy. Recently, I discovered this mother faced even more difficulties. After two years of coming for free therapy, she finally allowed me to drive her home one afternoon during a massive thunderstorm that frequently reconfigured our desert landscape during summer monsoons. We drove on the roads for a few miles and then went through cow paths, between the desert weeds, for seven or eight additional minutes in my four-wheel-drive vehicle. The entire time I pondered, "How on earth does she manage to walk to a bus with a toddler and a nearly lifeless child in her arms in this mud?"

What I saw is burned into my memory. She, her husband, and two young children lived in a lean-to shack made of pallets and a castoff tin roof. They had no water or electricity, and the space was not dry or insulated. All four of them were extremely thin, presumably because they lacked adequate food. Both parents had mentioned many times that the husband was unable to find work. They had also explained that the wife was unable to acquire help with basic needs or to find answers regarding how to help herself and her family.

Is it any wonder that families, especially those with disabled children, enter the U.S. as illegal immigrants? They seek sources of income, health care, educational services, and a better life overall. However, that option is not foolproof. Too often there is no dream realized in the U.S. for the first generation immigrant Latino children, legal or not. The entire family frequently faces continued poverty and amplified discrimination.

Only enlightened people who care enough to understand cultural differences will empower Spanish speakers. With understanding, their story can have a happy ending. Thank you for being one of those special people.

Physical Layout

This first chapter introduces the book and explains the configuration. The book design aims to enable the reader to easily pinpoint the reference material for use as a reference guide. There are also numerous examples and stories to help the reader grasp each concept more completely.

- Chapter 2 is filled with questions that are frequently asked regarding the education of Spanish speaking people of Latino descent.
- Chapters 3 through 14 contain elaborated supportive evidence.
- Chapter 15 contains the summary of answers to the frequently asked questions, with index page listings for each question.
- Chapter 16 provides a short discussion based on what the reader learned in the previous chapters.

The majority of the data are from my own qualitative and quantitative research in Central Mexico (my full-time residence). Additional data were gathered during 12 years of living, working, and researching with Mexicans on the Arizona-Sonora border. Less recent information was collected over 23 years of employment with Latino peers in food service positions in about a dozen different U.S. states. Other information was obtained over a lifetime of having Latino friends. Outside data came from studying others' academic research and referencing the sources. There are numerous examples and/or stories to explain the questions, answers, opinions and/or suggestions that have been and continue to be tried, revised, expanded, and improved upon as individuals and society change.

Reference and Novel Formats

This book can be read like a novel, but the design uses a textbook format to enable easy access to information. Some information is cross-referenced in more than one place, so that it could be easily located within each relevant section; the index is also extensive for that reason.

This reference book was written to enable you, the reader, to easily extract information and guidelines to follow. I call these guidelines *techniques of positive change*; they can help you empower students of Latino heritage, by acknowledging and enhancing their life experiences, in order to enrich their continued academic success.

Taking the time to look into the complex aspects of the Latino culture will make you a better teacher, business partner, peer and friend. We do not fear what we understand. That which we do not fear we can tolerate. That which we can tolerate, we can embrace. Those whom we embrace, we can love. The Latinos you meet may show you their friendliness when they take your hand, give you a very light kiss on the cheek, or grasp your palm firmly while telling you what an honor it is to meet you. What your greeting offers them may well depend on how deeply you have examined their culture.

Introduction

This book *will* alter your attitude toward the education of Latinos and change your understanding of Spanish speakers. Second-generation Mexicans, living outside of Mexico, most likely have never had an opportunity to see an analysis of their Latino culture. This analysis has finally been put into print with this groundbreaking book. Now the reader can look at the Latino culture and decipher it, as I have done by living in a native community (called a *campo*). Being a neighbor of subsistence farmers for nearly three years has taught me endless truths. I have also come to understand the source of misunderstandings, myths, and absolute lies about Latinos.

The results of my research will stimulate your thinking. You have in your hands the tools you need to change history by changing lives. Information within these pages will make your time with Latinos, as a *teacher, business person, peer* or *friend*, more satisfying and productive.

The specific target audience of this book is the unaware public, especially those who educate students, are corporate trainers, manage service businesses or farming, military services, and friends of Spanish speakers, or others who require clear, positive, and beneficial communication with Spanish-speaking people. This book would also be helpful to leaders, employees, or clients of Mexican people. Leaders, or people in positions of power, might include federal or state government officials, academic administrators, and CEOs of corporations, among others.

Administrators dealing with Latinos frequently appear to lack understanding about how these people think and act, regardless of which country those Latinos are residing in at the time. Authors have recorded countless stories of the complications of bi-cultural confusion especially in second-generation immigrants. The same confusion exists inside Mexico between the fourteen layers of social class; few in the administrative levels understand much of anything about the indigenous rural Latino.

The myths about Latinos are widespread; they have been retold so many times even those who imagine themselves to be well-informed are often incorrect due to a lack of available research based information. Additionally, administrative directives have been commonly put into place that have resulted in "dead wrong" ramifications for health, educational opportunities, financial security, and the social dignity of those of Latino heritage. Nearly all Latinos face inadequate income challenges, even highly educated adults. However, people from rural Latin America are usually in the lowest economic class; the bottom of the 14-level class system[1] is, therefore, economically and educationally disadvantaged to an extreme level. Rural, frequently indigenous, Latinos live at an economic level few North Americans could comprehend as a reality on this continent in the 21st century.

To add insult to injury, those in positions of authority or responsibility (often classroom teachers or supervisors) are often required to follow fatally flawed administrative directives that fail to accomplish positive results. Teachers who follow these orders are blamed for students' failures.

Teachers are failing to teach immigrant students of rural Latino heritage not because the teachers are incompetent, but because the administrative directives for teaching second-language learners are not research-based or appropriate for Native Latinos.

What is missing from this scenario is accurate and adequate information about what experiences and achievements the Latino student or employee is bringing into the classroom, and how to correctly scaffold[2] on those experiences and achievements in a culturally appropriate manner.

A culturally appropriate approach leads the student toward positive results, such as high self-esteem, engagement, active learning, academic success, and graduation from high school.

You might be asking yourself why information about the health, educational opportunities, economic status, and social dignity of some unknown number of people of rural Latino heritage would be of any interest to you. What does that have to do with your health, your knowledge-gathering options, or your financial security? If you intend to have a family of your own, or you have grandchildren, probably a great deal more than you realize.

You and/or your family may fail to find access to limited resources even though you have paid taxes to contribute to social services. Those who do not pay taxes are even less self-sustaining. In the U.S., advocates fight to ensure everyone's basic needs are met. Equality of providing social services often dissipates social services beyond those needing service. When that occurs, people miss out on much needed services.

Clearly, everyone needs to pay taxes. To make that possible, everyone needs access to positions of economic power, leadership, and social status, as well as opportunities to significantly contribute to the welfare of the society. More equal opportunities to get a good education, make a sustainable living, and pay taxes will benefit all citizens. Helping marginalized people gain skills helps everyone.

Educating the uninformed U.S. public about traditional learning styles of rural Mexico could create a win-win situation inside and outside of the classrooms. The acquired insight will allow American educators to set realistic expectations for immigrant Latino children living in the U.S. Additionally, these children would benefit by being able to learn more quickly and retain more information. Likewise, if urban Latino education administrators gathered some of the same insight about traditional teaching styles practiced in rural Latino homes, more children from the ranchos might become academically successful.

Time is running out to make positive changes in the education of Latinos in the U.S.

- As of 2002, 30% of the current U.S. population was born in Mexico.
- The number of Latinos born in the U.S. doubled between 1990 and 2000.
- Nearly 22% of babies are born to non-native English speakers in the U.S. each year; many of these babies learn Spanish as their first language. Thus, it is easy to see why statistical projections tell us that half of the U.S. will speak Spanish by 2024.[3, 4]
- Spanish is the second most common language in the U.S. after English.
- Vastly more Mexican immigrants are from low-socioeconomic-status rural areas of Mexico than any other region.
- Statistics inform us that Latinos have a higher fertility rate than other cultures.[5]
- Federal and state government officials, academic administrators, CEOs of corporations, and educators working with this population must act quickly using research-based focused methodology to achieve the best overall results.

I accepted the responsibility of living this emic (an anthropological term used when the basics of the cultural phenomena are researched, and often reported, by a participant who is living within the culture) life. I used a mixed methods research approach and meticulously recorded

This is a front view of a typical preschool in rural Central Mexico. Note the bright colors and extensive outdoor space. These characteristics are nearly always present in rural preschools. Children are normally in uniforms; Normally they are unisex smocks in matching cheerful colors.

what I learned. This passion for absolute accuracy developed because I observed what those of rural indigenous Latino culture lacked. The majority had no educational opportunities to achieve academic success either in Latin America or elsewhere. Researchers predominately find that isolated areas of Mexico lack basic learning necessities.[6] The majority of immigrants from Mexico to the U.S. come from rural areas and/or the lowest-socioeconomic class.[7] U.S. statistics show approximately 25% of Latino immigrants quit as soon as they are legally allowed to drop out, while others stay longer and then fail to finish.[8] In Mexico, rural indigenous people fare far worse because fewer than 10% of them are even allowed to start classes at the high school level.[9] Several economic factors contribute to this situation.

I have dedicated my life's work to finding solutions to educating Latinos in both countries; I have found many creative and culturally appropriate solutions that are neither costly nor complex. Due to my employment in large food service corporations from 1966 to 1989, I frequently worked with undocumented workers from Latin America. Since 1986, I have been engaged in nonprofit leadership positions, often assisting Latinos. Since 1996, when I moved to a small rural Mexican town on the Arizona-Sonora border, I have incorporated interviews, focus groups, surveys, observations, and professional expert questioning to comprehend the influence of lifestyles, viewpoints, ritualistic views, cultural practices and other attitudinal factors of Latinos living in the U.S., as well as in Latin America.

Summary: How to Obtain Learning Successes

The opinions expressed in this book are the result of personal research, unless otherwise stated. Research is normally written in the past tense, as the work has been completed. However, in this book, **if what I have found continues to be a factor at this time, it is written in the present tense.** As Lessie Jo Fraizer states so well, I am "a scholar struggling to forge a place at a particular moment in history,"[10] and I am recording what I have found. I now publish that information so others might benefit from my detailed observations. My goal is to provide answers for teachers and corporate trainers of Spanish speakers. In the process of helping them, my information will also help Latino people, whom I have come to love as my own extended family, residing in my adopted country.

I have observed what harm is being done in Latin America and in the U.S. by uninformed authorities and other people in positions of power, and have taken the position that Latinos are frequently misunderstood. I align myself as a social justice advocate for Latinos. My goal is to promote healing in classrooms and training rooms by promoting understanding of the Latino culture.

Equine therapy is one answer to many physical, emotional, or mental challenges that children and adults face. Often, there are more questions than answers. Why do some people respond and others do not? Why does the therapy work faster and/or better for some disabilities and not for others? We don't have those answers. We simply offer the service, and like family members, we watch and wait to see how each person in therapy responds. The young boy reaching for the dog is the victim of Down's Syndrome. His normally developed younger sister, who is held in the lap of another family member, is looking on. In the background, another parent looks on as her child participates in equine therapy. They all have questions, but then again, so do we. The answers are often a complex weaving of information, effort, patience, and trust.

2 Questions From Parents, Educators, and Business People

"Free the child's potential, and you will transform him into the world."

—MARIA MONTESSORI (1870–1952)

The first 12 questions below are compiled from comments and questions from parents, teachers, trainers, and business people I have known. They were seeking a means to free a child's potential to become a self-sustaining adult. These questions formed the basis for my formal research and collection of data over the four years prior to writing this book; they are referenced appropriately. I have included some casual research observations collected over my lifetime of living near or working with Latinos, which are part of internal dialogue and are not referenced.

1. How do we best prepare the next generation of children for adulthood?

2. Why aren't Latino students motivated to learn?

3. How do I teach English as a second language to Spanish-speaking Latino students?

4. What is going on globally that affects Latino students?

5. How might our shrinking access to land and nature affect education?

6. What else might our shrinking access to land and nature effect?

7. What can we as educators do to make school fun, to keep students engaged, and to help children form a life-long habit of learning?

8. Do Latina mothers care if their children are educated?

9. How do Latina mothers see their children's futures in the U.S. or in Latin American countries?

10. If a child had special needs, would that child's challenge(s) change your expectations for that child's adult future?

11. Why is it so difficult for a rural Latino child to acquire a decent education through high school in Latin American countries?

12. Why is it so difficult for an immigrant Latino child to acquire a decent education through high school in the U.S.?

The following eight questions are *personal interview* questions with a former Mexican government official. The answers to these eight questions are transcribed in Chapter 10.

13. "It is my understanding that the integration of students with disabilities into the public schools' classes in Mexico was your job for seven years [dates withheld from an interview for confidentiality]. Is that correct?"

14. "Did you consider the program a success? Why or why not?"

15. "Todd Fletcher, Ph.D., stated: 'Entre el dicho y el hecho hay mucho trecho.' (Translation: 'There are a lot of distances between word and deed.') Does this occur because of a) inability to coordinate programs, b) lack of money, c) political infighting, d) shortage of technology or experts, or e) something else?"

16. "Are you saying that, whereas the U.S. has President Obama demanding more funding for education and individuals in the private sector, such as Bill and Melinda Gates, giving tens of millions of dollars for education, Mexico lacks both public and private patrons focusing on education?"

17. "Since childhood, my conversations about Mexico have always ended up with someone blaming corruption for causing a lack of efficiency. From where I sit, it seems that the U.S. is equally corrupt, especially in education. What is the difference in Mexico?"

18. "If you were the president of Mexico, what would you do to ensure equal educational opportunities for a) children with disabilities, b) rural children, and c) those so poor that attending school is an economic hardship for their families?"

19. "My research found that nutritional problems are the biggest reason that rural Mexican children do not excel academically. Do you agree that environmental shortages (including socioeconomic status), and not genetic issues, should be addressed in order to increase academic success within the public schools?"

20. "In my private school, on the Sonora/Arizona border, which was funded with public money, I served breakfast, mid-morning snack, lunch, and mid-afternoon snack. All meals were carefully developed for outstanding nutritional value—a full day's worth of nutritional value for a growing child. Do you think that the rural Latino children need a nutritional program within the public schools to provide breakfast and mid-morning snack?"

Sources of Analysis

PART II, titled *An Analysis of the Culture*, contains chapters 3 through 14. Those chapters contain the results of my own research data, as well as references to the works of other authors. I have included field notes, observations, and vignettes to help the readers draw their own individual conclusions. Reading all of the information will help you improve your relationships with Latinos both inside and outside of the classroom. I have also explained why, based on my experiences, I am passionate about reporting what I know to be the truth with regard to education of Latinos in rural Central Mexico and elsewhere.

Deficit Treatment of My Neighbors' Children

The majority of Spanish-speaking Latino children have rich backgrounds and bright young minds that eagerly anticipate learning. Yet in both the U.S. and Latin America, they often live in an environment where they are *denied* access to education. These students, particularly those raised in rural areas of Latin America, are short-changed by the deficit model that is being utilized to create learning curricula for the *economically disadvantaged*.[1] *Economically disadvantaged* is a new category within the U.S. No Child Left Behind (NCLB) initiative. In general, well-intending educators of the *economically disadvantaged* Spanish-speaking Latino children in rural Latin American countries and in the U.S. often lack an understanding of how to best offer both content and second language acquisition in a manner appropriate for these children. This is evidenced by the fact that the dropout rate is the highest among Hispanic students.[2] The deficit model theory, which describes the student as inadequate, is often the basis for teachers' professional development programs.[3] The psychological *fight or flight response*[4] is created as a result, because the students become defensive and start doing everything they can to protect themselves from pain and humiliation.

The educators' authorized curricula fail to use a method that builds on the students' background (scaffolding),[5] enhances their self-esteem, and empowers them. This is especially true for those students raised in rural environments. Acknowledging and enhancing their life experiences could enhance learning. Enhanced learning may create happiness[6] in the schools, and happy students are often more motivated to learn.

Developing students who happily learn and feel good about themselves is the only rational way to enrich learning and improve academic success. The *authorized curricula* are successful at applying the deficit model, which implies that the student lacks drive or has an individual or cultural deficiency— in contrast to failures or limitations within the educational system to meet the needs of the student.[7]

When educators set high expectations, their students will likely meet these expectations; conversely, when the message of the authorized classroom curricula points to a personal deficiency, students are set up for both academic and social failures. The later pathway is the standard currently in place. This pathway of failures is evidenced by high percentages of students in Mexico and the U.S. who do not graduate from high school.

Clear Social Class Distinctions in the Classroom

In Latin America, the teachers of rural students come from a higher social class, and their curriculum is composed of urban-focused academic material.[8] This combination in the rural classrooms sends a *personal deficiency* message to the indigenous children raised in agricultural communities. The students know that the teacher is of a higher social class.

In rural Latin America, teachers usually come to the rural community solely to teach; then they catch a bus home. The teachers lack a social class connection to the community. Their commitment to the community often appears as little more than a means to gain a paycheck.

In the U.S., a similar situation exists: The curriculum designed for the *economically disadvantaged* students sends the same deficit message—the teacher is not poor and is, therefore, basically different from the students.

These not-so-subtle deficit messages in both countries make students defensive; these messages enhance fears and intimidate students. Instead of the student embracing the opportunity to learn by building on what they already know (scaffolding), rural Latino students employ what they know best—their survival instincts—to shut down emotionally and to physically shut out what they fear.[9]

Poor Educational Track Records

Our historical records of success with educating Mexicans in Mexico or Latino immigrants in the U.S. are dismal.[10] Fewer than 10% of all children in Mexico pass the entrance exams to get accepted into high school ("prepatoria"), and only about 25% of those actually graduate.[11] In the U.S., about half of Latino immigrant students who enter high school earn a diploma.[12]

The complexity of the questions related to what can be done to change those statistics continue to haunt us as we continue to utilize the deficit model of looking at what is wrong with the students, instead of looking in the mirror to see what educators are able to do to empower students instead of discouraging them.

When educational administrators have been informed by assessments that the students are failures, their administrative response has been to continue to make rapid-fire, drastic, non-research-based changes, laws, and rules within schools that lead to even more failures.[13]

As passionate educators, we all want positive results, not failures.

I have taken the position that the time has come to step back from rapid-fire, drastic, non-research-based changes, laws, and rules. Instead, we should adopt a proactive view and explain some of the complex questions facing modern education administrators across Latin America and the U.S.

According to Robert Fried, teaching is a zealous vocation that can bring enthusiasm and inspiring philosophy into classrooms.[14] Researcher Andy Hargreaves refers to teaching as an expressive practice made up of "emotional, passionate beings that connect with their students and fill their work and their classes with pleasure, creativity, challenge, and joy."[15]

I taught in children's summer church camps during my teenage years, as well as in municipal and privileged summer school or summer church camps in the 1980s. In the 1990s, my nonprofit offered free children's summer camps along the Sonora-Arizona border. Then the passion to enable change with Latino children drove me back into teaching in public and private schools in 2003. My classroom was typically made up of socioeconomically marginalized, disabled Spanish-speaking students. Later, I had age-segregated classes ranging from infancy to 12th grade in several public and private school programs. The emotional impact of not being able to make the differences I had anticipated in the U.S. inspired me to research for definitive answers in rural Central Mexico. I, like Amanda Coffey, have come to realize "that the ethnographic self is the outcome of complex negotiations."[16] Passion drives my desire to identify factors that explain why only half of Latino immigrant children graduate from high school in the U. S. Emotional commitment to Mexican children brought me to Central Mexico to find some answers.

Comments are Educational not Political

This book is not a political commentary. It is a studious exercise intended to help educators or instructors of Spanish-speakers.

This book is based on a variety of sources, including my observations, research, interviews, and group meetings, as well as extensive study of publications by other authors, academic, and otherwise. Take what works and use it; ignore what doesn't work in your situation.

My vision is not through the eyes of a Latino; my heritage is Polish-Scottish. I was born in rural New Mexico and spent 23 years in food service with Latino peers. I also lived on the Arizona-Sonora border for 12 years and taught in public and private schools in the region. Now I live in the lowest-social-class environment of Mexico and have many opportunities to learn about education of rural and urban Latinos.

Understanding Cultural Differences (Not Deficits)

Historical, social, and cultural reasons may contribute to Latino students' frequent failure to attain educational gratification and honors in the U.S. and Latin America. Feuerstein's Mediated Learning Experience (MLE) theory,[17] the belief in human modifiability based on a sociocultural influence, was the best explanation I found to address why many students of Mexican heritage find academic success to be inaccessible in both countries.

The MLE theory includes regulation and control of behavior, feelings of competency (displaying what one knows), sharing behavior (teaching each other in groups), individuation or psychological differentiation (appreciating the similarities and differences in each other), and self-driven goal of seeking-setting-achieving-monitoring (a learner-based creation of each course syllabus); the students are responsible for creating their own syllabus[17]

Latinos are raised to take on adult responsibilities and activities at a very early age by using adult-sized tools and mimicking the observed mature behavior. In the classroom, much of that standard is left out in the U.S. and in Latin America. The challenge for teachers is to become aware of the potential for change and to search for novelty, complexity, optimistic alternatives, and feelings of belonging (MLE).

Feuerstein has stated that the feeling of belonging to a culture may be significantly reduced if the child is deprived of the mediated learning experience associated with his or her native culture.[18] The educators' lack of cultural awareness or acknowledgment of the students' valuable experiences may, therefore, be viewed as one logical explanation for failing these Latino students. How they had learned—outdoors by observation and by utilizing few words (MLE)—has been replaced with verbal instructions given indoors.

Rural Latino children's' conscience behavior may be influenced by mediated learning experiences associated with their native culture. In an agricultural area, most of the learning continues to take place outdoors by observing and mimicking the activities of adults.

In the outdoors, the students are using adult tools and are not overly protected or supervised. They are making and correcting their own mistakes, and learning from them. They are not following detailed spoken instructions typical of a sterile classroom.

Home and School Differences in Styles of Instruction

My observations and those of other researchers indicate that rural, predominately indigenous parents rarely give verbal descriptions to their children.[19] Instead, they anticipate a need and take an action, which the child is expected to see and mimic. Parents expect the child to comprehend what is going on and learn by performing the same activities as they are until the child's skill is mastered and correctly applied.

Research has confirmed that children and parents spend little time together in verbal exchanges. One-on-one discussions or detailed descriptions by adults are rarely directed toward children.

It is common to meet a mother who has never considered verbal or physical interaction with her child in her role as teacher. Infants are entertained, not taught. I learned that names are often not given to an infant for some time, simply "niño or niña" is offered as a first name. This is apparently because infant mortality is high. Infants are cherished as gifts from God, not as future adults needing guidance. Adults are normally not heard speaking to infants. In rural Latin America, verbal communication between adults and children of all ages is minimal in the home and outdoors.

Furthermore, Latino students living in agricultural areas experience a major disconnect between home and school. Even if they cannot read, they are expected to memorize specific information and recall it, almost word for word, in assessments. Little creative thinking is required for a typical school lesson, but creative thinking develops through students' exchanges with each other regarding the lessons.

In school, students are expected to copy endless pages of printed material by hand while sitting at desks, tables, or in other group settings where they can talk among themselves, comfortably walk around the room, help each other with lessons, solve problems together, and freely exchange ideas. This often takes place in a multi-level classroom. The classrooms are always crowded. The desks or tables are touching, personal space is very tight, and there are up to 55 students with one teacher.

At home there is no printed material, and no reason to hold a pen or a pencil. Children are expected to observe the adults; children observe what is going on around them, indoors and outdoors, and mimic it. While observing adults, the children also talk among themselves; however, they do not question adults. The children freely exchange ideas with each other in a helpful, noncompetitive manner. They are expected to be creative thinkers, to generalize the information they acquire and to apply their knowledge to numerous situations at home (actualize), in the community, and in outside business situations—but not in school. It appeared that creative thinking is not expected or assessed in school, other than through art projects; however, creative thinking nonetheless develops in all subjects due to the *student-driven* way in which the lessons are completed, often in groups.

Norma González, Luis Moll, and Cathy Amanti found that the use of the schooling model of punitive measures and time limits within learning situations "developed one of the few adult-child conflicts within the household."[20] These same three researchers, all of whom I know and with whom I have discussed the Latino culture, suggested that reduced self-esteem is an outcome of the schooling model of punitive measures, resulting from the *cultural conflict*[21] of expectations that counters the child-motivated style of learning found in Latin American culture.

In Latino houses, children are expected to ask questions of each other, practice learned behavior, function within a "non-stressful domain or neutral zone of comfort, where little criticism was expressed, and they are not faulted,...allowing self-evaluation and self-judgment"; they are also encouraged to take as long as they like to accomplish the task.[22] This is in sharp contrast to the continuous deadline constraints placed on children in the U.S. public schools.

U.S.-Latin American Differences in Styles of Instruction

In contrast to classrooms in Latin America, a teacher verbalizes instructions most of the time in the U.S., often in a language not understood by the students. In the U.S., teachers expect their students to summarize, in their own words, the content of the lectures. Typically, the students heard something verbalized by their adult teacher and placed individual notes on paper while sitting in silence. The only other acceptable behavior was to ask the teacher a question by raising a hand. Usually, the students lacked the necessary language skills to do so, but yet they were expected to speak in front of all of the other students.

In the U.S., students are nearly always working alone, in competition with other students, while sitting at an individual desk— not in a group setting that is common in Latin America. Additionally, in the U.S., the students are not allowed to talk with each other in class; they are not allowed to walk over to another student's desk to get clarification, information, or to exchange ideas. In fact, if the student asks another student a question, the one who speaks up and is heard by the teacher would likely be severely punished, and may even be accused of cheating!

Summary: Questions from Parents, Educators, or Instructors

Obviously, the raised questions are not simple, but they were questions that need accurate answers based on fact and not fiction, nor on popular theories. The information in this book is not based on speculation or theory. Real-world observations and interviews are the basis of this report. These observations occurred inside actual homes and schools of Mexican children living in the Central Mexican state of Guanajuato, on the Sonora-Arizona border, and in other Mexican communities. I have traveled by car or bus from the Texas or Arizona border to Central or Western Mexico more than 20 times, conducting research along the way.

Read this with an open mind, and you will find information to benefit your students, peers, and other Latinos. My remarks are made with candor. My statements frequently dispute popular theories about Latinos and the poor. Although professional development courses are available to instruct teachers on how to educate Latino students of low socioeconomic status, the presented information may not be accurate and the recommended methods may not be effective. I seek the truth, as well as correct, appropriate, and helpful information. Therefore, I thank you in advance for your comments or questions—both are welcome.

PART TWO

Analysis of the Culture

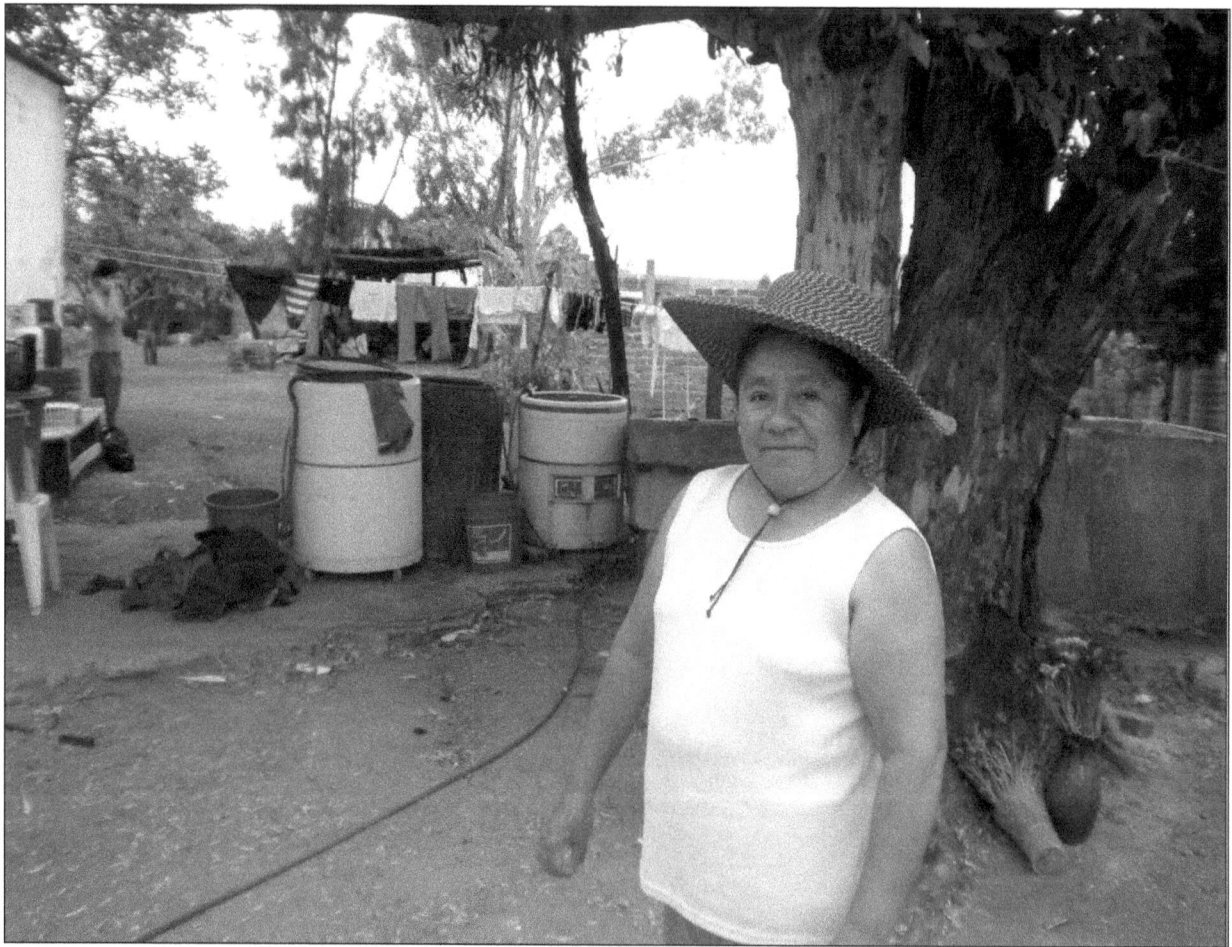

This charming, hard-working woman of faith, who always has time for her neighbors or visitors, is both a typical and an atypical campesino. She is typical because she starts work early in the morning, caring for her family, including her father-in-law (a widower) and two grandchildren who live with her. She is atypical because she is also the local church deacon; the weight of her accepted civic responsibility is enormous.

3

What Is a "Campesino"?

"Bowed by the weight of centuries he leans upon his hoe and gazes on the ground, the emptiness of ages in his face, and on his back the burden of the world"

—EDWIN MARKHAM

Economic-Geographic Characteristics

A *campesino* (com-pa-see-no) is briefly defined as someone of low socio-economic status living in a rural community, such as *campo, pueblo,* or *barrio* of less than 2,500 people. These areas are made up of predominately indigenous people living on very small ranches or in other tightly woven family units. Today most *campesinos* are subsistence farmers or day laborers. In general, these humble, hard-working, sincere, respectful people continue to do all they can to follow in the footsteps of their ancestors. They do that by working on the land and living in simple, unfinished, two-room brick, concrete block or adobe structures, often with stucco-only front and metal forms sticking out from the roof. Even that effort is getting more difficult. As family land has been divided, there is now limited land left to each adult child to sustain an additional family. There is also a lack of day labor jobs to sustain new families. As a result, many young adults are leaving for other parts of Latin America or the U.S. to find employment. This, in turn, often leads to more poverty in Latin America. If jobs are not found upon arrival in the U.S., then absence of emotional and/or financial support often leads to broken family units.

25

Housing Characteristics

My research, from early 2007, found that rural homes typically consisted of two rooms and were made of dirt adobe, brick, or concrete block. The floors were made of compacted dirt or bare concrete. Houses were literally functioning as sleeping structures, because most domestic activities, other than sleeping, took place outdoors. The house was cleaned daily; the concrete floor was mopped with a very strong disinfectant due to the non-potable tap, stream, creek, or lake water. Outside, the yard was swept with a broom and sometimes sprinkled with water to keep down the dust. The household tasks of cooking, washing, and maintaining hygiene were all accomplished outdoors using non-potable water. Domestic animals were also raised outside. Each insignificantly sized dwelling had an outdoor space set aside where laundry was done by hand all year round; it was hung on barbed wire strung across the yard. The dishes were washed in cold water in the same exterior environment. Some but not all of the dwellings had an enclosed area designated as a bathroom space. Only some of these spaces had flush toilets, and most had no sink. All family members took showers or baths outdoors with cold water.

"Housing is also an overwhelming problem. There are 116 houses with an average of four families in each house. Since on average each family has four or more children, statistically we can assume that about 700 people live in only 116 tiny houses. There were no social services for families in this community, nor a single home built here, out of over 11,000 free homes built by the government in the State of Guanajuato in over eight years. We saw over a dozen of these houses in another town (name withheld) on our last visit, but this town has none. It appeared that their claims of no help from the city government are valid."[1]

The living conditions of rural Latino residents reflected their socioeconomic status. Indigenous *campesino* residents lived in a world where burros, the standard beasts of burden, were piled so high with corn stalks that only their hoofs were visible to the on-lookers. Walking along dirt trails, the burros passed near roadways used by cars, trucks, and even earth-moving equipment. *Campesino* women shared a two-room, partially completed subsistence home with others; there were often five or six people in each tiny section of the frequently cold, dark, and musty non-insulated concrete blockhouse. Window and door openings were sometimes covered with loosely draped bed sheets instead of tightly fitted conventional wood, metal, or glass building products. Too frequently, adult females faced single parenthood; these families often included three generations of women—a grandmother, a mother and her daughter, all of whom shared a small two-room home.

Any child over the age of three was expected to share what they could earn outside the indigenous home.

Most houses in the campo are two-room brick structures. Rarely are they finished on the exterior or the interior. They are not insulated and may even lack windows or doors. Most bathrooms are separate areas; some are natural spaces outdoors.

Older siblings physically helped out the younger ones; any 5- to 10-year-old was likely the caregiver of toddlers and expected to solve problems and conflicts, as well as to negotiate without adult input. The oldest members of the indigenous family, the elders, also typically shared the small home, but they brought in no income or other assets to add to the family resources. Indigenous elders had used up all that they had to raise their own children in the *campo*.

These less-informed parents and grandparents were often victims of a multitude of disadvantages common to those living within the lowest socioeconomic conditions. This was an area where marketing was oral—from

Many homes took years to build. People share space with others in the meantime. They add to the structure as time and money allow.

a radio, a neighbor's mouth, or loudspeakers mounted on top of vehicles. The first two options offered some individual control, as one could be absent from a conversation or not turn on a radio; the third method was always invasive. Vehicles blared out sound from loudspeakers several times daily. The drivers mainly peddled tortillas, bread, or fresh vegetables. Sometimes the output was political information. External marketing for consumer items like the Internet, MP3 players, and other electronic items rarely found a way into these disadvantaged communities that lacked discretionary income for such items. Noise from loudspeakers was effective. The sound would even reach into a primitive bathroom shared by six or eight people. Ideally, a bathroom was a separate room where unheated running water would come out of a pipe or showerhead onto cold concrete floors that extended throughout the house. Radio was found in most homes, but television was not as common; therefore, realistically, most of the marketing ads did not reach rural communities. Additionally, the more the U.S. enforced immigration laws pertaining to Latinos, the less people were successful with legal or illegal emigration, and the less often locals saw electronic imports. Furthermore, registered aliens and undocumented aliens alike were finding it harder to find work in the U.S. due to the economic downturn. Therefore, fewer consumer goods crossed the border. Those items that did were subjected to higher and higher import tariffs; as a result, electronic items became even less available to those in rural communities. Basic human survival was so profoundly stressful in these communities that luxury items were a distant dream, not a realistic consideration.

Parents had no energy left in their lives to concern themselves with what children might have wanted outside of adequate food, dry shelter, and warm clothing for the winter.

These people lacked the ability to gain additional knowledge in various subjects for which they had no access. There were no rural public libraries, no free Internet and no means to gather information within these pueblos for anyone above elementary-school age.

The disadvantages included deprivation of overall basic needs, alcoholism, depression, incest, domestic violence, poor health, inadequate nutrition, and increased risk of illness.[2, 3]

Social Status Defined Legally

Recently I was told by a Mexican government administrator in the Department of Immigration that the federal government now defines indigenous as:

1. someone living in a *campo*;
2. someone following the traditional ritualistic lifestyle of native people;
3. someone speaking an indigenous language;
4. someone who refers to himself or herself as indigenous; or
5. someone whose parents are known as indigenous.

Oddly enough, the obvious physical characteristics of indigenous people are not in this list. Instead, these definitions remain easy to sidestep, and therefore, not difficult for the government to keep on the law books. Rarely, however, do they require economic actions. They were put into place to allow people of indigenous status to receive some additional benefits from the federal laws requiring such benefits to be enforced. The actual aspects of this offer by the Mexican government are multifaceted. On the fortunate side, a brilliant child might get more education if he or she and the family were to fight for the enforcement of the benefit.

Unfortunately, however, with 13 social status levels higher than theirs, few *campo* residents will embrace the title *indigenous. They are* humble people, with an overall fatalistic attitude. However, due to historic oppression of Latinos, they do not ask for and also don't expect any help from the Latin American government.

Detriments to Economic and Medical Assistance

The government provides some aid, because a lack of adequate nutrients is so common that both children and adults require nutritional supplements. In my research, I found that 30.9% of the 665 examined children suffered negative side effects from malnutrition; these findings are very similar to what others have found.[4]

The benefits program is called *Opportunities,* "Oportunidades." The paperwork was too difficult for most women to fill out appropriately; some did not have the required documents to get supplemental formula and protein for pregnant or nursing mothers and children under the age of five years. In Mexico, government-related paperwork in most areas demands numerous letters to prove that:

1. the rent has been paid;
2. utilities have been paid;
3. the actual place of residence is where the person says their home is;
4. the applicant actually knows the person whose names he has given as a reference; and
5. paperwork that cannot be located really does not exist (like your third grade report card or your dead mother's drivers license).

Many people share homes. Certainly, not all of the residents get a paid rent receipt or up-to-date utility payment receipts. Since rural homes rarely have an address, it is impossible to prove where a house is located. In many campos, residents are not literate, so proving a relationship with a reference can be difficult. Some paperwork simply does not exist.

A local minister who is an expatriate created the joke, "*And a copy of your second-quarter third grade report card is required.*"[5]

Too frequently, Latin American officials also claim no authority to be able to do anything without getting a "mordita," a bribe, tip, fine, service charge, or commission, from the person in need.[4] Dealing with public services is very stressful on the campesino who generally has limited financial resources. I personally know of two families who waited extensive times to get public water or other utilities in their homes—although the utility bill was paid, the mordita was not, and the paperwork simply stalled as the families waited to see if they could borrow money from other family members to provide to the officials as an incentive to finish the paperwork.

It is common knowledge in Latin America that all salaries to government employees are based on the expected direct contact with the public. Therefore, the employee usually collects the mordita while doing an already salaried assignment. Additionally, historical influences are so overwhelmingly ritualized that making a simple payment often means gaining approval by three or more people **in each** government office, bank, or some other linked institution that one must pass through to complete the task at hand. Due to historical influence, the entire system of consumer and government procedures is extremely inefficient; this is largely because there is a lack of trust among peers, bosses, or investors.

These factors explain why poor nutrition was the most common developmental delay problem identified in my research. Although there are government programs, unless an applicant can apply and get approved, the assistance is not forthcoming.

The indigenous caregiver simply cannot complete the paperwork adequately, nor is he or she able to pay additional fees, in the form of a mordita, for approval with errors; a bribe is often necessary to overlook an error or omission. Another contributing factor is the applicant's inability to fill out a form due to illiteracy; research data estimated rural illiteracy to be at 50%.[6] Lack of reading skills usually reduces economic stability, making the need for assistance greater.

There were other programs in place to overcome nutritional shortages, but they also required an application. One program gave 100 pesos to the parents of each child under the age of five years, which translates to about $8 a month. Another program gave each child under the age of five 30 bags of nutritional supplement meals; the same 30 bags of supplemental protein drinks were allocated to pregnant or nursing mothers. This program required that the mothers and the children have examinations in the health clinic every 30 days. Some mothers did not participate in the program because they could not get to the clinic every month or because their gain would be less than the effort required to put forth.

"Sadly, hungry, depressed (often very young) mothers get pregnant to get additional food or public attention and then cannot meet the paperwork requirements for food, have no money to get special seating for pregnant women on the public buses, and therefore, more malnourished babies are born."[7]

Special Needs and Educational Assistance

My research data were based on the theory that rural caregivers of some infants or children with developmental delays or special needs could benefit from my input with regard to what they could do to help themselves and their offspring. The health department also hoped that medical personnel would benefit from interacting with people trained in special needs. I theorized that traditional assessments might fail to take into account sociocultural factors present in indigenous rural Latin American farm or ranch communities, the low socioeconomic *campos*.[8 & 9]

Data suggested that Native Indian or indigenous Mexican caregivers struggle with self-esteem issues related to social class status and, thus, fail to advocate for themselves or their children in the U.S., as well as in Latin America.

Additionally, data from many studies implied that caregivers lack access to social services, including those aimed at working with developmental delays and special needs; the same was found to be true for programs aimed at children without disabilities.[10] Cultural factors maintained the status quo: The upper class held power, the middle class struggled, and the *campesino* continued to lose vital assets needed to meet basic human needs. The findings identified a disproportionate number of developmentally delayed children, mainly due to malnutrition or other environmental influences resulting from class status and/or lack of access to information. *Campesino* participants from 18 rural Central Mexican facilities were studied. Participants represented over 100 *campos*. My research utilized an emic ethnographic approach—an approach in which the researcher is an insider, employing both qualitative and quantitative methodology. Results indicated that factors related to community heritage status affected rural Mexican children's ability to acquire the basic nutritional intake. Caregivers had limited abilities to improve the quality of life for their *campesino* children. Adequate nutrition is necessary to achieve academic success and/or social elevation in Latin America and elsewhere.

My research was composed of mixed methodologies, qualitative and quantitative, that were tailored specifically to indigenous people living in the Central Mexico *campo*. According to K. Pike (1954), two perspectives are used in the study of cultural systems: the "outsider" (etic) or the "insider" (emic).[11] As an "insider," I only had to enter people's homes to learn.[12] I also moved into their lives and into a home amidst their houses in rural Central Mexico. To the best of my knowledge, every aspect of my new life was comparable to my neighbors—including sharing the drought-torn toxic environment, where untreated sewage flowed down the dirt road that we all had to cross to get home. Every three days out of seven, raw sewage flowed from that road into the public water reservoir— the reservoir that I could see from my kitchen window. That reservoir supplied the water flowing into my kitchen sink. I lived in a place where I had to use poisonous non-potable water inside my home and to consider how to keep my family safe from disease.

In addition to trying to find clean water, rural mothers living near me struggled to meet their families' basic needs for food, clothing, and shelter. The men would practically offer their souls for a single day's worth of wages to save personal pride and ease family hardship. The women's will, strength, stamina, and ability to adapt to hardship were observed by this curious gringo woman, who was eager to understand and record what was observed and said.

I undertook this research and lifestyle with a high level of commitment because I was seeking to understand the ever-changing Latin American sociocultural influences on human development. Admittedly, the factors I think I understand will continue to change. Researcher Barbara Rogoff explains that sociocultural influences on human development "can be understood only in light of the cultural practices and circumstance of their communities—which also change."[13] Similar to a housewife's circumstance, this type of research can never be finished, as it continuously evolves.

This research team consisted of Jolene—my translator, soul sister, and fellow teaching volunteer—and me. We worked side by side on our third joint research project related to Spanish speakers. This was a way of being in the rural Mexicans' world, a cultural world far different from our own. We were there as their community adapted to changes imposed from the outside world.

We learned that a lack of special-needs services in rural educational settings could contribute to motivating parents to immigrate to the U.S.; parents want appropriate academic programs for all of their children, including exceptional services for those who fall outside of normal ranges in one or more areas of development.[14] This study's data implied an unexpectedly

The author and Jolene Gailey are in the field in early 2009. The two young girls, 11 and 16, respectively—who lived in this adobe home—were unable to come to the clinic for evaluation. Their mother and grandmother care for eight children; the father had abandoned the family. The younger girl has been unable to walk since the age of two due to spinal meningitis; she also had received treatment for hydrocephalus. Her older sister lost her sight at the age of 12, when a tumor lodged too close to her brain stem had been removed and her optic nerve got struck. Their medical doctor, who walked the researchers to this home, took the photo.

high number of indigenous children with special needs, and statistics have also documented this trend; this may explain some of the motivation of parents to emigrate to the U.S. The emigration trend by Mexican parents in search for better educational exceptional services has occurred for years. If it were accurately tracked, the number of identified special needs students in Mexico likely would be higher than the current documented levels in all areas of disabilities. Perhaps educational resources for children with disabilities in Latin America would have been made available sooner if so many had not left. As it stands now, the lack of services still encourages parents to travel to *el norte* with their disabled children.

Latin American parents immigrating to the U.S. risk everything to give their children a better academic opportunity. They are frequently disappointed. The statistics for Hispanic students show that these students are twice as likely as their Caucasian peers to be identified for special-needs educational services in the U.S.—and not in favor of getting more of what they need.[15] Additionally, a special-needs **label** in their school records might offer them inappropriate exceptional resource services that lack

Parents often emigrate to the U.S. as a means to access educational services for their children with unusual challenges or disabilities. Although the numerous laws ensure that all children will get special education services if they need them, the reality is often a disappointment for parents and teachers alike.

cultural awareness, might lower their self-esteem when they are still learning to speak English like their peers, might reduce their likelihood of academic success due to feeling less than capable, and might result in their being treated unfairly. The public schooling system is already economically stressed in the U.S. Bias related to Latin Americans may interfere with creating a positive educational outcome for immigrant Latin American students, disabled or normally-abled (a term used in the special education field to describe a child who does not have special needs). Studies have shown that academic success is often not the outcome of emigration from Mexico for children with or without disabilities.[16]

Statistics have shown that nearly half of all Latin American immigrant children living in the U.S. and attending public schools did not graduate from high school, although they were expected to complete the program.[17] Other studies have shown that many Mexicans were motivated to finish since they had set life goals that relied on graduating from high school. [18]

Many of the existent myths related to Latin American's lifestyles or sociocultural influences are clearly due to a lack of understanding of the Mexican culture, especially in indigenous rural areas. The rural area that was researched was rich with indigenous groups: Guamares, Chichimecas, Guachichile, Otomíes, and Purépecha or Tarascan, which includes

Celaya, Acámbaro, and Yurirapúndaro. The only living indigenous language in the state was Chichimeca-Jonaz, but it has been said that the people of the state "have inherited the genetic legacy of the original Indian people."[19] With so much native influence, life in rural Latin America is a blend of sociocultural influences that are embedded in the society's day-to-day existence. Communities face challenges from bombardment by external environmental factors and influence, may bend and finally change their rich indigenous Latin American cultural practices, for example when the community loses their sacred tree due to development. Some of these outside factors may influence a change in cultural practices as elders struggle to keep the deeply held indigenous Latin American traditions. Life in a rural Central Mexican *campo* lacks access to a continuous stream of world-view updates, but people living there also have a strong desire to retain traditions. Both external environmental factors and internal community practices reflect components of myths related to both lifestyles.[20] Misunderstanding is likely two-sided—coming from those living inside the *campo*, as well as those living elsewhere. Perpetuated myths may be due to ignorance, a desire to create a more captivating story (manipulation), or an outright desire to control another group of people as a means to elevate one's own group identity.[21]

The word "sociocultural", according to Lev Vygotsky, is "the genetic law of cultural development—any function of a child's cultural development that appears on a social plane while simultaneously appearing on a psychological plane is sociocultural."[22]

As a researcher from the outside of the Mexican culture, I conducted my research to evaluate the physical and emotional development of children residing in remote Mexican *campos*. The question of researcher's bias, lack of understanding of the heritage, and other factors skewing subjective assessments were considered.

Sociocultural influence on indigenous children residing in rural Central Mexico is composed of a complex web of historical, as well as the current, variables; it is also affected by the repeated roles of people whose cultural heritage is scripted and inherited.[23] Researchers have found that sociocultural influences affect everything in the lives of children:

- from breast feeding patterns[24] to specific learning disabilities;[25]
- from meeting developmental milestones[26] to birth weight or other nutritional factors;[27]

- from learning styles[28] to overall school success;[29]
- from social class status or class status biases[30] to family dynamics;[31]
- from career options[32] to educational opportunities;[33]
- from gaining literacy[34] to self-esteem;[35]
- from ways of handling stress[36] to second language acquisition;[37]
- and from alcoholism[38] to single parenthood.[39]

The list is broad and seemingly endless, yet only a few of the reasons are illustrated here. The fact that Latin America has "impoverished areas that include rural, indigenous, and poverty-stricken" communities have already been documented; this research was conducted in such documented regions.[40] Nearly all factors found to be significant in my research are environmental influences that could possibly be overcome through early childhood intervention and caregiver educational programs.[41] This investigative approach was necessary to reveal the reality of sociocultural influences on indigenous children born into and/or residing inside the rural Central Mexico *campo*. Research makes records of reality, and in doing so it provides findings that often replace myths. If we already knew the answers we would not call it research.

When individuals using the U.S. standards to evaluate a *campesino* child, by asking seemingly bias-free questions, they may actually skew the results due to their cultural ignorance as the outsiders. This is why choosing which assessment to use was a difficult decision to make; appropriate, tested, and unbiased materials are very hard to find. By steeping myself in the culture, I discovered that both parties (Mexican caregivers and I) held their own culturally influenced expectations regarding the roles of caregiver and teacher. The U.S. standards often suggested that mothers taught certain skills, while the *campesino* caregivers expected teachers to do all of the teaching outside of the domestic or ranch chores. My research found that, as a group, *campesino* mothers did not understand the concept that they are their children's teachers—both socially and academically—from birth onward. Unless a mother starts teaching at an early age, there exists almost no reason for her child to expect her to be a teacher at a later date.

Socially Acceptable Behavioral Norms

From our visits to clinics within *campos,* we found that both younger and older women reported looking for emotional, social, or educational help to solve problems. Their problems mainly dominated three areas:

(1) domestic, child care, and self-improvement options; (2) social class issues and access to financial assistance, career options, or informational services; and (3) academic concerns and access to knowledge. One asked for money, while fewer than five asked for a direct asset like a book or tuition; the vast majority was desperately seeking self-improvement options. They often appeared to be in a position of *generational hopelessness.*[42] Social class structure and cultural influences were predominately difficult due to rigid gender roles.[43]

Having no social security or retirement provisions appeared to cause the women to expect absolute obedience from their children, in order to instill the belief that caring for elderly parents was absolutely paramount.[44]

Data implied that a father's social standing appeared to be untarnished if he left his wife and child. However, not caring for an elderly parent, even by a man, appeared to create social upheaval. The overall impression during my research and my background studies was that respect for the elders was of more value than any other moral commitment or personality characteristic.[45] My research found that mothers could accept physical and mental disabilities as fate, regardless of the age of the relative, but could not accept behavior outside normal expectations of children or teens (in either gender), or of female adults. The concerns regarding children and teens related to hyperactivity or signs of disobedience (Table 3.0). The concern regarding adult females related to getting older and becoming the primary family leader.

Summary—What is a Campesino?

Most of the *campesinos* I know are industrious, friendly, family-oriented, and exceedingly generous with their knowledge. Innovation is their middle name. They place the needs of their family unit far above individual wants or needs.

They are usually not well nourished; they spend a lot of their disposable income on snack foods, sugary treats, and Coca-Cola. All of these items are expensive in Mexico, but they are status symbols. Observations confirmed that *campesinsos* wanted a better life for their families, especially for their children. Although food might be a basic, obvious, immediate daily need, those interviewed implied that it was also valuable to appear higher on the public hierarchy scale. In the same way that lighter skin color has historically helped African-Americans in the class structure, appearing more elevated on the social ladder through the use of status symbols is thought to have a long-term effect in assisting *campesino* children socially in Latin America.

Most mothers are extremely involved with their children, walking them considerable distances to activities, keeping them clean, and doing all they know how to do to keep them healthy. Respect is the paramount lesson taught to all children by their mothers. Fathers teach trades to their sons. Parents honor their own parents, their children's grandparents, to a fault and hesitate to step into unknown ways of doing things that are different from those they were taught. Things are often done the old traditional way among these subsistence farmers and their families. To the outsider, it may seem like a contradiction to want a higher status for the children who are being taught to do things in the same manner as their grandparents have done.

Table 3.0: Parents Emotional Behavioral Disorder (EBD) Concerns in Children by Age Groups

#	Age	EBD	Total Percent
51	1–60 days	5	3.6%
138	2–6 months	16	12.6%
127	6–12 months	25	37.3%
67	12–18 months	24	34.0%
47	18–24 months	16	38.3%
49	24–36 months	19	38.8%
42	36–48 months	14	33.3%
44	48–60 months	17	38.6%
71	over 60 months	26	36.6%
636		162	25.5%

The local church only one house lot away from my home is a very active place. Although there is no resident priest, the space is occupied at least fours days a week. Every year in mid-January, after about six weeks of daily fireworks through the December holidays, the dancers arrive for our Virgin of Guadalupe Community Festival. Everyone for miles around attends the festivities where the local rituals are perfomed with limitless joyfulness.

4 Defining a Ritualistic Lifestyle

"There is a time for everything, and a season for every activity under heaven: a time to be born and a time to die, a time to plant and a time to uproot, a time to kill and a time to heal, a time to tear down and a time to build, a time to weep and a time to laugh, a time to mourn and a time to dance,"

—INSPIRATION FOR "TURN, TURN, TURN" BY THE BYRDS

Bright Children Face "Hopeless" Futures

Hopelessness penetrates the atmosphere in the area of rural Mexico where I reside. Historical records state that is the norm in Latin America.[1]

"Hopeless" was the adjective that best described what I heard from adults.

Hopeless is the word mothers used when expressing their feelings about not having enough nutritious food in the house. It is also how men feel about scrambling to their boring work each morning, how old women feel about having no money for propane to run their marginal cook-stoves, and how mature men feel about their joint pain from years of manual labor. Even young girls' dreams are clouded by the realization that the boys they admire do not notice them because the boys dream solely of leaving for the U.S. The youthful boys see the expensive tennis shoes, flashy cars, or money for a fancy house as a possibility only pursuant to working in the U.S. Interviewees explained that all boys imagine themselves with those costly items, but they ignore the knowledge that most men who leave end up sending back sad excuses with little cash. Few actually return with fine treasures, because just as the proverbial

41

rainbow does not literally have a fortune at its end, the reality of finding well-paid work in the U.S. is far from the myths shared among boys.

Religion Is the Most Powerful Influence in the Indigenous People's Lives

The way these disillusioned people cope is by practicing their faith. All that occurs here, especially in areas which those from other cultures are quick to criticize (for repeated births, silent suffering, absolute obedience of women to men, abject poverty, lack of an education, little access to healthcare, poor nutrition, and more), is due to the Latin Americans' unrelenting devotion to faith— predominately the Roman Catholic faith. My observations were of a lifestyle dominated by religious traditions, which incorporate ritualistic, most likely pagan, practices with more recent Christian doctrines. My theory was confirmed within the country when I twice visited the Museum of Archeology in Mexico City, where the English translation stated that this transition had occurred all over Mexico. Both pagan and Christian traditions practiced sacrifices; today, this translates to the modern practice of giving gifts. Although the gifts are predominately cheap imports from China, the cost of those gifts is a sacrifice for these families.

I have a theory that, as humans, we yearn for the comfort of religious rituals or expressions of faith. We profess spirituality or other means of acknowledging a "higher power" as a way to comfort ourselves with the knowledge that we are loved and have value. At some level, we are assured that no matter how far away joy, success, admiration, or prosperity might seem to be, if we are loved, we have enough hope to make it through another day. Fortunately, the depth of faith found in rural Latin America is so powerful that it helps people to overcome much of the emotional heartache, even when their babies' bellies remain empty.

Life in rural Latin America has ritual woven into most aspects of living. People use faith to overcome adversity and tragedy.

The Roman Catholic faith has encouraged formation of large families by prohibiting the use of birth control, and the Latin American government has also encouraged reproduction due to its public honoring of pregnant or nursing mothers. On public busses, there are seats designated specifically for pregnant or nursing mothers. It is common to find parking spots reserved for the disabled around the world, but in Latin America, they are also labeled for pregnant women or mothers of tiny children. Historical fluctuations in family size and other social network changes in Latin America have often been a direct result of the governmental policies;[2] Latin America government tends to either encourage or discourage larger or smaller families through legislative changes. Social pressure also appears to be exceptionally strong; several teachers have told me that nursing a child or being pregnant is the highest form of achievement for a girl, as becoming pregnant is easier than attaining a higher social status. This occurs because academic success gains nothing socially for either sex until the third generation has repeated the pattern. This cultural norm is explained by the following interview.

Maria's Story

A woman I will call "Maria," participated in a research project[3] at a school on the Arizona-Sonora border. She has raised her two daughters, one son, one niece, and one nephew, without much assistance, predominately as a single parent. She leads her family within her faith—as an example of her beliefs, by inviting participation in worship, but not by beating her religious ideals into the young ones. Her example of a faith-based life is exemplified by the fact that her every breath comes from a deep place within her soul, and where she accepts every hardship as how a way of life occurs. Additionally, states she carries no resentments. She has a decidedly level head and a heart so oversized that it is a wonder that she can stand upright.

Maria is a true workaholic, working 12-hour days at the school and another four to eight hours on weekends. She relocated her nail and hair care salon to her own house, replacing her living room. She is always busy and gains clients solely by word of mouth. Maria usually has her head tilted downward, "talking care of business" either right next to the school director Esmerelda during the day, at home when Esmerelda is off, at home when she is running her beauty business at night, or at either place when she is caring for a child. Looking down toward her work does not mean she is unaware, however: If a child cries, she takes off like a shot! It must be the same way at home, because the five kids she is raising alone are always happy and self-assured. Her house is spotlessly clean, and the kids help her to keep it that way. It appears that she creates a "nest" of safety—physically, emotionally, and spiritually—for anyone who comes near her at the school or at home. If pressed by a direct question, she will tell you that her deep faith keeps her going and renews her energy.

Maria's friends said that "she appeared to have an invisible stream of love and trust radiating out from her." Many of the other women in the school showed the same qualities that stem from religious faith.

Nothing Carries the Social Value like a Person's Name

Another ritual practice is the retaining of both the mother's and the father's surname. Birth dates are not important, but names have elevated value. Names are used to define social status. Even medical personnel pay little attention to birth dates.[4] The two last names, with the mother's name following the father's name, provide the information of value—the data used to identify a person. Other cultural customs, like not giving children a first name for weeks, months, or even their entire childhoods, may seem odd to those from the U.S. In the U.S., the first and last names must be recorded on a birth certificate within hours of birth. However, delaying choosing a first name is widely accepted within the Latin American society. Names consistently appear to be of great value, and they are chosen extremely carefully. The final choice is usually confirmed during family conferences, which often take place months after a child is born but before a religious blessing, such as baptism, takes place. Additional names most often pertain to favored relatives, dear friends, saints, or other valued choices. There are also more names given during life transition markers. New names may come after completing the catechism course in the Catholic faith. When a couple marries, however, both people retain their own names. Each person, therefore, retains his or her own social status.

Children are given a long string of names, usually five or six of distinctive value. That unique combination makes them very unique and identifies them specifically and individually.

Locals explain that this characteristic is beneficial for specific identification, (1) to embarrass someone in the newspaper when arrested, or (2) to announce a wedding or other positive event. The following is from my field notes:

I inquired about the dates of birth of the two children I had just examined. The medical doctor made every effort to go through lots of files but still was unable to find the birth dates of the children within any of her medical records. The doctor said that sometimes even the mother cannot recall birth dates.[5]

Travel to Maintain Relationships is a Necessary Expense

The stress of bias and low socioeconomic status can affect the parent-child relationships,[6] but the practice of a ritualistic lifestyle requires family visits. Educational policy, the road out of low socioeconomic status in the U.S., is biased in Latin America. Perhaps the 220 years under Spanish rule, when Native Indians were not allowed to be educated, followed by 100 years of a dictatorship and gender inequality have all contributed to this difference between the countries in regard to education and position on the social class scale. [7]

If a family manages to have three generations of people gain both a professional education and financial success, only then does the social status of the family improve. Those I interviewed agreed that the higher-class social acceptance must be based on common elements of economic stability, education, and career title, and that at least two of these must be present for at least three generations.

The social status of a family improves only if the family manages to have three generations of people both gain a professional education and gain financial success. Those I interviewed agreed that the higher-class social acceptance must be based on common elements of financial success, education, and career title, and that at least two of these must be present for at least three generations.

Numerous interviewees in the teaching profession in Latin America[8] stated that there is a lack of benefit for the first one in the family to be educated. The following explains the factors behind this phenomenon:

1. less motivation in Latin America to gain an education than in the U.S.;
2. no access to student loans, because a better position in society with higher paying job is not likely to occur in order to repay them;
3. a different attitude toward time, which in Latin America is not conceived in a fashion that would plan three generations ahead.

This lack of immediate benefit may be viewed as one more reason to immigrate to the U.S., where post-graduate or college education elevates the individual's social status.

When moving to the U.S., Latino people of lower socioeconomic status make life-threatening attempts to cross the border. While living on

It would be an unusual day not to hear the sound of children playing in the background. All over the community children are free to walk, run, and play without interference; many watchful eyes make sure they are safe. The outdoor sounds change if there is a death or another community event requiring everyone's immediate attention. Relationships always come first; most families are interrelated.

the US/MX border, I have witnessed this many times firsthand. They take these chances in order to gain some hope for their families.[9] Often the dreams behind the hope include education, which in the U.S. provides a way to elevate social status by gaining professional title, position, or financial success.

The crossings occur no matter how futile the reality of making that trip may seem. Stories told from the experiences within families are passed around among friends. A young Latin American girl may be absolutely sure that she is *the one true love* of her same-aged Latin American boy and that he will *stay with her forever*. The reality of what occurs is often a lot different. Many single heads-of-household mothers have learned this the hard way.

During my research of 18 rural communities, I found that there was often only one old man residing within the community, as all of the other males had left to seek work elsewhere. My family lived about 10 miles north of the Mexican border for 12 years. During that period I observed that economic and social reality, day after emotionally endless day, as men "jumped" the border seeking employment. When the mothers whom I interviewed in small rural health departments asked Jolene and me for advice, we had none to offer them. The fact was that these women had already married, started a family, and needed financial resources.[10]

Mexican people still make the journey to *el norte* (the U.S.) with optimism.[11] Additionally, leaving employment in the U.S. for a Christmas journey south to visit the oldest family female is a part of the annual ritual. Even if death is the result, the effort is considered worth the price. Cultural rules dictate that when the matriarch must be visited by the whole family, even those working illegally in another country must come.[12] The deep traditional importance of these trips can be further appreciated by examining statistics, which show that 42% of rural heads of household of one-adult families live in poverty.[13] Where the funding comes from to make these sojourns for a holiday is anybody's guess.

Summary: Defining a Ritualistic Lifestyle

Unlike in the U.S., there is never an apology for speaking of activities related to the practice of a religion or for taking time off to tend to matters of faith (funeral, holiday, wedding, birthday, blessing, etc.), because all social, governmental, and national business calendars function around holy holidays in a totally matter-of-fact manner. Church bells ring several times during the week to announce church business meetings, youth or adult faith-based classes, and/or public religious services. Faith-based parades routinely stop traffic. Most children continuously wear religious symbols on their bodies and leave home every day with verbalized blessings. Unlike the common practice of attending religious services once a week in the U.S., faith-based practices in Latin America appear to have a much higher priority than employment, education, or even family obligations. From my observations, the Latinos who do not actively practice faith appear to have to take a hard stand to maintain their rejection of faith-based practice and status quo. Regardless of their declarations or non-belief, their words seem to fall on "deaf ears"—the rest of the community still invites them and expects them to participate in religious events, as though they had never said anything to excuse themselves from such activities or from those invitations.

All family members share the job of raising children.

5 The Focus of Life: Family

We all grow up with the weight of history on us. Our ancestors dwell in the attics of our brains as they do in the spiraling chains of knowledge hidden in every cell of our bodies.

—SHIRLEY ABBOTT

Nothing Comes Before Family

Defining family structure in rural Latin America is no easy task. I will draw from the knowledge of anthropologist Ruth Behar, who wove the story of how she had searched for her Jewish-Cuban roots through ethnography (a social science or anthropological method of research where data is gathered on human societies/heritages through observations, interviews, questionnaires, or similar field study methods) by "exploring the embedded nature of personal experience within the ethnographic process." Her search for the memories she had lost at the age of three, when she had left Cuba, drove her to collect the stories from the "abuelas" (grandmothers)—because she wanted to tell *stories about real people in real places*.[1] She was driven to find stories even though she did not know if they existed. Our work is similarly driven; however, ours is not a personal conquest, but rather a group passion to set right a moral and ethical misconception—that the disadvantaged lowest socioeconomic class of Latinos lacks access to education in both Latin America and the U.S. We uncovered the attitudes of women we interviewed, and are offering here to help explain current literature regarding life in Latin America or in some Mexican-American immigrant homes.

49

In the U.S., people who need assistance enjoy many advantages; how-ever, it is hard to imagine a high level of optimism from women who live in Latin America, where many of these advantages are lacking.

When an educator or an instructor is working with those from the Latin American culture, privacy issues must be kept in mind. Degrading any family member by publically voicing a family secret will create an impenetrable barrier to communication.

It is the high regard for children in general and the cultural view in particular that compel all adults within the extended family to care for the children.

Strong cultural values create this environment (children are clearly the benefactors).[2] Researchers have shown that parental attitudes have a heavy impact on the children's ability to achieve academic success.[3]

Family Teamwork is the Norm

Researchers of Latin American bilingual families have found that close family ties within the home result in a quiet acceptance and deep joy for all members who do their part to help the whole family.[4]

The extended family provides cooperation and mutual support. What works satisfactorily within the family unit will work equally well in schools if lessons in each subject are a cooperative effort.[5] Do not assume this extends into the community. The defined family unit is inwardly focused.

If a Latin American family can afford the construction materials, the members build a high wall around their family unit. If no physical wall exists, a symbolic wall separating the family from the community is still present. There are few instances of volunteering in the community, because the focus is on the family or the extended family, not on the neighbors. The concept of volunteering is not understood. The Mexican government is working hard to encourage the concept of working as a team to clean up waste and recycle, but it is difficult. Community pride and teamwork are shown with the yearly celebration—and that is about the extent of the commitment, because caring for the family takes all available assets.

Written Communication

The inability to read community notices often adds to the lack of com-munity involvement. The home frequently lacks printed material in any language and, therefore, lacks the tools necessary for parental involvement in helping children with homework.[6] There are no opportunities in the home to practice reading in order to become a more capable reader. Immigrant Latin American family members are often Limited English Proficient (LEP) and cannot help with English homework either. In all cases, written communication is restricted, which limits written interaction inside and outside of the home.

Health is Always a Major Concern

A Lab Test Story

Yes, there really are awful creatures who take up residence in the guts of people living in or visiting Mexico. The medicine required to kill these creatures costs about $18 (USD) for six pills and needs to be taken once a day for three days every three months. That is prohibitively expensive for a family living in rural areas. Nevertheless, cost is only the beginning of the problem; finding out what bug needs killing is a major hurdle that a rural person also cannot overcome.

My own personal lab test experience from when I was quite ill further explains why staying healthy is so hard in Mexico. To find out what "bug" I had, I needed to produce a stool sample and have it examined by a lab technician. Everyone told me that such an examination would cost about $7 (USD). I went to a lab owned by my doctor's friend. I was told that the owner was reliable, but I was very disappointed when she asked for three times the average $7 rate—equivalent to the cost of a day's pay for a construction worker. I also had to drive into her clinic to pick up a special cup, as a sterile glass jar was not good enough to use. So, I had to make two trips. Each took an hour and two gallons of gas. I was given no written instructions.

After I dropped off the first sample, on my second trip, the owner asked if the sample was over two hours old. I said that it was, and then she refused to take it. So, I returned the following day with a fresh sample. However, once again she asked for another sample. She finally accepted my third sample, delivered on the fourth trip.

I asked what day and what time I might get the results; I was feeling quite anxious as I was pretty sick and had been for several days. She replied, "four o'clock" and held up four fingers. By that afternoon, I had made six trips and used 12 gallons of gas. I stood outside her office, in the hot sun, for an hour before she arrived. I was feeling very ill. My gut was letting me know that my blood sugar levels dropped too low, because I had not eaten properly due to the illness. The lab lady asked for my original receipt, so I went outside into my car and brought it back. She took it but refused to give me the results; she also refused to give the results to my physician over the phone or to e-mail them to my physician. She explained that a lab official would sign the results sometime before 7 P.M. and only then could I look at them! Words cannot describe the emotional upset I felt at that moment; I was too sick to think rationally. I simply left, physically shaking.

Why did she say to arrive at 4 P.M.? I have no idea. Why did she not explain the process upfront? I have no idea. What I do know is that I made a total of eight trips, that each trip took an hour, and that I paid for the lab work. It cost about $66 (USD), or the equivalent to a week's worth of wages for a Mexican, to find out what kind of a bug was inside me. Had I come by bus, as most Mexicans do, I could not have captured the sample and made it to her lab in less than two hours. Furthermore, had I been the parent of six or more children, I would have not had the time or money to treat my illness. This is why rural people lose ground in the race toward getting or staying healthy. Trying to deal with a medical issue under such impossible conditions is a pet peeve of mine, because I know that my neighbors have no options. I had options, and yet even I could not get treated humanely.

Obesity is a Big Health Problem

Health is undermined in the U.S. by sedentary indoor activities resulting in childhood obesity. Lots of Coca-Cola, snacks, and sugar have made Mexico the second-fattest nation as of September 2010.[7] Obesity and its resulting health complications of that trend often reduce alertness in school and happiness elsewhere.[8] There is a big difference between being well-nourished and being fat. The former produces healthy bodies and alert minds, while the latter comes from too many calories that may or may not be beneficial to the human body or mind. Lack of a well-rounded education due to being unhealthy, and being unable to access or retain information can undermine both wealth and happiness.[9] Fortunately, the rural students and adults walk a great deal daily, which helps them to maintain a healthier weight; the city students do not fare as well, as they ride a public bus most of the time.

Other Health Considerations

One disorder, attention deficit hyperactivity disorder (ADHD), is asymptomatic when the child is outdoors.[10] As interviews and my research showed, there is very little ADHD in Mexico. Family therapist Michael

Gurain states that 70% to 80 % of children are able to adapt to overstimulation.[11] Are the other 20% to 30% in special education or detention classes? ADHD is not a problem in Latin America in a way it exists in the U.S., since the children are often outdoors. Additionally, ADHD symptoms are socially unacceptable in the Latin American culture. Now that we know that the brain adapts to culture and modifies itself based on the culture where the person is living, it makes sense that different cultures have unfamiliar medical or psychological conditions.[12] This medical discovery further explains why my 2009 research found only one child with ADHD symptoms out of 665 examined children.[13]

Environmental and social problems affect a child's life in many ways. Because we are aware of the far-reaching negative health effects of water and air pollution, reading about these effects is very common. Light pollution also has far-reaching negative effects on people, but little has been written about it in regard to animal migration habits. And what about the constant distractions of noise pollution? Richard Lovu quotes a child stating, "In the city you can't hear anything, because you hear everything."[14] This is how modern urban children grow up. It is only in the outdoors away from cities that children can enjoy any semblance of silence.

Another factor to consider is there are more serious restrictions, even laws, against touching another person, both in schools and in the workplace. Nancy Dess warns of the harmful outcome resulting from these restrictions when she points out that among primates who lack touch, infant mortality increases and adults have more aggression.[15] Perhaps that is one of the reasons behind anger in modern urban U.S. schools; it might also explain what I have observed in non-urban Mexican schools: a lack of anger, far fewer competitive activities, a willingness to work without supervision, and an eagerness to be helpful in group efforts with classmates—even "slow" classmates. I have continuously observed this behavior over the last six years while working with rural and urban Mexican school children. Although my experience teaching in a large urban city was shorter, I was interacting with low socioeconomic Mexican neighborhood schools each time. The behaviors involving social skills among the first generation immigrant students were nearly identical to the rural schoolchildren. Second-generation immigrants do not tend to exhibit the same social behaviors as rural raised or first generation students.

Understanding the advantages that Latino children, who are raised in agricultural environments, bring to the classroom might help teachers to engage them into school lessons with less effort. Understanding what children are thinking based on where and how they are raised—indoors or outside and with or without touch—may help parents, teachers, and peers find alternative methods, inside and outside of the classroom/training room, to increase health, wealth, and happiness as adulthood outcomes.[16]

Teachers in Latin America are always touching Latino children; this probably helps the children to overcome some emotional challenges that exist. Immigrant Latino students must be confused and disoriented in U.S. schools, where touch is prohibited in educational environments.

Self-Reliance Improves Student's Health

Mexican students have some major emotional development advantages, because as children they have adult responsibilities that increase maturity. They spend a large portion of each day outdoors, which increases their attention span. They spend little time in front of a TV and even less on the Internet, which decreases distraction due to outside stimulation.

Science has made it clear that the problems facing U.S. parents and educators are significantly different today than they were a century ago,[17] and solutions are often far less obvious. Even a decade ago it would have been hard to imagine that "the most serious threat to the continuation *of the health in the human species is the direct result of overprotection of the young children*" of today.[18] Research informs us that many parents are guilty of allowing technology to be both the babysitter and the mentor to their children.[19] These children are kept physically "safe" indoors, in front of a television or a computer, while being deprived of experiences in nature—the primary teacher and healer for any human being.[20] Rural Latinos do not face this dilemma.

A 1998 Carnegie Mellon University study found that spending only a few hours a week on the Internet resulted in higher levels of depression and loneliness in all ages of users;[21] this information confirms that an electronic babysitter is not a good alternative to developing our eighth intelligence, the naturalist intelligence.[22]

The media is responding to a scientific fact. A *Parade Magazine* front page headline stated, "Special Report: Raising Healthier Kids." The subtitle read, "Learn about the exciting new theory experts believe may solve many of your child's ills."[23] The *Parade* cover showed a woman and child, who were appropriately aged to be mother and daughter, both dressed in green sweat suits; they were hugging while standing on a computer-enlarged pair of green leaves.[24] In the same month, the cover of *Instructor Magazine* had a picture of two students, an Asian girl and an African-American boy, painting their white, blonde, European-descent teacher with green paint; the wall, the desk, the floor, and the blackboards were also partially covered in green paint. The issue was titled, "Be a Hero for the Planet," and the title for the lead story read, "How Green Classrooms are Reconnecting Kids with Nature."[25] This positive trend may be the response to comments by scientists regarding climate changes and the resulting increased awareness of the pressing need to teach eco-literacy. Many developing countries, including Latin America, have surpassed the U.S. in being informed about nature.[26] School is the perfect place to start teaching about the outdoors; physical education and field trips should not be limited. Keep in mind that Latin American children shine in this area of expertise.

Privacy in Social Matters is Paramount

How Latinos conduct their social lives with friends and family varies a great deal from how they behave in social situations with the outsiders. Latinos are very shy about home matters in the workplace or at school. In the U.S. special-education classes, especially for severe and profoundly disabled students, helping students to function at home is a major focus of each school class. Educators and instructors intend to help the students transfer what is learned in the classroom to the workplace, to the home environment, or to a higher-level class; home practice will make the learning more permanent. When a teacher or a trainer is working with those from the Latin American culture, the privacy issue must be kept in mind.

Researchers have applied methods of training people in workshops with the expectation that performance within the workplace will mirror the workshop experience. They have found that cultural factors interfere with that transfer process.[27] Relating to the existing funds of knowledge helps overcome that problem.

Special-education teachers refer to this transfer from the classroom to the home as *a generalization,* something very difficult and sometimes almost unattainable for children with severe cognitive disorders. The learning of a task like pouring tea from a metal teapot in school is not transferred to the use of a ceramic teapot at home, because the teaching of "generalization" of an activity to other objects is not completed by the teacher inside the student's actual home. Cultural issues of privacy in the Latin American home may interfere, because life inside the home, as family custom dictates, is often kept from the public eye.

Care of the Elderly is a Social Expectation

Social norms for indigenous Latino adults dictate that children are raised to be caregivers of their parents later in life. This is the obvious solution, as there are no social security, retirement, or other similar programs in place to help the parents. For this reason, it is vital that children are absolutely obedient to parents and grandparents, a trend other researchers have also noticed in other Latin American communities. This expectation is reflected in where people live, whom they marry, what employment they accept, and whether or not they continue their education.

As a result, a Latino adult's or child's level of interest, ambition, or involvement in matters of business or social life outside of the immediate home is often negligible; it frequently does not even extend into their local community.

A Striking Discovery

The phenomenon of social security is something I discovered as a consequence of analyzing data related to extreme concerns of caregivers regarding their children's stated inappropriate behavior. This seemingly strong overreaction by caregivers to behavioral problems implies that good behavior assures *social security* for the elders through respect for the elders.[28] There are no social security, retirement, or other similar programs inside Latin America to provide for aging parents or other elders; to fill the need for elderly care, children are raised to be absolutely obedient to parents and grandparents.[29]

The data implies that generations of offspring are expected to remain respectful their entire lives, always staying in or near the community to care for their aging parents or grandparents.[30]

The children's behavior, observed by Jolene and me, appeared to include normal childhood activities and actions; it fit well within the expected ranges of U.S. standards. The described behavior outside of health clinics appeared to involve normal childhood adventures and other behavior expressed by a healthy child. With that realization, I looked for validation or rebuttal to explain why Latino children's behavior was expected to be so mellow. I questioned the indigenous people who had left the *campo* lifestyle, who had become well-educated, bi-lingual, and had expanded their social standing by frequently visiting the U.S. both for business and social reasons. In each case, I was assured that social security within the *campo* was maintained by raising lots of children to be well behaved and dedicated to caring for their family for a lifetime.

All interviewees stated that they lost status within their family by moving and focusing on a world outside their campo.

The interviewees' continued attentiveness to the family's needs did not compensate for the expectation of physical presence, at all times, to care for the elders.

Summary: The Focus of Life is Family

Life in rural communities is hard for everyone, but there are some distinct advantages. Although people of all ages seem to live in heightened survival mode, adapting to life with amazing agility and resourcefulness, they also receive all of the benefits of living in nature. These are benefits not found in urban environments. Quality tools for any job are simply too costly to be acquired, and people expect to spend a portion of each day repairing something. As a result, they are more adaptable. They have a great deal of "common sense" as they adapt to both natural and artificial challenges. I was always stunned to see how they react to various challenges without expressed anger. Adults from the U.S. typically expect mechanical and electronic items to function perfectly most of the time. Residents of rural Latin America have learned that there is no way to avoid things breaking; instead of blaming poor quality of workmanship, they accept fate and find more and more innovative ways to make things last.

The agricultural Latin American residents appear to mange hardship by emotionally supporting each other, using their relationships for extensive networking, and making a strong effort to look on the bright side of life—while living in an environment that scholars frequently describe as *generational poverty*.[31] In my opinion, the lessons learned by rural Latin American children from their close family ties in a natural setting are priceless assets to their lives. These lessons should be shared in the classroom or the workplace to help other people learn to cope with challenges with a similar means of adapting.

Don Mackenzie, the volunteer work foreman in the background, is overseeing the laying of a wide, sturdy foundation for a two-story community center. Mexican men who are in the construction trades have highly developed mechanical thinking skills, specifically related to the raw materials they use in the mountainous areas. Granite rock, other natural stones, concrete blocks, and bricks are predominately used as the foundation. Concrete is reinforced with linked metal wires. The work is very labor-intensive and slow, but the result lasts much longer than the life of the builder.

6 The Role of Fathers

This gave me occasion to observe, that when men are employed they are best contented. For on the days they worked they were good-natured and cheerful; and with the consciousness of having done a good days work they spent the evenings jolly; but on the idle days they were mutinous and quarrelsome, finding fault with their pork, the bread, etc. and in continual ill-humor.

—Benjamin Franklin, Autobiography, 1771

Social Expectations of Mexican Men

Keep in mind, when reading this chapter, since 1996 I have incorporated interviews, focus groups, surveys, observations, and/or professional questioning of experts to comprehend the lifestyles, ritualistic views, cultural practices and/or other attitudinal influences on Latino adults. Throughout this book, I often compare the results of research I gathered on the Arizona-Sonora border to help the reader understand the culture and the resulting lifestyle of *campo* men and women in Central Mexico. I also refer to additional research I have done in Central and Western Mexico in *campos* and in cities.

The *campo* men are taught from birth that they represent Jesus to all Mexican men and women, and, like Jesus "raging in the temple at the moneychangers" or doing something less honorable, their behavior is accepted. My data is included to help the reader understand why. The male dominates his wife and children. He also dominates any single female family member—a sister, a maiden aunt, a widow, or any other unmarried females or children who are relatives.[1]

Domestic violence and incest are often overlooked by both sexes and the public as a "normal" aspect of life in Latin America.

Incest is more common in the rural areas because it's difficult to obtain any assistance for the victims. Transportation costs money, child care is not easily accessible, and people cannot take time to travel far without drawing attention from the community. In fact, oppression in rural areas is harder to overcome because assistance is physically further away and may require money. Additionally, asking for help carries negative stigma.

The clearest observation of gender bias is the common observation of a male child wearing a helmet while riding a motorcycle or bicycle, while his father and his sister ride helmet-free. I have yet to see any female child wear a helmet while on a motorcycle. Another common sight is the oldest male child in the passenger seat sitting next to his father who is the driver, while the mother and all younger siblings are sitting in the back seat.[2]

I often see Latino boys aged 8 to 12 driving older women around, but I have never seen a young female doing the same thing in rural communities. Latino boys of all ages ride burros or horses every day, some selling milk out of buckets that hang off the burros and others driving home straw-covered burros. They also use mules to plow in the rocky fields. Normally, they do these activities without any supervision. I have seen one young Latina female, under 15, on a horse without supervision. The only other time I saw a nationalized girl on a horse in Latin America was at our annual horse show event. The queen of the event made a short pass through the riding area with everyone coming in behind her; there was one bronco rider who was a female, in her 20s or 30s, but she did not appear to be of Latino descent, as her hair was light and her build was tall and large-boned like that of a foreigner—she certainly was not indigenous.

Gender-Biased Outlook

Anticipating my move to Central Mexico from the Arizona-Sonora border, I was shocked to learn the extent of gender bias toward young females in the state of Guanajuato, the exact center of all of Mexico. Many research participants have stated that Guanajuato is an extremely conservative state. In the town by the same name, there are some legal options to help women with issues related to gender; however, in the rural area where I live, as in other agricultural communities, there are typically no options outside of family emotional support or defiance, depending on the family's outlook.

Several people I interviewed told me that 12 was the standard age of consent for a girl. Therefore, unless a girl is younger than 12 years of age, she is presumed to have agreed to have sex.

A recent article in *National Geographic* in Spanish interviewed Veronica Sanchez, who runs Las Libres in Guanajuato, Mexico; Las Libres is the central legal option for gender issues in this area. Veronica offers advice to abused women. Her life is constantly threatened.[3]

When I questioned "Helena" about gender differences within the Mexican culture in 2007, she offered the following summary of that lifestyle:

The woman gets the family ahead (i.e. she becomes the family leader, head of household, [and] takes charge) after the woman gets pregnant and the man leaves.[4]

This woman had an associate's degree and two years of medical training. She was the mother of two boys too young for preschool, had a stable marriage to a successful Latino man and lived in the U.S. She was 32 years of age.[5]

Then I asked her, "Does unconditional love have a down side?" She informed me that these Mexican women universally identify with the gender bias favoring males. The women agreed that the unfortunate outcome of unconditional love for the male children—as well as low expectations of them as children and adults—is the males' irresponsible, yet socially acceptable, behavior.[6]

An interview I recorded in 2007 with Maria, just over a mile from the Arizona border, summarized the role of the females, half of whom walked to daily jobs in the U.S. from their homes in Mexico. Maria was very clear that asking male parents about their dreams for their children's future was a waste of time; she suggested that we instead ask the mothers, the grandmothers, the sisters, or the aunts. "Ask those who are caring for the children," she explained.[7] She elaborated by saying that by asking those who know the children, the women, I would receive truthful answers. "Do not bother asking the fathers anything about how they see their children's future, because that question [has] never occurred to them," she continued.

The following statement was agreed upon by 11 out of 13 women in a focus group:

The Latino male can leave his family, leave his job, not attend church, and behave in a manner inside his community that is less than honorable, and yet his social status is relatively unharmed. It is not their responsibility to think about it [their behavior], do anything about their behavior, or take any credit or blame for how it turns out.

Maria was speaking for herself, but in a sweeping manner she indicated that a Latina female has one job: caregiver. "The way she rates her success is how her children turn out; period. " Maria went on to explain that, "Latino men have only one job, to earn a living; some do [earn a living], other's don't [earn a living], but that is their only job."[8] In the same way, the boys expect their needs, like getting help with homework, to take precedence over the needs of the girls.[9]

Observations of Male Employees

Our *campesino* male neighbors are subsistence farmers, carpenters, metal workers, or stonemasons; they work in an outdoor environment and are in touch with the earth nearly all day, every day. Their wives are also outdoors a good share of the day—cooking, caring for domestic animals, washing clothing by hand and hanging it out, walking to buy groceries or to visit other women; these are the cultural expectations for women during the day.[10] Greenwald and Banaji state that "social behavior often is expressed in an implicit or unconscious fashion," instead of being under conscious control. [11, 12] That thought process explains why childhood experiences are so valid in any environment and, perhaps, why a bond developed between people living and working outdoors is different than the bond formed between those who are normally indoors.[13]

Teamwork in outdoor environments is seen throughout the workday.

Teamwork develops critical thinking skills when team members face interactions with animals or situations in nature that require quick problem solving and rapid responses. Men frequently work in close cooperation with others. Research has shown that people in the U.S. often lack exposure to nature[14] and, therefore, have limited opportunities to develop critical thinking skills under those conditions.[14,15] Perhaps the skills that have developed in rural Central Mexico, especially by the males working outdoors, are not well known in places where people interact in work and domestic environments that are predominately indoors. It may be

A handmade adobe brick wall being built in 2011. The man is the father of five young children. He nurtures each one at home and when they stop by his workplace with his meals.

that conditions that require specific critical thinking skills are more likely to exist in places where children and adults spend a great deal of time outside.[16] In these rural areas, children (usually males) are often responsible for moving livestock from one pasture to another, which takes many hours a day. Other children (usually females) are responsible for washing clothing and dishes, taking care of the younger siblings, and cooking outdoors.[17] The men build the indoor sleeping and outdoor working spaces for the females.

In urban and rural areas of Central Mexico, children walk to school, have recess and two meals outdoors at school, and spend afternoon and evening hours outdoors in recreational activities. In outlying and city areas, both sexes often are the authority over younger siblings, frequently outdoors, tasked with a level of responsibility inconceivable by the standards of more developed countries. Teamwork and a strong relationship factor, especially within the extended families, are evident throughout each day in the rural villages.[18]

Juan's Story

The first day we moved to the village, a young man named "Juan" asked for employment. We hired him, and he continued to work for us nearly every week for over a year. Juan was very proud of having fathered two daughters; the oldest, Lupie, 12, was academically gifted, while the youngest, Karin, 10, was unable to read anything until fourth grade. Lupe had nearly mastered English already, while Karin struggled. Juan's wife, Maria, was four years older than he was but looked 10 years older than her years—as do most of the women in rural areas. Maria had few skills related to anything other than domestic activities. She was considered to be a good mother, wife, sister, and aunt; her time was willingly spent helping the members of the family. Juan said he worked two jobs to keep Maria and the girls well dressed; Maria said he worked because he liked beer. Their two-room, unfinished block house, with an outside bathroom, was always open to us for visits and celebrations.

When we needed to buy something or when we needed information, Juan would bring in a relative, find us a good price, or tell us where to go. When we were out of funding for two employees and needed to cut back to only one, Juan offered his position to his older brother, "Jose," who was grateful to take the offer. Jose had a bigger family, a heart condition, and not as much youthful energy. He was the father of five children, including 1-year-old twins. Jose greeted us each day with an open but shy smile and a firm handshake. He had extensive architectural experience and outstanding critical thinking skills. His children visited to bring him food once a day on days when none had been prepared prior to his leaving home early in the morning. The family lived within a walking distance of our house and became a part of our extended family.

The following transcript is from a morning conversation with Juan:

After our typical morning introductions, he became solemn as he told me of the events of the evening before: a child of three had died. My sadness deepened as he explained that the mother had gone to Guanajuato and left her 6-year-old to care for the younger child in her absence. Apparently there was an open cistern (due to water storage) with stairs from the house leading to the top of it. The 3-year-old climbed up the stairs, fell into the water, and drowned, and the 6-year-old never heard a thing. A neighbor was called later, but it was too late.[19]

The following transcript is from an evening fiesta at Juan's house with Jose and their mother in attendance. Their mother is the head of the family. Her husband left for the U.S. 23 years ago; since then, he has visited his wife and eight children only twice.

As the sun began to sink behind the horizon, I moved closer and then even nearer to the fire. I had spent all evening near the family matriarch, so enjoying her company and Jolene's translation of what I missed of her conversations. We watched her patiently make over 100 tortillas and more than two-buckets-full of cornmeal mash, as more and more people arrived to eat and join the festivities. One couple that arrived just late enough to go easily unnoticed in the evening dusk was not ignored. They were clearly higher on the social scale. It was immediately clear to us from their clothing, demeanor, and others' reaction that we were in the presence of welcomed guests and not local family members. The woman handed Maria a cake and remarked about being happy to join her to celebrate her saint's day. What we learned later was that the couple had employed Maria for about two years as housekeeper three days a week. Juan announced, after several beers, that both he and his wife were honored to have both of their patrons at home at the same time. Don looked at me and stated that he had never imagined himself a "patron" to anyone.[20]

This morning I thought about the evening we had spent last night at Juan's house, in his yard, with his family. I am experiencing an ethnographer's dream: acceptance by those I wish to study, service, and record for others.[21]

Latino Fathers as Caregivers

The comments under this heading may seem very strange in context of social acceptance that Latino males are not expected to be responsible parents, but that is exactly why viewing fathers who assume the role of caregivers has attracted so much attention from this observer.

Unlike fathers in some other cultures, Latino fathers seem to have no hesitation showing their feelings about their children. It is not uncommon to see one of these fathers with tears in his eyes as he discusses his children.

This father clearly
adores his young son.

Fernando's Story

Fernando, who is in his mid-40s, is handsome enough to be a model. His wife is equally attractive. They both have traditional Native Indian physical features that are highlighted by their radiant personalities, which confirm to onlookers their deep roots in Mexican culture.

They met in high school, married soon afterward, and seem to be totally in unison with their life goals. His stable, quiet, loving wife has been a kindergarten teacher for about 25 years. They have three daughters: 12, 14, and 20 years of age. All three girls radiate a deep respect for their parents, as well as individual self-confidence blended with respect for everyone they meet. They seem to be a carefree family with clear goals, to which everyone is committed.

They serve as role models for Fernando's birth community, where his father had been a prominent landowner until he sold off what he had in order to support his 14 children. The father's first wife had died after giving birth to three children, and his second wife gave birth to 11 children; she still lives in the same community. Fernando was the first son to graduate from high school and the first sibling to attend college. He is a voracious reader of Spanish and English, a model life-long learner.

Although he is self-employed and works extensive hours doing physical labor, his life's focus is his bright, caring, and goal-oriented daughters. His employment affords him a moderate income, yet his oldest daughter is in medical school. His two younger daughters learned English from spending a semester in Texas with their aunt and uncle and studying it hard in Mexico. They dream of attending college in the U.S. To help them reach their goal, Fernando has managed to become a U.S. citizen and is working toward helping them do the same. When his wife retires, they plan to live in the U.S. until all of the girls finish college. Every time I see Fernando with his family, I admire his role as a strong, stable family man who is totally in tune with his position as family provider and role model to his children.

Alberto's Story

"Alberto" is the name I will use for Fernando's younger brother. Both boys attended high school and college in Mexico City while staying with a relative. The brothers are emotionally close—like twins. As adults, they share life and caregiving roles as strong, stable family men totally in tune with their positions as family providers and role models to their children.

Alberto's wife is an equally committed member of the family unit; she is only eight months shy of finishing her law degree. They are currently raising three girls, two of their own plus a niece. Their oldest daughter, 11, is highly self-confident and enthusiastic; she is an outstanding student and appears to need the attention of the stereotypical only child, which she was for many years. Their youngest daughter, 2, suffers from congenital health problems that cause her to have seizures several times a day; her doctors are now considering brain surgery. About eight months ago, they took in their 6-year-old niece after her mother had died of cancer. The niece's father is incapable of caring for her, as he is never sober. His alcoholism likely damaged his daughter *in utero*: The girl is unable to learn or retain information, which makes schoolwork an unattainable challenge. Alberto and his wife are feeling the strain of taking on too much caregiving at a time when their own family demands are emotionally and physically overwhelming. An observer cannot help but be in awe of such generous community members, who reach the upper limits of cultural expectations for family care.

Jose's Story

Jose is in his late 30s or early 40s. He is from a very large family, but his father had left for the U.S. 23 years ago and just returned recently. He only visited twice in the 23 years he was gone, so Jose's mother had to be strong and make her children self-reliant. Jose is probably her greatest success; he is very emotionally stable. Perhaps "blessed" with a weak heart, he, unlike his siblings, does not drink alcohol. All of the money he makes apparently goes into his home and for his family. He even owns a Volkswagen Beetle. Car ownership is a very rare accessory in this community.

Jose is often seen carrying, feeding, or dressing a child. He is a natural role model as a protector and plays no macho role in front of his children or the public. Although he is an accomplished engineer, stonemason, and construction leader, he is, nonetheless, always humble. He quietly works long and hard, and without complaining about the fact that he has five children to support.

His small-framed wife gave birth to twin boys one year ago; the next child, another boy, is six years old. The fourth child is the only girl; she is 10. Their firstborn is a boy of 11. Like his father, he is a quiet, humble young man willing to assume responsibility for being the oldest. The following field notes share what life is like for Jose's children living in a predominately indigenous village and rarely seeing life outside that village. This is a wonderful tale of three children who experienced for the first time in the summer of 2010 how others live in a city in the 21st century.

Jose is the head of his family; his wife's name is Lupe. The high self-disciplined standards set by Jose are reflected on his children. Far more mature than his years, tall, slender Marco is a model example of refinement and class at the tender age of 11. He works hard to dress older than his years in a more formal style, excels in his schoolwork, and always watches out for the younger children. The only girl, Fernanda, reminds one of a beautiful butterfly. She is a wisp of quiet and extremely polite beauty, a vision just quietly floating by before one's eyes, never assertive or aggressive. At 10 years of age, she looks like a carbon copy of her mother. Fernanda is more dedicated to reading than is common in the campo. The long-time baby of the family, Alfredo, at 6 years of age and with a square build, is a visual miniature version of his father. The identical twin boys, whom I will call Norieto and Norbeto, will turn 1 year on August 3. They are much bigger than the other three children were at the same age. They look just like their dad and mirror everyone's quiet nature.

We learned early in our living among Latinos that gifts are an important part of the culture. It has been our habit to give gifts to the families of men whom we employ. Therefore, Jose's twin sons have had the food supplement that Lupe likes to have to augment her breast milk. This has been possible, even though it costs what Jose earns as one day's wages, because we have provided it as a bonus to him. The beginning of the school year is a major expense for all the families in the campo. Last year we bought winter coats for nearly a dozen children of those fathers who worked for us and for another nonprofit, whose construction project we had been overseeing. This year, with just two fathers working for us, we planned to offer more help to fewer children. Therefore, Friday afternoon I asked Jose if the family had any plans for Saturday, since my husband and I had errands in Leon and wanted to take the three oldest children along to get them some school clothes. He was agreeable but warned us that Alfredo often "runs around." I assured him that I had many dog collars and leashes; he laughed as we settled on 10:30 a.m. as a good time to pick up the children.

We arrived in the ravine below their house at 10:30 a.m. I walked up the grassy side of the hill, past the rabbit and goat pens, wandered among the free-range chickens, ducked under the laundry hung on barbed wire lines low enough for Lupe to reach and headed toward their house. I hollered "Hola," the customary greeting usually translated as a casual "Hi." There in the doorway stood all three children, spotlessly clean and wearing their best clothing overshadowed only by their bright smiling faces. All three greeted me with wide-eyed anticipation apparent in every aspect of their body language. Lupe greeted me, and I handed her two knit shirts I had found on sale the day before for the twins. She thanked me. I told her that we had many errands, so I was not sure how long this trip would take; she assured me that it was no problem.

Like the Pied Piper, I led and the children followed me back to our SUV and eagerly but quietly entered the back seat that must have seemed very big to them. I had laid out an appropriately colored knit shirt for each child. Each child sat down, waited, and listened carefully as I explained how to use the seatbelts. I helped them get fastened in; each of them was cautious as they placed the folded shirts on their laps, gently examining only the corners. Not one of them opened the shirt until they got back home in the evening; they simply grinned and thanked us many times.

The hour-long ride took us out of the ravine, along the dirt road toward the closest town, over the yet-to-be repaired open sewer line that dumps into the city's drinking water, and toward paved roadways. Within 15 minutes, we were driving on pavement and 20 minutes later we were on a four-lane highway. The quiet voices in the back seat were in sharp contrast to the enormous eyes looking outside. When asked, they all said that they had never been to León, Guanajuato. Alfredo fought to stay awake during the whole trip to the city, stretching his small frame so that he could see everything outside.

We entered the mega-parking lot of the Home Depot, Office Max, and Costco and parked. Not a sound came from the back seat as the children carefully put down their shirts and joined us outside. Each took the others' hands and with caution followed toward one store's entrance outside the mall. My husband left us there and went to the Home Depot alone, while I started upstairs to the children's clothing area. The walk was very slow, because the children were in shock as they looked at shiny furniture, appliances, cell phones, sewing machines, and household electronics. We started up the stairs in silence. As soon as we arrived at the top, a saleswoman greeted us and sized up the situation: a mature white-haired lady with little sun tan holding hands with three black-eyed, dark-skinned children who appeared in a state of shock. She obviously trusted that the children were in my care, because she inquired if school clothes were the business of the day. I assured her that this was our mission. She hailed a friend to take Fernanda to the girls' clothing section and our work began.

Alfredo wandered about four feet away to look at shiny plastic backpacks, but quickly returned to my side. I checked the size tag in Marco's jeans and then watched as he grinned full-faced when I asked him to choose if he'd rather try on acrylic dress pants or blue jeans. The dress pants won out, and off he went with the saleslady and four pairs to try on. Turning my attention to 6-year-old Alfredo, I discovered that his way-too-big jeans had a four-inch cuff, so checking sizes didn't help. We checked out dress pants and jeans, but his eyes "popped" when he spotted the cargo pants. We settled on one size 4 and one size 5 in the same color and style before we turned toward socks. Marco picked out a three-pair set of two black and one white; all very mature in style to go with his two pairs of navy-blue colored slacks. Fernanda was back with her saleslady asking questions, when Alfredo spotted the single red, white, and matching color pairs of loudly printed socks, which he chose. Then we all turned to join Fernanda in the girl's area, where the shoes were also located.

We picked out shoes for Fernanda first. There were about 12 pairs to choose from, and that was simply too many. The saleslady's help was priceless, as she knew that narrowing it down to two pairs was far more manageable. Fernanda agreed that just a little bigger would make them last longer. The black Mary Janes with a Velcro strap and a heart on the side was her choice. I lifted Alfredo onto a chair seat to see the 20 pairs he had to choose from; he was not at all intimidated and got just the pair of slip-on blacks with Velcro closure that he wanted. Like Alfredo, Marco knew exactly what he wanted to replace the highly stylized, and too-large, shoes that he was wearing. I noted that each of them chose very sensible black shoes with gripper soles that make walking in the campo so much easier; not a rhinestone or fad design in sight. The children were unable to locate tennis shoes to fit them in a style they liked, so it was over to the backpacks instead.

Marco wanted a poor-quality blue backpack that said "America" on it, and Fernanda wanted a very cheap one with Tinkerbell (and the Disney logo). I placed each of the backpacks they chose on a table surface with the much-higher-quality ones beside them. Marco picked up the black back-pack with multiple compartments, a water bottle holder, and a separate cell-phone sleeve. He rejected the poor-quality blue backpack. Fernanda left the Tinkerbell backpack in favor of one with a lovely blonde girl on the first of many compartments, a water bottle, and a separate cell-phone holder. The two of them helped Alfredo to make the same wise decision, as Spiderman was overridden for an unnamed "monster-boy" backpack with many compartments, a water bottle, and a compartment for a phone.

Time stood still as we all waited for my husband, Don, to come back from the Home Depot. Don had asked that we allow him to make sure that each of the kids got good-quality shoes before paying, so we waited for him upstairs and downstairs and outside, and finally he joined us. He carefully examined each item and double-checked shoe sizes and quality. Once again, the saleslady was invaluable. We made three piles on the counter for shirts, pants, socks, shoes, and backpacks. The two check-out clerks were clear that three bags must be supplied. Don and Alfredo looked at the adjoining toys as we checked out. Each of the children ap-proached to take their own bag of school clothes, and off we went, won-dering if Alfredo was going to make it down the stairs with a bag nearly as tall as he was.

Don took the bags to the car after each of the children assured him that they were not hungry. Don explained that we needed to eat, and that they should walk with me to the food court while he took everything to the car. Again we moved along, but this time into a busy mall. All of the children were clearly stunned at the quantity of items within their range of view. The passage of time was significant, as they paused to look at the array of items for sale. The fact that none of them had ever been in a mall before was evident in their amazed gazes.

Once at the food court, I explained that the 30-plus shops offered many different items, including ice cream. Fernanda spoke up that she wanted ice cream. I assured her that it was coming. Don joined us just in time to see us walk past McDonald's, at which point Alfredo's single finger digit pointed at the sign, but he did not say a word. At the end of the row of stores, Don and I settled on the green salad bar. When I questioned Marco, he sang out "Pizza!" and Alfredo agreed. Fernanda said "ice cream" again, but at the pizza stand she decided on pizza, too. Marco ate two really large pieces; Alfredo and Fernanda had one each. Alfredo had ordered Pepsi with confidence. Marco had apple juice. Cleanup of the table ended with a trip to the bathroom, where Alfredo was very stunned. He had learned about seatbelt buckles today, and now he was faced with gender-defined bathrooms, too. He was still perplexed as he followed Don and Alfredo. I reassured him that it was correct.

Automatic water into a hand-washing sink was really odd to Alfredo as well as to Fernanda. Don was as delighted as I to observe Alfredo investigating the auto-water system in the sink. Furthermore, Don could stop that diversion with another: an automatic hand-drying machine, which was a real treat for Alfredo. He came out of the men's bathroom talking about a mile a minute about the auto-hand-dryer to Fernanda, who had waited beside me outside the men's room.

Our last stop was the ice cream shop; Fernanda picked the one she wanted out of the two visible ice cream stores. Don, anticipating leftovers, realized that he would have none to eat (he was right). We sat at a new table, and Alfredo almost finished his small cup before offering it to everyone else. As we sat watching them delight in sweet frozen cream with fruit, I asked Don if he liked playing grandparents to these lovely children. His grin was as big as the children's had been all day when he admitted that watching the "first time" through others' eyes was a deeply satisfying experience. Like me, he saw this day's events as a rare opportunity to share a very intimate time with some extremely special young children, who were having several initial experiences far later in life than our modern world might imagine possible.[22]

Summary: The Role of Fathers

If we are to understand the culture, then it is imperative we refrain from being judgmental and expecting gender equality. Gender equality is not a part of the rural Latino culture. Very few women have been able to gain a foothold in the social network and/or in business. Veronica Cruz Sanchez is the major exception. She runs a health service, which is free for women. She arranges abortions, speaks out against violence toward women, and, because of her work, faces death threats on nearly a daily basis. [23]

Few women in this culture are willing to accept the role of speaking out for and protecting women's rights.

When a self-improvement class is offered at no charge, the females of all ages want to attend. Those who can manage to get away from their houses will attend, and others might ask for feedback later. Even if the class might help bring income into the home, the husband is likely to resist—making money is his job.

Making inroads to equality in education, employment, or domestic affairs is unlikely to have a major change in the rural areas, except in cases where some enlightenment has already taken root. The man is the head of the family, and if he is gone, the woman takes her place behind the oldest son. That is the norm.

I have pointed out a few exceptions to this rule in the stories about some of the caregiving fathers whom I know. There are many more who are exceptions to the norm, but it is important that the reader understands that educators and trainers should not expect a 21st century equality, which is not a part of this rural Mexican culture.

"Abuela" (grandmother). This is an original 12" × 16" oil painting by Jolene Gailey. The older women in the community are usually less than 5 feet tall, generally bent over, still active, and highly respected.

7

The Role of Mothers

"The house does not rest upon the ground, but upon a woman"

—MEXICAN PROVERB

Social Expectations of Latina Mothers

Research found that the resourcefulness of the indigenous mother is nothing short of awe-inspiring. Her creative skills are fine-tuned by basic survival efforts. Living in the *campo* every day is a test of physical, mental, and emotional endurance, the level of which is not imaginable to mothers in non-third-world countries. A mother in a developed country worries about getting the latest electronic gadget (a new laptop) for her teenage son, paying car insurance premiums for her college-attending daughter, or helping her son prepare for his middle-school Latin final. A *campo* mother has daily worries about whether there will be enough clean water or cornmeal to make tortillas to fill the bellies of her six hungry children, whether she will be able to pay the equivalent of $4 a month for her electric bill to keep the single light bulb in her house working, and whether her daughter's only school blouse will be torn by the barbed-wire clothesline during a windstorm. All mothers have concerns for their children's welfare. However, *campo* mothers are fighting for their children's basic physical survival, while mothers in developed countries are negotiating for their children's social standing. The social status concerns of a mother in a developed country are perceived by her as being strongly connected to access to educational opportunities and elevated social status.

These two types of mothers are really worlds apart, and *so are their children*. Understanding this difference is a major factor in comprehending why academic success for Latino children is frequently a significant challenge.

Single Head of Household

All too often the indigenous mother's absent husband forgets to send money; he might stay away for years, while she waits. It is her fate as the caregiver to simply wait—that is the role the females born in the *campo* assume. Mothers, with or without husbands working locally, stay home and work from early in the morning until late in the evening every day to care for the family. The level of care taken to clean the houses is excessive by U.S. norms, perhaps because the water is not potable and always cold. Mothers spend seemingly endless hours scrubbing both the insides and the outsides of their houses with powerful disinfectants. Most houses are cleaned with a single strong product; the smell of "Fabuloso" permeates the air each morning in the urban cities.

It is not appropriate for life-skills educators or trainers to assume that rural Latina women know how to clean a house or a business in urban areas or per the U.S. standards. If the school is teaching life skills or a job includes cleaning, then training on how to clean a modern house or an office should be provided.

It's vital that a helpful, culturally sensitive person explains what specific cleaning items are used for and how to use them correctly. Typically, rural Latina women do not understand that the outside of the refrigerators, electric appliances, garbage cans, file cabinets, shelves, and the like should be cleaned, because these items and the products used to clean them probably do not exist in these women's houses. Another item not likely to be present in their houses is kitchen counter-tops and glass in windows, doors, or cabinets. Trainers need to explain which chemicals should be used for each of these items, as well as for cleaning a desk or a table and even for scrubbing a bathtub or toilet. The rural Latino simply has not had any experience with sliver polish, brass cleaner, furniture polish, upholstery cleaner or freshener, electronic equipment dust cleaners, computer monitor or TV screen cleaners, spray starch, and/or a vacuum cleaner. Just imagine a house in 1760: If a cleaning product did not exist then, it's a really good idea to provide clear instructions to the Latino person assigned to use the product. Additionally, the adult may

Mother and her children are begging on public city streets. This is not an uncommon occurrence.

have never seen a mattress or a pillow cover, an extra blanket at the foot of a bed, two pillows for each adult, or cushions on a couch. He or she may also have not seen an afghan hung over a rocking chair, a chest of drawers, clothes or a broom closet, and/or a vast number of other items incorrectly assumed to be a part of living in the 21st century. When this information is clearly understood, then one can realize why rural Latinos, who have different life experiences from those in developed or urban settings, often appear to lack understanding; in actuality, they lack experiences. Your job as a teacher or a trainer is to give clear, complete, and detailed instructions with specific guidelines, which is necessary to get a positive result.

The Women's Struggle for Healthy Families

Despite great care and caution being taken to keep intestinal parasites out of the food, children often get very sick. Other researchers found that the Latina mothers interviewed "promoted and protected the health of their preschool children by taking care ('el cuidado') and by being mindful ('el pendiente') of balancing the health of their infants', children's,' and youths' bodies, minds, and souls."[1] I discovered that by understanding this personal cultural outlook, it might be possible to design *culturally sensitive health programs* that would reach toward and build on existing maternal strengths. If urban and rural women were reached in a heritage-appropriate manner and if the offered programs acknowledged their children as the national treasures, the living assets, and the future leaders of Latin America, then the women might be able to understand the value of exerting a greater effort toward preventative health care. They could, for example, learn how to reduce the use of sugar, restrict processed foods, and increase home vegetable gardening. My observations and suggestions are consistent with those of other researchers.[2]

The rural medical personnel I interviewed verified that in spite of mothers' best efforts, malnutrition is a regional epidemic. Additionally, most children have acid reflux and intestinal parasites.

Being healthy and well-fed is frequently a challenge in the *campo*. Animals either run loose all over the dirt yard, or they are tied or hobbled (two legs tied together on a very short rope) in the yard. Yards are covered in animal feces, which most mothers sweep away at least once a day into a pile in a corner of the yard. The fly problem is extremely difficult to control, because houses do not have screens on windows or doors. In Central and Western Mexico, the inside ceilings of rural houses and exposed food items are covered with flies night and day from March through December.

Caring for Children with Special Needs

Many unique problems exist in the *campo* making educational special needs more common in children and adults. An educational special need is defined as anything that makes learning more difficult. For example, having one leg an inch shorter than the other is a disability but not an educational special need. In the *campo*, mothers of children with special needs, educational or otherwise, face numerous challenges.

Frequently, they struggle alone; even if they are not officially single, absentee fathers leads to a lifestyle similar to single parents. Additionally, providing proper nutrition for themselves and their children is often impossible. They do not receive enough help from others and are not able to get any outside help due to transportation hurdles.

Researchers suspect that, due to being economically marginalized, mothers have to deal with nutrition-related problems and other health issues in older children; they also often forget what they were told by the medical personnel when their children were younger. Nutritional problems are often the result of a lack of income for adequate food; forgetfulness often is the result of having the responsibility to care for too many children with very few resources. I have observed medical employees often reminding a mother of what supplements were given to one of her children earlier in life.

Overworked mothers teach their Latina daughters nearly from birth how to be good mothers; the daughters' help is needed within the family. If a woman's child is born in need of special services, then the normally-abled daughter's help is even more imperative, because little outside administrative help is available to guide the mother in raising a special-needs child.[3] Mothers have come to expect this lack of resources and the necessity to adapt from within the family.

A major factor in getting help for the special-needs children is the need to use public transportation to get to the facility that might be able to offer some help. As mothers do not have cars, public transportation is the only option. Often, however, whole communities have no access to public transportation; they may only have access via a nearby community. "Nearby" might be defined as an easy walk for a teenage boy, but a mother of five might have an entirely different viewpoint regarding the phrase—she has to manage the trip walking with her young brood or having to carry a baby.

Access to transportation is a major factor in determining the economic positioning of an entire community.

Transportation issues are even harder for parents with special-needs children or elderly adults in need of medical care.

Caregiver is the Rural Latina Mother's Central Role

The social expectation for the rural mother is to be the caregiver, primarily of children. She is expected to be wholly committed to her role, with or without a partner. Mothers appear to have clearly defined roles as caregivers of their children; very few work outside the house, drive a car, or are involved in any activity other than staying in the house or walking to the house of another relative to care for him or her.

This narrow domestic assignment is not a shared responsibility with the husband or a son—only with a daughter, sister, or another female.

In my 2007 research on the Arizona-Sonora border, I interviewed thirteen women who lived either in Mexico or in the U.S.; all of them worked in the U.S and were Mexican nationals. These women's statements will help clarify for others the lives of women in a Central or Western Mexican *campo*. Eleven of the thirteen women completely agreed with the following statement:

The Latino male can leave his family, leave his job, not attend church, and behave in a manner inside his community that is less than honorable, and yet his social status is relatively unharmed.

According to these women, the Latina female faced an entirely different role. One of the women, Maria, elaborated on this with her explanation:

I am much harder on my girls! I have to be, because our culture expects so much more of them. They have so much more responsibility than the men. All the man has to do is earn money.

She later added:

The grandmother is the leader of the whole family, often living "out back" after her husband dies so that she can be consulted and cared for by the entire family in her later life (i.e. even by the younger men). The focus of the culture is the family, and the hub in that wheel of life is the mother or grandmother.

My research data suggested that all mothers expect their children to be obedient, and that only the females are also expected to be helpful inside the house. Domestic chores require an exceptional amount of time and hard physical labor, because the well-known "labor-saving devices" are not available to these women. The research participants I interviewed consistently expressed that the mother's job was also to keep the entire family healthy; the theme of health is heard daily in both casual and serious conversations.

The women within the scope of my research lived outdoors for a large percentage of each day—cooking, eating, bathing, washing clothing, caring for domestic livestock, walking to school or neighborhood vendors, socializing in multi-generational settings, worshiping, and interacting informally with peers. Women are always caring for others, but they are not learning any new ways to accomplish this task.

The often-jealous Latino males, my female interviewees stated emphatically, met any activity outside of these parameters with suspicion. The men appear to fear any deviation from the domestic norms their own mothers followed.

Once again I offer Maria's explanation regarding the difference between the role of men and women in the Latnio family:

> *For Latina women, the role is far more complex, truly multi-faceted. The Latino male may or may not play the father role, or even the husband role; very little stigma is attached either way. The Latina female is expected to be the head of the household, the provider for anyone in the immediate or extended family, an outstanding mother to anyone who is in her house, a cool-headed leader no matter what might occur in her house or community, the teacher of all cultural or religious activities done in the house, the one to shoulder any responsibility that might be asked of her, a giver of advice and labor to anyone who asks that of her, and the one who is always in control. There is no high stigma if a girl is pregnant and unmarried,[4] as long as she is a good mother, but not caring for her children is unthinkable.*

The female school bus driver, whom I will call "Anita," explained,

> *I never expected to only have one man with me my entire life.*

That pronouncement by Anita was followed by,

> *Mexican men are expected to earn money—that is their total job—but the Mexican female creates the family and preserves it.*

Latina Indigenous Women Rule the Home

In her interview, Maria stated:

> *Women show the right path; they are the leaders of the home. Both (parents) may help with values, but the mother is the leader. Whatever the Latina mother says, that is what is going to be!*

Later in her interview Maria emphatically stressed,

> *In the U.S. the paycheck is everything, but in Latin America it is the family; and it is the woman who heads each of the families—whatever it takes.*

Maria said several times during the interview:

The woman must do whatever it takes to care for the family, to keep the children safe, to make the home—whatever it takes. That is why all Latina women must be strong.

None of the other interviewed women disagreed with this last paragraph, although they were directly asked.

Gender differences within their culture were also discussed by the focus group.[5] It was "Mona" who summarized:

A man is "Dad" in name only; the mother is the actual head of every Latin America household.

The other focus group members nodded their heads in agreement. Mona continued:

The men do not clean, do not cook, and are spoiled all over Latin America by their mothers. They have a machismo attitude, because all they have to do is work outside the house. It is OK for them to leave the family, to drop out of school or out of the family.... The culture is always harder on the women.... In Latin America, we are the heads of the families. It may not be right, but if something bad or something good happens (in the home), it is (the responsibility of) the woman.

The women have to watch their kids.... The women have the last word in the world, even if the men might not say so.

When the focus group, including the women I called "Mona," "Sadie," and "Jetta," were asked about the Latina women, they spoke out in agreement:

Everyone expects more. The women are expected to cook, to clean, to work hard, and to always, always care for the children—no matter what, to care for the children.

As an afterthought, one of them added,

And you know, we do not see any autism or ADHD in Latin America.

"Alice" lived in Sonora, Mexico, and walked over the Arizona border to work at a U.S. school every day. She was one of the older women at the school, probably in her mid 50s. When asked about the difference between raising girls and boys in Latin America, she replied:

They (Latin Americans) love the boys more. It is the girls who raise the babies and run the households.

When the same question was asked of another Sonora resident, "Patty," who also walked to the same school on the Arizona-Sonora border every day, she replied that she thought things might be changing a little in one tiny aspect of life, "because it is more equal about going to college now."

As a young woman just out of high school, Patty said that she knew several female friends from Mexico who were attending college.

The woman I will call "Esmerelda," who was employed at the school, made the most telling statement about being successful outside of the home when she said:

I would never have been able to be this (a director of a school) in Latin America. I would not have been given the opportunity.

Every day, the private school bus brought in one junior-high-age girl and two high-school-age girls—all volunteers (two of them were Esmerelda's girls and one was Maria's daughter). They arrived with the grade school students who stayed at the school each afternoon. The girls had to help with the lessons for the "big kids" at one end of the large (2,000 square feet), open, multi-purpose building, while the preschoolers worked at the other end just a few feet from the kitchen. Maria had explained to me that young women needed to be prepared for the responsibility they would face as adults in their Latin American community.

In a town with such large-scale unemployment, when one family member had a job, he or she would inform other people in the family about possible employment opportunities. Every day at about 5:30 P.M., Esmerelda's boyfriend's son arrived to clean the school. He would finish by 6:30 P.M., when the whole 5,283 square feet of indoor space and almost as much outdoor space fell silent. Silence continued until 6 A.M., at which time the bus full of students pulled in again.

Boys would never be asked to help with anything that the women were doing, but it was common to see the women help the boys with cleaning.

Six adults piled into the private school bus at the end of the work day; after the final run, Esmerelda took it home for safekeeping, because she lived in the U.S. If she did not do that, the bus owned by the U.S. school might be taken at night, illegally, to Mexico.

Mexican indigenous women's position of power within their homes seems to develop momentum with age. The women may have been raped at the age of 10 or 11 and had four or more children and an absent husband by the time they were 18—life presents them with such challenges. If these women live to become grandmothers, however, they likely have become very wise with age. Their survival instincts have kept the bellies of their children full; have kept the roofs repaired so that rainwater, snow, or hail could be kept off the bedclothes; have fought off reoccurring intestinal parasites or perhaps malaria; and have ensured that at least two generations of family members have something clean to cover their bodies. The level of commitment expected by women is shown in the following journal entry:

> One mother of 14 children had been living apart from her husband and the children's father for 23 years. He only visited three times in all those years, but he always sent money. Therefore, when he suddenly moved back from the U.S. to Mexico, when he was elderly and could no longer find work in the U.S., he entered the home without resistance—since her position of power was considered socially to be less than her husband's.[5]

I knew these women thoroughly from having hired and trained each of them as school employees. I questioned them about how their commitments to their heritage influenced their individual value systems, knowing that they were comfortable enough to give me open, honest replies. These were questions that someone who knew them casually could not ask. A casual friend might not have known to ask such questions, and even if they asked, they would not have received an honest reply.[6] The intimate bond of affection between me and my interviewees was partially the result of them knowing that I had worked side-by-side with them (in the school) for up to 14 hours a day for over a year.[7] I knew that everyone was equally capable of handling whatever situation might develop.[8] Caring for children implied that any situation could occur; therefore, having a "sixth sense" about the children was imperative for all of the employees.[9] Trust had been tested on many occasions.

The following interview question was asked of the focus group:

Do the children of these Latina women always expect to be loved and cared for by a female?

The answer was unanimously, "Yes," and included a complete examination of just how much work it took to fill that role.

When Esmerelda was asked how things were going at the school, she replied: "Good! I could never have done this without them (the other employees), they are incredible!"

Eleven women from the focus group agreed that the typical Latina female's key role was that of a capable caregiver. The following events are just a sample of what these women took for granted and what they were able to accomplish without any ongoing training:

- In the second week after the school's opening, a 2-year-old child developed a slight fever, went into convulsions, and stopped breathing. Quick-thinking employees saved that child's life.
- In another case, a mother would drop off her child when she was too self-medicated to care for the child. No employee ever asked the administration if non-payment should be used as a reason to turn her child, or any other child, away.
- In the third case, two siblings came in extremely dirty and hungry. Nothing was said. The children were bathed, fed, and cared for as if it were a common occurrence. The sadness of the subsequent events affected these strong women: The Department of Economic Services was 33 minutes late in letting the school know that the paperwork had been put in place prohibiting the father to take the kids; by the time the department phoned the school, the father had already picked up the two children and left for another state.
- On one occasion, when another father was legally forbidden to pick up his child, he threatened three female employees with physical harm. Similarly, there was another incident where a father with a criminal history often walked past the school and looked in to spot his children. In both cases, the employees were calm and professional. They did not overreact or under-react; they simply protected the children under their care.
- One day a young boy crushed his finger in an outside gate as he moved from one playground to another. The blood was gone and the child was taken away in an ambulance before I finished making a

quick trip to the post office just three blocks from the school. All of this rapid-fire thinking, acting, and getting assistance was completed by another employee who took on the role of the leader without hesitation; these women thought fast and worked well as a team. We had in place clear levels of leadership hierarchy when anyone was gone, but such planning was rarely needed—the women were cooperative and always put the needs of the children first.

These are examples of how Latina women think fast, work as a team to develop decisions, and put children's well-being as the main priority.

Qualitative data told the same story—that as each woman started her shift at the school, she took the time to greet every other woman with a hug and a kiss on the cheek, and then to inquire about their respective families. The culture dictated this form of physical and emotional contact.

Intense phone calls were common for the school—a person, usually a child or another relative, calling into the school to speak to the female head-of-household. No time was spent considering the stress that the female was already facing both at her job at the school and at home; she was the leader of the family, period, and needed to be reached right away. All of the school's employees were female, and most were heads of households. They were employed because they wanted to reduce reliance on public assistance.[10] This choice meant that they had to work very hard to juggle both a job and the responsibilities of being leaders of their families. These women were usually single and living in poverty, yet they faced whatever problems arose with dignity while internalizing additional psychological stress.[11]

Maria's Statements

The following is an excerpt from Maria's interview:

QUESTION: So, could I say that you feel like you've really succeeded in your life, that you feel really good about your life?

MARIA: I have succeeded, but I have not accomplished yet what I want for them (the children)—but I think I have succeeded.

QUESTION: It is (through) them (i.e. how they, the children, are doing in life)—that's how you rate yourself. It's (through) them, is that right?

MARIA: That is how I rate myself. I knew that since they were small, a reflection of me was going to be in them. I know that each one of them has to be them (an individual), and that is the way I want it.

A typical parade in city streets is religion-based. The female icon is most often used in worship services, parades, and rituals.

Every day, the school breakfast was served from 7:30 A.M. to 9 A.M. Children of all ages would pass in and out of the arms of six or seven female employees during that time period. Stories were shared among the women, because each had suffered so much in life, had accomplished a great deal, and had raised many children. Many mothers had adult children and then helped raise relatives' or friends' children. The majority of the women had accepted extreme levels of responsibility, had fought for everything they had, and had crossed the Arizona-Sonora border hundreds of times. A significant number of the women had a relative or a friend in jail. Having this strong network of emotional support helped them keep their dignity. The women had accomplished everything as single parents. They often remarked that they carried a deep faith in God.

The women I interviewed in the Arizona school shouldered a collective understanding of how deadly the road they walked along and lived on really was. This road, commonly referred to as the open wound, was on the border between the U.S. and Mexico.[12]

The *campo* women in Central Mexico also know of *the open wound*, because the men they love are attracted to that legal line. The *campo* men dream of crossing over the U.S.-Mexico border and finding work on the other side, especially when work is unavailable near home. The men dream of then returning to their homes deep in Mexico with riches made in *el norte*. The reality is far different than the dream: Families are separated; men do not find good paying jobs; and old relationships are replaced with new ones (thus creating more mouths to feed). Families are torn apart, and the riches are not forthcoming. The reality of the border is a sore that will not heal; it is referred to as *the open wound*, because it is always festering.

Lack of Quality Sleep is Common

After classes, snacks, outdoor play, and lunch at the border school came the nap time. Day sleeping was especially important for those children who slept poorly at home. Many children had disruptive home lives due to self-medicated people in the home who kept the nights from being peaceful. The school caregivers gently rubbed the backs of the children who were the most restless.

Each child at the U.S. school was patiently held, rubbed, or verbally soothed, while soft music played in the background—no one knew what physical, mental, or emotional challenges that tiny soul faced elsewhere. Eventually, all of the children would fall asleep; they always did. Some children who experienced challenging home lives slept for 2 to 3 hours in that place of love and safety, while others slept for just 30 to 40 minutes.

Latino culture makes evenings and nights the *family time,* so children are often up very late: often until 11 P.M. or 12 A.M. It is also normal to have music playing very loudly or firecrackers going off all night—especially inside Latin America, where noise and fireworks are not regulated. Therefore, Latino children in the U.S. or in Latin America tend to miss a great deal of time that might otherwise be set aside for sleeping. It is typical for immigrant Latino children to be at low ebb from lack of sleep while in the classroom. It is just as common for adult employees to be sleepy during the day at their place of employment. I believe this habit of missing sleep is used as a means to compensate for long hours of hard work needed to meet the demands of caring for a large family. I think that the desire to replace concerns over mental and physical survival by allocating time for joyful celebrations shared with others is how people adapt. Unfortunately, these times of joy, which occur at night when there are no other obligations, and can result in sleep deprivation.

Sisterhood

In the U.S. border school, while the children slept, the women employees would gather at tables, eat, and share stories about the community, their families, and *the open wound*.[13] Frequently, someone that they knew was arrested, fell ill, or lost a loved one to drugs. Often, one or two of the women would make place markers for a local Quinceanera (15th birthday celebration for female Latina girls: a transition to adulthood) or for a funeral, while the others talked and ate. Later, items would be laid out for the afternoon's lesson. Through it all, there was no one shouting orders. All activities would just go on as planned, because these women had always worked as a team *taking care of business*—family or community business, it made no difference. The women accepted the responsibilities without hesitation.

This pattern continues in the *campo*. Women accept every hardship as a fact of life and are supportive of each other. The women carry no obvious resentments, although it is apparent that their emotional pain is deep.

The women in the campo, work as a team; most are related, or have been related at one time or another. Collectively, the women find a way to keep a level head because of their strong faith in God and each other. Their hearts are always ready to accept yet another child who needs them.

Most of the women take little time for themselves or for anything other than the simple material gifts that they often meticulously select and give to each other—small samples or travel sizes of hygiene items, jewelry or purses made in Mexico, homemade food, or handcrafted items. How they buy numerous gifts with so few dollars and give the items with such sincerity is beyond comprehension. The respect and love lavished on others is the only consistent absolute within a community where *the open wound* is always on the horizon of men's minds.[14]

Showing respect to others and to property is a common trait among Mexican women. My research was an affirmation that the women of Mexico had respect, taught their children about respect, and acted toward others with respect. A caring culture apparently thrives on the characteristics of past relationships that have been propagated into the 21st century. There are visible signs of children receiving unconditional love,[15] of a grandmother or other relatives caring for children belonging to others[16] and of unquestioning respect for each other.[17]

One of the main golas of Mexican women is children must not be lost.[18]

Housework and Feeding the Family

Cultural code dictates that women work in the house doing all domestic chores, as well as caring for the children and the husband or other male provider. This job is expected of the women. It is both honorable and pure drudgery, because society demands that all women must do it and must do it their entire lives.

I have yet to hear anyone say that domestic obligations are easy enough to allow women time for anything additional, like paid employment. Women are not encouraged to earn an income outside the house. Many men will not allow any work for income, like sewing or baking, to be done in the family house.

Some women clean others' house, but few. Comments that I hear are that women's work is considered to be a time-consuming and vital job—the perfect role for women. Mexicans appear to realize that "modern conveniences" for domestic chores do not exist in rural communities. Additionally, it seems that all people realize that caring for a house is a full-time job. This could be because *family is first* or because the expectation level of cleanliness required in the home is so high that women must be there to sweep and mop every day.

They sweep inside the house and outside on the grounds in front of the house. The entire interior is mopped at least once a day "until the stripes come off the tile," as the local expatriate saying goes. While most houses are cleaned once a week in the U.S., the Mexican standards dictate daily mopping, dusting, and attention to home cleanliness. This occurs in rural areas even though the walls are exposed brick, the floor is just compacted dirt or exposed concrete, and the toilet is outdoors. The family house is expected to be cleaned every day, top to bottom, inside and out. Women are expected to work inside the house; they are thought to be already overwhelmed with the work in front of them and are only excused if another family member temporarily needs them. If that occurs, then all is put aside until the needs of that person are met.

This is a stark contrast to the expectations of women in the U.S. for themselves and by others.

Ruth Payne describes the poor as *lazy and living in female-centered authoritarian families who are chronically unemployed*.[19] This statement is a gross misrepresentation of my observations of people living in rural Mexico.

Typically the Mexican women awake before daylight to begin cleaning, cooking, and getting children set for the day. An infant is usually fed in the family bed before the mother gets out of bed. The infant is strapped to the mother's chest, side, or back with a "rebozo," a long thin scarf. That same style scarf is used to carry children (in youth) and groceries (in old age), in addition to keeping out the sun's rays or keeping warm. Wearing a rebozo is a badge of honor, as well as a practical accessory.

I have speculated that the per capita consumption of brooms is 12 a year, with mops coming in a close second. From morning to night, indoors and outside of the house or business, women are seen sweeping. Mexican women in rural communities are fastidiously clean, as are their urban counterparts that sweep and sometimes mop the sidewalks in front of their houses. The minimum expectation by a woman for a job as a housekeeper is three full days a week. Normally, expatriates in the U.S. hire Mexican women to come in for about four hours a week to clean an average house. The Mexicans think of this as an unacceptable option, since cleaning the home is a daily activity, as is doing the laundry. Mexican cooking is prepared from scratch and eaten in family groups at least twice a day. After eating an early morning "desayano" (breakfast) before 8 A.M., "almuerzo" (a mid-morning snack) is eaten at about 10:30 A.M. The snack usually consists of a leftover from the day before. In public schools, this includes substantial food, typically consisting of a burrito or a taco with meat and cheese—not a lot of food is provided, but it consists of substantial food, not sugary snacks.

"Comida" is lunch, usually eaten between 2 P.M. and 4 P.M. It is a leisurely mid-day meal of rather large proportions, which are often carried to the men at work by their wives or children. The relatives walk to the job site with or without an infant being held in someone's arms along with the food being carried. "Cena" is the last meal of the day; frequently only fruit is eaten, but a white bread sandwich is another option. The four typical meals are augmented with Coca-Cola and both sugary and/or salty snacks, especially in mid-morning and throughout the afternoon. The highest per capita consumption of Coca-Cola in the world is in Mexico, and the Coca-Cola in Mexico has the largest cane sugar content and the most calories.[20] Undoubtedly, drinking so much Coca-Cola contributes to high national levels of obesity and increased tooth decay.[21]

Neuropsychologist Helena Todd of Santiago, Chile, has spent her entire adult life studying predominately indigenous Spanish-speaking mothers.

Dr. Todd has determined that the only way to create literacy in marginalized Spanish-speaking children is by creating literacy in their mothers first.[22] I completely agree with her.

For their children to have access to an education, it is vital for Latina mothers to gain access to knowledge first and to maintain such access on an ongoing basis. Educated mothers educate their children, even if only by the children's observation of their mothers reading or doing a math calculation. Uneducated mothers are unable to help their children with schoolwork. Even though the culture does not encourage mothers to accept the role of an educator, educated women will influence their children's education in a positive manner.

Mexican mothers stay behind and care for the children all of their lives, while the fathers head north looking for work. University of Arizona playwright Ochoa O'Leary found similar statements made in interviews of women who attempted to cross illegally into *el norte* by themselves. These are women who had made arrangements with their mothers to care for the children, because Mexican women are always mothers, even if they are grandmothers. Some women make the very painful decision to cross and leave their children behind. This is not a decision made lightly, and the women suffer greatly, as do their children; they do it because leaving is better than slowly starving. Many stories I have read say exactly that: leave to find work or stay and starve over time are the two choices many Mexican parents have to make. It's rare for a woman to take that route, but it does happen when they are alone and have no other options. Women, although most married, consider themselves single mothers.

These individuals are highly motivated. They have whole families. They are trying to find a way to support them.[23]

Regardless of what choices a Latina woman makes, her role is always that of a mother, and her desire is for her children to have a better life than she has experienced. Nearly every mother in Latin America I have ever questioned put quality education first on her list of what she wanted for all of her children. Too bad Latin America has not had a female president, because then there might be more of a budget allocated for education. Regardless of the current budget trends, rest assured that Latina mothers want their children educated.

Summary: The Role of Latina Women

It is hard to remain unbiased when observing Latina girls, women, grand-mothers, and the role into which they are born. Their culture demands youthful domestic responsibilities at a very early age and unimaginable responsibilities of motherhood, but does not allow equality with the males. At a very early age, frequently by 4 years of age, girls are wobbling on rather high heels and wearing red lipstick with tight jeans and dangling earrings, because that is the norm within the culture. As mothers, they often look totally worn out due to bearing many children. By old age, they have lost height due to physically carrying anywhere from eight to over a dozen children both inside and outside their wombs, as well as emotionally carrying much domestic responsibility. They are, indeed, to be both admired and assisted, but only when they specifically request help. They are proud women and deserve the utmost respect and the most culturally appropriate emotional, educational, and physical support.

Two young primary school students are working alongside the adult males, building in concrete, stone, and adobe in their rural community. They are learning the trade and developing a work ethic at an early age. Because they are being raised in a cooperative society, they have no expectation of being paid for their time or labor.

8 Raising Latino Children

Don't handicap your children by making their lives easy.

—Robert A. Heinlein

Cultural Differences in Infant Care

Most young parents acknowledge infants are not born with a set of instructions; if they were, I am convinced at least some of the "standard operating procedures" from the rural Latino neighborhood would be included in the manual. It seems every child there is treated as a *blessed event*.

Kingsolver remarked, "What I discovered in Spain was a culture that held children to be its meringues and éclairs."[1] The same is true in rural Latin America, where children are *participants in dynamic cultural communities*, where they are constantly held, admired, and highly cherished.

Exhausted mothers do not put down a new infant. The child is simply handed to another family member—a sister, grandparent, father, or sibling. The child is held or is lying in the family bed with one or more people beside him or her 24 hours a day. Although the "taco babies" (a common reference) wear many layers of blankets around them and are tightly bound, they experience a lot more skin-to-skin contact than U.S. children. Children in the U.S. grow up in car seats, infant carriers, strollers, and/or cribs, while the Mexican infant is constantly being touched, shifted, or checked on while hearing another's heartbeat.

The Latino infant is constantly being touched, shifted, or checked on while hearing another's heartbeat. Additionally, if children start to cry while being held, their needs are met immediately to help them stop crying.

I observed that unlike European-American *packaged* babies, Latino infants often have skin-to-skin contact with a caregiver, appearing to feel more secure and crying less frequently. Latinos I interviewed confirmed that this is all part of a process of developing a *lifetime responsibility to the family of origin;* other researchers have discovered the same phenomena. [2]

Such lifetime devotion may be an intended social return on the family's investment in each child. This admiration of children is also why so few Latino children are orphans, even though early parental deaths are more common than in developed countries. When necessary, family members take in the children without hesitation and raise them.

Mattie's Story

Over the last year, I personally observed this custom. Within a month of moving to the *campo* I met a young child I will call "Mattie," who looked to be about three or four years of age. She appeared to be indigenous and learning-disabled, and had characteristics that I had seen in children identified as having the fetal alcohol syndrome. Mattie accompanied her mother, a house-to-house seller of fresh vegetables. At first, Mattie came to my house with both her parents. Soon I learned that others, along with me, had never seen Mattie's father sober. After a few visits, Mattie came only with her mother.

Mattie's mother explained that she chose to keep Mattie out of school, since the child had been so unhappy there. I discussed this with her on many occasions. Nobody could deny that Mattie was generally unhappy regardless of where she was or what she was doing. She wore a frown most of the time and was very suspicious of everyone. I observed the same behavior in Mattie that her mother reported.

Jolene and I visited their house several times. They lived on the edge of the lowest, dampest part of town in an adobe shack in very poor repair with no utilities. Mattie's mother had one skinny dog in bad health, no other children, and few assets in or near the house. The father was never present when we visited, but I did frequently see him around town completely inebriated.

Mattie's mother developed a fast-paced cancer; she was dead within a year of diagnosis. Immediately upon the mother's death, her cousin, who already had two girls of her own, agreed to take in the motherless 6-year-old. The woman and her husband did that to ease the strain on Mattie's father and grandfather. Both grandmothers were already deceased.

One of the couple's girls, a 2-year-old, is disabled. The family frequently came to my house for physical therapy for the 2-year-old girl and/or advice on how to parent a disabled child. The toddler's diagnosis was inconclusive, but she was clearly challenged with a serious neurological disorder.

I was close to the couple making the generous parenting offer, having met them on the very first day I came to this *campo*. We often spoke about family matters. The minute I had seen their then 10-month-old daughter, I knew that she had special needs and offered my services. A year passed before her parents learned from a physician what her challenges were; they had not known that she was disabled. As a trusted friend, I counseled these new parents on what to expect from Mattie, how to shelter the other two girls from possible behavioral challenges, and how to preserve their personal pride as accomplished parents. I advised them that their love and parental skills would not *cure* Mattie's observed symptoms or learning problems. I wanted to be sure they were not overly critical of themselves. The transition to being parents of a third daughter had been very hard. We often discussed options for helping Mattie, the couple, and the other two girls.

Independence, Development, and Crawling

Infants are held day and night until they walk, which means they are not allowed to crawl. I observed this phenomenon in cities, in villages, in health clinics, and in homes from all socioeconomic levels. I questioned parents, medical personnel, and teachers to make certain I was correct; all agreed crawling is not culturally sanctioned. A female physician, the mother of six who was educated in the U.S., allowed me to interview her about crawling. She assured me that keeping Latino children off dirt or bare concrete floors is probably only one reason for not allowing children to crawl. She explained that cultural tradition requires that an older person physically controls an infant at all times. She confirmed my observations that infants are rarely out of a parent's, sibling's, or another relative's arms night or day; infants are normally wrapped tightly in layered blankets that allow restricted movement. She explained that only one of her children had crawled. She elaborated by saying that quizzical stares toward both her and her infant confirmed that people found both the child's behavior and her allowing that behavior to occur very odd. Additionally, she added that in her lifetime, she had never seen another Latino infant crawl; she was nearly 40 years of age at the time.

Researchers vary from having very strong proactive opinions to site concerns about infants not receiving benefits from crawling. Research results are mixed related to developmental movement therapy programs that incorporate crawling or crawling-like behavior by children or adults (long after learning to walk). Most experts agree that crawling increases muscle strength, balance, and eye-hand coordination. Additionally, crawling stimulates brain activity, the ability to perceive and comprehend the depth (an understanding of edges, ledges, and falling), left and right brain coordination, and increased oxygen flow throughout the body, specifically to the brain. Emotionally, it increases independence by stimulating the crawler's willingness to independently explore the surrounding environment.[3]

Crawling certainly increases independence and personal decision-making. Latino infants are nearly always held. Traditionally, they do not independently crawl and explore on their own. Therefore, their level of independence is reduced compared to the U.S. standards, and they have almost no decision-making opportunities. Educators or instructors should consider that this might have some positive influence with regard to family bonding and some negative influence with regard to independence.

Talk Between Parents and Children

Oddly enough, the infant in a rural, predominately indigenous environment does not receive much verbal or visual stimulation. The child is an extension of the mother's life, a receiver of massive amounts of attention to detail, and a participant in all of her activities. The infant is *usually at her eye level* but rarely hears verbal comments directed toward him or her. The baby also rarely experiences eye contact with the person holding him or her. U.S. parents tend to "chatter" a great deal to their infants, looking them right in the eye and continuously eliciting a response. I have observed that urban Latino parents in the U.S. and Latino parents of higher social status in Latin America engage in the same behavior with infants as U.S. parents, not like rural Latino parents interact with their children.

I observed that speech in rural Latin America is generally saved for other adults. Teamwork in outlying Mexico is coordinated visually more than verbally. Even among adults, fewer words are used than is common for verbalizing in other cultures in their home countries.

The history of Mexico is one of oppressed people and scarce resources; even speaking is an effort if there is no need. Life is in general about basic human survival. My research found that 30.9% of 665 children in 18 rural communities were malnourished (see Table 3.0). There was no time or reason for philosophical discussions; having sufficient food to eat and beer for occasions with friends and family was seen as enough of an actual blessing. It seemed logical for a mother operating under such extreme survival conditions to ask, "Was there something else important to say to my children?"

A Comparison of Teen Attitudes

When I posed a question to a teen in the U.S. as a teacher, I often received a "Who cares?" reply, a flippant attitude, and a glaring "I dare you" stare. When I pose a similar question to a teen in Latin America, I generally receive an immediate respectful eye-to-eye gaze and a humble reply, usually followed by a shy, but warm, smile. I still find the contrast startling. It became clear to me that a different parenting approach was being applied to raising children in a Latin American home. One could assume that the lack of economic resources in rural Latin America would be a factor; however, I came to realize that the contrast between the attitudes of U.S. and Latino teenagers is too complicated to be attributed to simply the socioeconomic status.

Being a Mother is Always First Priority

First, the reader must appreciate the depth of a Latino female's commitment to all of her children, even to the point of self-sacrifice. Scholars have noted that Hispanic fathers have a greater denial of their children having a disability than either African-American or Caucasian men. However, the Hispanic mother was unwavering in her acceptance of any disability and any child.[4] Many cultures lack the supportive commitment to children that is so common in the Latin American homes, as I observed. Maybe that lack of supportive commitment to children is a factor that has resulted in children being abused or neglected in a multitude of ways in other cultures.

Perhaps if all Latina mothers could overcome economic woes, so that none of their Latino children would have to struggle so hard to survive, there would not be horrible drug gangs and resultant gang violence among Latinos. Living in absolute poverty or even observing poverty in others is not an excuse for illegal or immoral behavior. Generational poverty can breed deep-seated resentment. Resulting defiance from extended hardship experienced by self or others is the only answer I can find for why a few people raised by Latina women appear to lack any remnant of a conscience or respect for people or property. The majority of Latino children are polite and well behaved; they remain so as adults.

After spending some time in the *campo,* I could spot the *street-smart* kids who adapted to their marginalized state by not trusting others. They also were the ones who were more likely to be dishonest in dealing with others, usually by exaggerating the truth, or telling outright lies. The majority of Latinos I have known are happy, well-adjusted, respectful, and honest; they are people who place a high value on other people and property. In my opinion, those characteristics are a positive reflection of their mother's care.

Educators or instructors of Spanish speakers should consider that a lack of supportive commitment to students might be a deterrent to creating a positive learning environment.

The Latino Dream

Latina mothers appear to have an innate knowledge of how to make a child feel loved. Latina mothers want their children to have high self-esteem, to have self-love, to develop a deeply rooted sense of responsibility to succeed in school, and to become capable, humble, accepting, and productive adults.

The word that was lacking in that description was *happy.* I observed that Latinos worked to find joy, because they lived in a fatalistic society. Unlike the American dream, where anything is possible, the attitude overwhelmingly apparent in rural Latin America was: *Today was hard and tomorrow may never come.*

Seriousness of the Caregiver Role

Apparently, each newborn child makes one simple request: "Be my caregiver." Fulfilling that request is the hardest job on the planet. Latina women know, yet appear to welcome that role. I was blessed to be on the receiving end of that deeply engrained trait. I perceived that role through having lived around Latina women as a child, having worked side-by-side with them in restaurants for 23 years and in classrooms for another seven years, and from doing research to identify the bicultural and bilingual attitudes of Latina mothers. I was examining all Latina mothers' attitudes, including how they felt about children who faced one or more challenges—such as physical, mental, or emotional challenges, poverty, teen pregnancy, and/or Limited English Proficiency/English as a Second Language (LEP/ESL) hurdles.[4]

I found that those Latina women who felt that they had failed as mothers left sadness and emptiness in their wake, as though their lives were only half-lived.

Adult Attitudes and Responsibilities in Children

The children who live and work within this rural Mexican social network appear to acquire mature attributes at an extremely early age, pursuant to social expectations. For example, I observed conscientious behavior in the form of respecting others and meeting social responsibilities which, according to Daniel Goleman, are signs of both emotional and social intelligences.[5] Joseph Forgas defines social cognition as having some of the same mature qualities that I have observed.[6] Howard Gardner defines interpersonal intelligence as having the knowledge of how to handle relationships in an experienced manner equal to what I typically observe in the *campo*.[7] These mature attributes are very similar types of behavior or intellectual expression. They may be the result of extensive exposure to unveiled information about family business as well as exposure to nature.

In nature and in a primitive camping style of daily living, children develop an increased demand for cognitive thinking skills.[8] This development appears to be the result of needing to react quickly in order to survive potentially life-threatening situations.

Surviving a potentially life-threatening situation in nature or in a primitive home, both known as *outdoor education*, enhances self-esteem and, therefore, enables a child to develop hope for survival and other challenges inside and outside of the family.[8] Enhanced self-esteem changes behavior; confidence is an observable trait.[9] The majority of *outdoor education* research has been done in Europe, where it is gaining a lot of respect. In the U.S., schools are applying *outdoor education* in small areas, because little more than the fact that ADHD is asymptomatic outdoors has been acknowledged. However, "Outward Bound," a program designed for seamen who need to develop cooperative teamwork in life-threatening situations, has been used as a training tool by the U.S. corporations.[10] There is a self-help program for parents called "Tough Love," which is designed to make teenagers accountable for their actions, in order to give parents back some personal power inside their own homes.[11] Tough Love is often used before parents choose to send the misbehaving child to a group program like Eckerd Youth Alternatives, as a means to restore a more normal home life by actually removing the offending teenager from the home and into the hands of professionals for some period of time.[12] The most invasive *outdoor education* option is moving the youth to an inpatient facility or a similar establishment that has had success with treating teenagers for drug, alcohol, and/or emotional problems; these facilities may use some nature walks or art therapy in the outdoors as a means to reach the troubled youth. The least invasive means is probably equine therapy, which is always held outdoors. It is the most productive means to heal physical, emotional, or cognitive challenges in infants through adults. Having raised a son with bipolar disorder and ADHD, I have had more experiences in the areas listed above than I care to remember. The Eckerd Youth Alternatives was the most effective option for my son and for my family. I believe it was because my son lived in a national forest 100% of the time and faced life or death challenges at least once a week from actual encounters with wild animals. I camped with him for a few days as part of a parent program. During that time, I had a crocodile touch my canoe a few inches from my hand. I will never forget that experience, and surviving it changed me. Therefore, my theory is that rural Mexican kids have developed skills that are being overlooked in the classroom; sharing their special knowledge and experience would assist everyone, even the teachers working with them.

Children living in the U.S. are suffering from what the National Recreation and Park Association has identified as a critical trend of our time called "Nature-Deficit Disorder," a lack of exposure to nature.[13] Therefore, the Mexican immigrant child in a U.S. classroom is an expert in an area about which the other students may know little or nothing about; my observations have found that the urban child living in Mexico may be equally lacking in outdoor experiences and, therefore, may also have a deficit in this area. In either case, a smart teacher or trainer will enhance the classroom experience for all participants by allowing the people with outdoor experiences to share their *funds of knowledge* with everyone else.

Educators or instructors need to understand that time spent outdoors has been reduced a great deal in our time.[14]

This new symbolic demarcation line suggests that baby boomers—Americans born between 1946 and 1964—may constitute the last generation of Americans to share an intimate, familial attachment to the land and water.[15]

Near the beginning of his book, *Last Child in the Woods*, Richard Louv stated that contact with nature may be equal in importance to adequate sleep and good nutrition in order to achieve mental, physical, and spiritual health, and that the health of the earth is at stake as well.[16] Louv cites numerous researchers who acknowledge that health and nature go together.[17] It may be that the development of mental, physical, and spiritual health is magnified by the *campesino* lifestyle.

Contact with nature may be equal in importance to adequate sleep and good nutrition in order to achieve *mental, physical,* and *spiritual health. The health of the earth is at stake as well.*[18] It may be that the development of mental, physical, and spiritual health is magnified by the rural *campesino* lifestyle. Those facts might explain the ability of your students to win the struggle for survival and care for their families and extended families, even with an otherwise overwhelming sense of hopelessness.

In January 2004, I wrote a thesis titled *Outdoor Education for the Development of Responsible Youth* at the University of Arizona. This exercise was frustrating because there was a shortage of research material available. Fortunately, a copious amount of academic material related to *outdoor education* exists today, as many researchers now agree on the value of time in nature for mental, emotional, physical, and spiritual health.[19]

This fact alone serves to reinforce my theory of untapped human resources available in agricultural communities in Latin America. Rural residents appear to have all the right ingredients for success in life; they are simply starving for access to knowledge of life outside the campo and for opportunities anywhere.

Children in rural Latin America have a great deal of exposure to nature, because they live predominately outdoors. Nevertheless, they are not experiencing nature in an entirely positive manner; they struggle for survival while living in dwellings with fewer amenities than a camping tent. Mothers are unable to provide enough food, nutrition, and/or supplemental vitamins to enable the children to concentrate in school without having to try to stop their stomachs from growling—a significant distraction.

My position is in accord with other researchers: All rural low-socioeconomic-status children are students who have educational special needs that need to be addressed, but not necessarily labeled as such.[20] Some children have severe and profound needs that are obvious, like mental retardation, autism, or Down syndrome while others may have subtle unique challenges that do not need to be labeled, but that need to be identified in order to facilitate the learning. The broad category of reading disabilities is generally an invisible challenge. Some researchers take the position that reading disabilities in Latin America are influenced by numerous variables, such as gender, language development, food intake, frequency of perinatal risk factors, and neurological soft signs.[21] I agree with those researchers. The good news is that learning disabilities—including extreme struggles with reading, spelling, math, or other areas of learning—normally can be overcome with years of hard work.

My 2009 data suggested that *campesino* children were educationally marginalized because of their cultural status in addition to their economic situation that resulted in a lack of appropriate nutrition.[22] Additionally, there was limited, sometimes non-existent, access to social welfare resources, such as in-person educational training programs for caregivers or children, or online self-help information.

The data confirmed that the *campesino* caregiver raised children in a multi-generational, non-competitive, and interdependent format. This process occurred predominately outdoors, where the young mimicked the activities of adults and took on adult roles and responsibilities at an extremely early age. It was not uncommon to see a *campesino* toddler about the age of three tending a herd of goats or controlling a 1,000-pound horse. By the age of seven or eight, rural Latino children were driving vehicles by themselves within the community. There were few behaviors among rural Latino youth that mirrored what might be found in high schools in more developed countries; by the age ten or twelve, a rural Mexican boy would be spending his days behaving exactly the way an adult in his community behaved—by working long hours in a strenuous manner. It was not out of the ordinary to see Mexican children from agricultural communities plowing the fields with mules, moving feed with burros, or performing domestic activities, including caring for several slightly younger siblings without adult supervision. They did these jobs with ease acquired from experience.

Worldwide, three- to five-year-old indigenous children *largely care for them-selves*[23] and often at least one younger sibling. If a child has had all of that responsibility from the age of three or five, is it any wonder that being treated like a helpless and irresponsible young child as a teenager generates anger and resentment?

The following journal entry describes a typical situation in rural Latin America:

> *The young girl was about seven years old and had an infant propped on her hip as she walked down the dirt road; a toddler of about three years followed behind her. I stopped to ask if she needed a ride, but she declined, saying her grandmother lived only a short distance further down the road.*[24]

Polite rural Latinos usually accepted rides only if the distance was great; they did so with the same amount of respect that is seen when sick people (of all ages) wear face masks to protect others from exposure to the germs.

Children characteristically matured more rapidly when they were acting as caregivers due to their varied adult-like experiences. Their situation provided a stark contrast to the following quote written in reference to over-indulged teenagers or young adults living in the U.S.:

We (U.S.) have the most prolonged adolescence in the history of mankind. There is no other society that requires so many years to pass before people are grown up. Adolescence is nurtured and prolonged by educational processes and by industry that has found a bonanza in embracing the teenaged population and fortifying "adolescent values." This prolongation of adolescence robs the country of the population group (currently the Millennial Generation) having the most risk takers, and the highest ideals.[25]

Some Mothers Crumble Under Social Demands

Examining the castoff children abandoned to the streets by their mothers targets additional research pertaining to the lowered status, the gender bias, and the resulting perceived lack of self-sufficiency by single mothers in Mexico. Researcher Post has identified female children in Mexico as marginalized due to a lack of effective social-welfare programs for mothers functioning alone that could help them become independent heads of household.[26] I have personally verified the marginalizing of single mothers in Mexico through (1) living for over a decade on the border of Douglas, Arizona, and Agua Prieta, Sonora, Mexico; (2) working in schools with Mexican women, many of whom were single; (3) spending six summers in Mexico during Study Abroad programs; (4) visiting a Catholic priest who is caring for nearly 300 orphans without any help from governmental social services in Central Mexico, and (5) living in a rural Mexican community.

The overwhelming feelings that make a woman abandon her child usually occur when she has no support system or when the law is not on her side. The women of Guanajuato have both of these factors against them. In the summer of 2005, I met a University of Arizona (UA) graduate who taught me about the struggles of women in Mexico. Since that time, I have learned more, often firsthand. I was so pleased to know that a fellow UA alumnus was a volunteer for abused women in the state of Guanajuato, Mexico. She elaborated on the levels of abuse toward women and kept me updated with newsletters about the struggles of Mexican women before I moved to Mexico. These newsletters had articles on abandoned children and other relevant facts, including information about the efforts of a local group, Los Libres, in helping women. Los Libres has affirmed that abuse of women is a reality in Central Mexico. [27]

Los Libres also affirmed that not only do women get desperate and run away, but sometimes they do not run soon enough. They are subject to wrongful imprisonment without cause, which may be another reason they might abandon a child—because they are in prison or fear going to prison and not being able to care for a child. Several Los Libres legal aid groups worked for years to help women wrongly imprisoned. [28]

On September 8, 2010, seven women were released from prison. Each of them had served three to eight years for murder. It was explained that the women, who had miscarriages, were accused of having abortions in an effort to scare other women away from any thought of taking such an action. It was reported that the longest sentence was 29 years. Every one of the seven women was a native indigenous woman with no economic means to defend herself. [29] This level of abuse makes a strong emotional impact on women who seek gender equality.

The Realities of Second Language Acquisition

Choosing to relocate my entire family and my research into an environment where my first challenge was going to be learning the language was done to gain a better understanding about the deficiency model of minority groups.[30] I became the minority language learner struggling with daily conversation and academic content—"the ignoramus" researcher.[31] Similar to a scientist who experiments on himself, I felt that in the end I would develop a better understanding of what was being asked of immigrant children socially, politically, and academically in the U.S. schools and communities. Fortunately for my ego, Latino people were far more patient than those I had found in other places; I was also not working toward passing standardized testing in a second language.

Like the Latino immigrant child in the U.S., my family offered me first language (L1 or mother tongue) stability at home; but unlike the immigrant child, my second language did not threaten my first. A serious breakdown of communication occurs in the U.S. when young immigrant Latino children must act as language brokers, translating English into Spanish for adult relatives. Sometimes the child may have to translate sensitive information, like a message from an unpaid bill collector or shocking news that a relative had been killed. The child, therefore, may wish that he or she was not the translator. The child retains the first language but may wish that he or she did not have bilingual abilities. Some researchers have found that this adult-level responsibility to translate information for adults may induce emotional stress that can lead to poor academic results.[32]

Researchers Norma González, Luis Moll, and Cathy Amanti found that the use of the schooling model of punitive measures and time limits within learning situations "developed one of the few adult-child conflicts within the household."[33] These same three researchers suggested that reduced self-esteem was the outcome of the punitive measures model of schooling, because of the cultural conflict of expectations that opposed the student-motivated style of learning of the Latino culture.[34] Educators or instructors would do well to rework the student syllabi to be more student-friendly or to develop student-driven learning syllabi.

Children were expected to ask questions and practice the learned behavior, functioning within a "non-stressful domain or neutral zone of comfort, where little criticism was expressed, and they would not be faulted." As a result, "this more relaxed approach allowed self-evaluation and self-judgment."[35] The students were also encouraged to take as long as they liked to accomplish the task, which was a better approach for Latino students.

This was in sharp contrast to the rigid time restraints placed on all children in public schools in the U.S.

Role Models Set the Stage for Learning

My casual and formal research evolved into observations of survivors: powerful women who stood as mentors and role models to their children, their grandchildren, their relatives, and their communities. Bridges were built between women "even when separated by race and class."[36] They were the ones who expected to be called on as the problem solvers for any problems within the family; they told me that they expected and welcomed this role. They were idealists who engaged in the daily goals of caring for the children and preserving the family and the heritage. They did this by quietly and universally taking the role of family leader and protector of the culture.

My research participants in 2007 were working for a private bilingual school located right on the Arizona-Sonora border and were paid minimum wage; half of them were the sole wage earners within their families, as well as heads of households with children. I uncovered their cultural patterns, their self-described role within their heritage, and their definition of personal success. Maria's, Esmerelda's, and others' comments on their expectations as Latina mothers have been included throughout this book. They all considered the role of the matriarch to be paramount, both personally and culturally.

The goal of my 2007 research project was to capture opinions of those Latina women and learn how they functioned within the Latino culture. Each woman had stories to tell and was happy to tell them openly and honestly to someone they already knew and trusted. Many Latinos face bias in the U.S. The women knew that I, their interviewer, was biased toward them in a positive manner because I knew them so well. The women knew that I would accurately record what they had to say. Many transcribed statements in this book are from that research.

Mothers Expect Children to be Perfectly Behaved

During my time in Central Mexico, I found that Mexican mothers were less tolerant of misbehavior, compared to the mothers I had met in the U.S. while living on the Arizona-Sonora border. During my 2009 research in Mexico, mothers often reported any behavior outside the rigid standard of perfection with an alarming urgency and with hope of finding a permanent and rapid solution. That included any issues related to signs and expressions of anger in infants, children, and youth. The mothers frequently reported that parents expected their children to be quiet, to sit still without distractions (toys, MP3 players, etc.), and to be well behaved and respectful of the family and other authority figures.

The parents reported that children were expected to speak softly and infrequently; any other behavioral pattern was an alert of grave concern. I expected children to be talkative and active with adults or other children. How I expected a child to communicate and act in the presence of an adult and how I expected a child to behave when playing with another child were far outside of the parameters expected by rural mothers.

Interviewees in both the 2009 study in Central Mexico and the 2007 study in the U.S., who came from all walks of life, stated that the Latina mother ruled the household. I have observed this to mean that the Latina mother typically demands from her children an unquestioning, absolute respect. Assuredly, there is a qualifier to that statement: If a young mother is living with her husband or another adult male, her decisions may always be overridden by the adult male living in the house. This statement is especially true for decisions pertaining to male children. Fathers are less likely to interfere with mothers' demands of daughters than of sons. Fathers frequently step in and override their wives' discipline methods and expectations of sons, especially after the boys reach the age of ten.

The tenth birthday, particularly for males, signifies the end of childhood in Mexico. This might be compared to the significance of the twelfth birthday in the U.S. By the age of ten, a Latino child is considered to be generally self-sufficient; although, as previously stated, the amount of responsibility that a ten-year-old in Latin America assumes, male or female, is vastly greater than that of any twelve-year-old in the U.S.

Infrequent Talking to Children is Standard

The parents interviewed in 2009 in Central Mexico implied that children were raised in a culture in which it is not customary to talk a lot. My experience living in the *campo* has confirmed this. Conversations are expected to be limited, especially adult-child conversations. I am alarmed at the limited verbal communication and the lack of emphasis by a parent to perfect children's speaking skills. Parents are concerned if their children do not speak at all, but they do not assume the role of making them verbal. Parents have informed me that teachers or language therapists are supposed to assume the role for educating children to speak correctly.

Lower-than-expected reading skills among the caregivers may mean that reading out loud to a child might not produce satisfactory communication for either party. Reading aloud by adults is a very labored activity, and the child may have difficulty following the material being read. Repeating the reading activity is unlikely, even if teachers or others suggest that the caregivers try it. Parents whom I have observed seem uncomfortable reading aloud. Additionally, the child is unlikely to respond to a photo of an object in a book if the parent refers to it, because there has been no generalization instruction or even training regarding such an object by caregivers or other relatives. The donated books I use with neighbors for reading classes often lack photos of objects found in the *campo*. Additionally, children are not used to having an adult read to them. The children might appear highly timid and look away, because their culture expects them not to look into the eyes of adults; children normally learn by imitating what they see, not by being singled out for attention or by being instructed.

This is another example of how cultural expectations having a direct influence on personal, social, religious, and political activities and expectations of the norm within the *campo*. This is a good example of heritage norms affecting behavior.

If a child does not talk and a specialist perceives this to be a verbal disability, this may be an invalid assessment. Instead, cultural influences or other factors may be present.

Summary: Raising Latino Children

The difference between raising children in the developing region of rural Latin America and raising them in a technologically advanced environment of the U.S. is really vast. One must remember that different is not bad or good—it's simply outside expectations.

What educators or instructors must understand is how to help each student, regardless of age or social status, to reach his or her maximum potential at home, in school, or in the workplace.

This young man works in town every day, selling sweet breads instead of attending school; he is probably ten to twelve years of age. It is common for bread vendors to carry their wares on their heads.

9

Let's Talk Business

The first rule of any technology used in a business is that automation applied to an efficient operation will magnify the efficiency. The second is that automation applied to an inefficient operation will magnify the inefficiency.

—Bill Gates

Educators or Trainers Must Comprehend the Complexity of Business in Latin America

The difficulty of doing business in Latin America is legendary for a reason. It is true that doing business in Latin America is nearly always mystifyingly difficult. It matters little if the process involves buying a taco from a local vendor or completing a foreign visa application; the process is repeatedly complex and frequently unsatisfying. Nearly all business activities by rural men or women are related to family businesses. Because children are involved nearly from birth in making an income for the family or at least observing how an income is made, this must be understood by educators or instructors of Spanish speakers. The role of a child may be giving change to someone buying a product inside the home, helping to feed a goat to be sold, making tortillas in the family kitchen to sell in the community, or walking to their father's job site to deliver a meal; the norm is for the whole family to be involved in the earning of money. Frequently, children are also involved in observing how money is put aside to be used for the business in order to keep the business running. The hard lesson of saving money to buy inventory for selling is learned at a very early age in Latin America. Therefore, it is imperative that educators or instructors of Spanish speakers understand the complexities of business in Latin America.

Business History Differences

Puritans, a very distinctive group of people, settled the roots of the current government in the U.S. The Puritans were a group of people who held that the spoken word was a legal contract: *Your word is your honor.* That attitude formed the basis of the way business is done in the U.S. The concept of a democracy was sold to the people. There was a great emphasis on fairness and political correctness. Contracts were upheld and employees were expected to be team players. The path to financial success was, by all appearances, *based on hard work and honest contracts.*

The fact that activities going on in the U.S. government today have been found to be corrupt has nothing to do with what is being addressed here. My statements have everything to do with the *appearance* of how business is done in the U.S. and have almost nothing to do with what is actually taking place. The appearance is one of a teamwork and trust, just as the concept of *innocent until proven guilty* is the basis of the U.S. justice system.

Mexico has a totally different history. After Spain conquered Mexico and took control from Native Indians, other countries were expected to steal the "New Spain," Mexico. The governments of Spain and other neighboring countries were, for hundreds of years, under the rule of a very complex hierarchy of monarchs. These monarchs were absolute rulers, conquers, and warriors.

The public message was that *people who overpowered others and took their property increased their own and their country's wealth.* The means to financial and business success appeared to be to advocate pillaging from others with total disregard for others' property.

Mexico is a democracy, a political system with the individual freedom vote and the option to engage in family economic endeavors with limited restrictions. It is true that there is a holdover from the Spanish rule, as well as from the rule of other conquerors and warriors with dictatorship attitudes; this is evident from extreme social class differences between the employer and the employee. Observations confirmed that *overpower others* attitude in business conduct was alive in Mexico. Interviews with Mexicans revealed that foreigners were often thought to be *a little stupid,* because they might accept the first price requested for an item being sold or pay an employee before the contracted work was actually completed. The custom of politeness and spoken words of respect between people apparently fooled foreigners. What appeared to be happening was not what actually was going on. There was a lack of trust, fairness, or equality between an employee and employer. This is observed as business as usual in Latin America.

Even in a business that was only slightly bigger than a walk-in closet, there were often three employees, two of whom watched the other one. The employees double-checked each other on every transaction, while being paid next-to-nothing in wages.[1] My statements have everything to do with the *appearance* of how business was done in Mexico regardless of what was actually taking place. The appearance was one of believing everyone to be a thief. That was why the business cash drawers were nearly always empty; an employee rarely handled any cash. Buying from a small vendor on the street or from Home Depot or Wal-Mart, even on a Saturday, often resulted in an extensive wait, as someone had to get the change; this was applicable to transactions of any size that required coin or bill change. Most cash drawers were emptied every couple of minutes in bigger stores and handled only by the owners in smaller establishments. The lack of efficiency when making a purchase in Latin America, due to employees not being trusted to handle money, was a constant amazement. An observer of Latino business practices must keep in mind that *guilty until proven innocent* is the basis of the Latino justice system.

The cultural makeup of the U.S. and Latin America is very different. The U.S. is a vast melting pot of numerous diverse cultures either clinging to heritage roots within relocated small communities or thinning out heritages through integration and intermarriage; Mexico has remained far more homogeneous. Both countries started out with Native Indian cultures, but the U.S. welcomed immigrants from all over the world for many years. In contrast, small Mexican communities struggled to preserve their Native Indian cultures while sharing their country, their land, and their businesses with the Spanish conquerors. Today the joint market consists of tourism or export of items processed or produced in Mexico, like food, animals, tin, gold, and sugar. Tourism trade and/or exporting may put each group in competition with the other for the same market share.

This business environment is inefficient for the economic growth of a country as a whole: Too much focus is placed on watching the competition at the retail level and not enough on external customer service, internal quality control, design and development of new products, inefficient operations, marketing, and other executive functions of a successful business model.

Tax Structure

Mexican government tries to collect taxes from the public; the collected taxes help the government to pay for social services. However, it seems that the Mexican public tries harder to avoid paying taxes at all costs. Getting a receipt in a small store, a national store chain, or a professional's office is next to impossible, because no one wants to pay the taxes due on a sale.

Logic dictates that a government that cannot collect taxes cannot supply adequate services to the public.

Observations confirmed that if a retailer agrees to provide a receipt for a sale, there is always the question of "factora o recibo?" directed toward the consumer beforehand. A "factora" is an invoice that shows all taxes paid. A "recibo" is an invoice that shows the total amount paid without itemization. By making a purchase, it becomes possible to understand the complexities of Mexican business. Even employees in large international corporations will ask consumers if they require a simple proof of purchase ("un recibo") or if they need a legal receipt that itemizes all taxes and fees ("una factora"). If they request "un recibo," the transaction is completed in a flash; if they request "una factora," however, then the amount due can increase by about 17% to 20% and the waiting time may be considerable. The same is true of contractors, housekeepers, or other casual employees; they all want to be paid in cash without any record of their employment and without making any payments to social welfare or governmental taxation programs.

Chapter 10 includes an interview with a former Mexican government official that will further explain the inner workings of the economic system in Mexico; that interview will shed more light on the subject of why taxes are difficult to collect in Mexico. If all citizens fail to pay taxes or other fees needed to fund programs, there are going to be shortages, and the Mexican government will be unable to provide basic needs to the most disadvantaged citizens. It takes an income to fund programs. To this observer, it appeared that almost no one was paying taxes in Mexico, yet the U.S. public media reports about corruption inside the Mexican government but not about the failure of the Mexican public to pay taxes. These factors made it very difficult for me, an experienced and educated businesswoman, to determine what was actually going on with the economics in Mexico. Mexico is rich in land, resources, and people, but determining what economic changes would best benefit and serve the entire population is a challenge.

Employment

Rural Latin America citizens are so short of physical and economic resources that their lives are nearly always intertwined and dependent upon outside forces, including but not limited to the economic situation in the U.S. or in Latin America, seasonal employment patterns, immigration issues, political changes, or other changes related to acquiring income. In addition to other hazards of being lower class citizens, these financially disadvantaged people face constant challenges related to living in third-world conditions, including poor hygiene, few physical or time resources, lack of potable water, limited access to special-education services, lack of unemployment insurance, and no social security disability or other retirement services. They also face environmental hurdles, both internal and external to the agricultural communities. Just as cutting trees leaves the land barren unless new trees are subsequently planted, Latin America has natural resources—like ore and oil reserves—that need careful management to preserve them. Determining who owns these reserves, internal Native Indians or the external federal government, can cause conflicts.

Much of the rural Latin Americans' lives are intertwined with both internal and external cultural, social, political, and religious events, because there is a "trickle-down" effect within this economically and socially depressed society. Economic and/or social changes in the upper classes have a direct effect on the lower classes. What they do not lack is creativity and innovation.

Due to the lack of welfare or other social service programs, rural Mexicans stretch themselves to the outer limits in their effort to make money and to otherwise be self-sufficient.

Career Titles

The power of a title must be clearly understood. If a person has a paid position in a private or a public organization that requires him to do the same job over a period of time, he will have a title. He will also have a uniform with an embroidered logo and his name embroidered below the logo. He will have personal power and almost unquestioned authority. That regular-paycheck position carries more status than can be imagined, even if it is only as a cleaning person in a well-known hotel.

People with a continuous income appear to stay in their career/job position until death—that's why their name is embroidered below the logo. Personal power over clients or customers—not over fellow employees—and almost unquestioned authority are the prizes given to people in lieu of a decent salary.

Recognizing Power in Business

No matter the title, that employee is expected to be totally in control of any situation. The uniform (to go with the title) would be made of high-quality fabric, and the employee would keep it completely spotless and pressed. If a hat is included, it would also be in perfectly clean and neat condition. There are 14 class status levels, and the observer is always expected to assume that the person being observed is of a higher status than they actually are—every effort is made to convey that impression.[2]

In transacting business with Latinos, it is prudent to be attentive to the type of uniform and size of *rubber stamp used. A large rubber stamp* is a very important status symbol in Latin America. The larger the stamp, the more authority the employee holds within his position of power.[3] The stamp is often used with excessive force when hitting a page—perhaps the loud sound is intended to make the stamp appear larger.

My advice is to be humbled by the embroidered uniform and to be even more so if a large (2-inch square or bigger) stamp is sitting nearby; otherwise, there will likely be problems that will bring all business transitions to a halt.

Government Inaction

At some point, rural people take matters into their own hands. For instance, if sewer lines break and sewage leaks into a lake used as the local water source and no city political official orders a repair, then illness would occur in the community. The illness, resulting from a lack of services from a nearby city, is a direct internal event that influences the rural community. After waiting for a while, the locals will make the best repair that they are able to with limited resources.

Our road has raw sewage rushing down most of the time. The sewage runs over the road that people used for walking to/from a nearby town and then leaks into the public water supply. The community leaders tried to get the government to repair the broken pipes, but they were not successful. Periodically, the locals take matters into their own hands by taking shovels and stone and making a temporary fix. Passersby hand the local residents a couple pesos for trying. Raw sewage running between houses is a horrid health hazard, but because putting food on the table is usually a higher immediate priority for the families, the raw sewage continues to flow down the street. In the meantime, my neighbors try to "peddle" food or some other product to each other for enough profit to buy tortillas for their family dinner. Additionally, any item donated to those helping with the sewer problem in lieu of cash, like food or other items bartered with labor, is a welcome addition to the dining room table.

Efficiency: A Word That Does Not Translate

The lack of efficiency in processing paperwork and the overabundance of workers nearly always available to help customers in Mexican government offices were shocking to anyone who normally anticipated a business to be run with an eye on efficiency and reduction of labor costs. It was not at all uncommon to walk into a very large old building with the dividing walls of the interior made entirely of glass, enabling one to see everything that was going on. Examining what was occurring, from an efficiency standpoint, was easy. Seeing excessive numbers of employees moving around in a less than an efficient manner was common. Perhaps because labor was cheap, overcoming that extra expense had a low priority. It appeared the nepotism of people in hiring positions, who wanted to keep relatives employed, also contributed to a lack of concern for efficiency.

The Domino Effect

Another factor to consider is distant economic situations. When the economy changes, there is a ripple effect from higher class to lower class. A man from rural Mexico who is a subsistence farmer or a day laborer and does not have a steady position of power or a continuing paycheck is vulnerable to those changes. No matter how far away from the *campo* he is working, the money he sends home stops if he is out of work. As a result, life in his home community would immediately change due to an indirect external event causing changes in a distant economy. The effect on the rural Latin American resident is quick, harsh, and unpredictable. Latin Americans lack the ability to use executive functions.[4]

Executive function is the ability to plan ahead in a linear manner, like using a Gant Chart, a drawing that visually shows the time line of a business activity and estimated dates when supplies or labor would be needed to perform a job without delays. In Latin America, my observation and observations of those whom I interviewed confirmed that if a job site anticipated needing more concrete on Monday, the order would not be placed until Monday morning. If work had progressed faster than anticipated and workers were ready for the additional concrete on Friday afternoon, the concrete would still not be ordered until Monday morning. Then everyone would sit around and do nothing while waiting for the concrete to be delivered. None of the employees would see this situation as odd, wasteful, or inefficient, because this approach has always been used in construction work. Everyone accepts this lack of pre-planning, ordering, and organizing in a linear manner as *standard operating procedure*. People interviewed about this pattern explained that the need did not exist until there was no more concrete left. I have been assured that this was ingrained into cultural norms because "something" might happen. If time was allocated to another activity, there might be no need for the concrete until Tuesday, so why order it on Friday? It appeared as though there was absolutely no apparent comprehension of the fact that people would be getting paid to sit around on the next workday waiting for the supplies or the tools of their trade to be delivered. As a former certified member of the American Inventory and Production Control Society, I was deeply mystified by this acceptance of a lack of preplanning in the construction trade.

This thought process was not limited to common supplies. The same thing would occur if what was needed was a bulldozer, even if the order for the machine needed a three- or four-day lead time. Until the day arrived that the bulldozer was actually needed, it would not be ordered. Any delays meant that workers would take off work, without pay, and not come back for three to four days. They would be losing a steady paycheck in the process and would have to look for another job. Since that was the way it had always been done, those questioned assured me that there was nothing unusual about this pattern of doing business, and that it was normal in any business, even outside of the construction trade.

Due to life being so uncertain, only what was needed for today was purchased for today. Rarely was there planning ahead for the following day's meal or for the next step in a construction project.

Paid to Watch Each Other, Not Paid to Produce

Employees were expected to watch each other to make sure that nothing was stolen and that no one ever made a mistake. The primary business focus seemed to be on employees monitoring each other, not on customer service, creating a dissatisfying experience for clients accustomed to US business efficiency.

Additional people checked the work completed by the first employee at least twice before moving on. There was no margin of error planned into business practices in Latin America.

Perhaps that was exactly why an abundance of errors occurred outside of anticipated errors. Observation clearly showed that fear was present in every employed person. Employees were so afraid of making a mistake that they looked at every situation inside, outside, and backward—to the point where what was finally accomplished made even less sense to a common observer than to an efficiency expert. An efficiency expert would consider the lost time expenditure a great deal more of a financial burden—due to paying direct overhead, like the cost of labor, and indirect costs, like training the employees—than the overall loss that a mistake would produce.

Getting Federal Health Insurance Story

Recently, we applied for state health insurance. The process took about two hours in Room One of one building. There were two pages of request forms to fill out, and our paperwork was looked over. Requested paperwork nearly always included the U.S. Passport, one of the Mexican visas (FMT, FM3, or FM2), a housing contract, power/water/phone bills with "paid" stamped across them, two or three recent color photographs of a specific size (without the subject wearing glasses or earrings), plus any additional items specific to the request. There was only one other customer in Room One. Checking that customer's paperwork took nearly two hours: The forms were lost; many employees stopped by; and everything was checked numerous times. I have been told by Mexicans and expatriates that employees are expected to "watch for suspicious activity" to make sure that the client is worthy of getting whatever it is that he or she is requesting from a government office.

After the first approval finally came, we had to go upstairs to Room Two, where the paperwork checked again by three more people. Then we were handed a slip to take to the bank. We then had to walk to a specific bank, which I will call "Room Three," to pay the fee and get several more receipts to bring back to Room Two. Each receipt from the bank had a big rubber-stamp mark on it. Those receipts were carefully examined before we were granted approval to return to Room One. At that point, we got our health books with one photo inside, extra photos, and a receipt to take to Room Four. We went to the other side of town to Room Four, stood in line, and then learned that clients could not take that next step in the same calendar month as when they applied. Therefore, we had to wait over three weeks to return to Room Four. Upon our return, we easily handed over our health books, had photos attached to file folders with our names on them, and then had our health books returned to us. We were finally done!

Some people have reported being required to take a physical and have lab tests done on every family member in Room Four, but other people, like us, have not had that additional step. This difference might have been up to the person in command of handling our folders, or the rules might have changed. It is common to have numerous unknown factors in a transaction like this one in Mexico.

In the future, the annual approval process will likely be easier for us. That is the typical pattern: The initial application is extremely difficult, while the renewal is easy. The initial process is similar in every government office, and until it is completed, all exchanges will take lots of time, and changing offices, rooms, or buildings—and, therefore, moving between numerous employees who appear to be checking each other's work—will be required.

Anytime a person can get in and out of a bank in less than one hour, something very unusual must have occurred.

No matter how small the bank transaction, the process takes an hour of standing in line, being observed for any suspicious activity, having the transaction double-checked, and finally getting what I came for, maybe. If I asked for change, I would not get change—because people cannot "buy" change at a bank in Latin America. If I needed change, then I would have to go to a toll booth ("cuota"), a place on the highway where cars have to pay a toll using small change, not to a bank; there were no alternatives. The same was true for trying to get a check cashed.

You cannot get a check cashed in Mexico— there is always a reason found to turn down cashing a check. One expatriate actually wrote someone a check at the bank in front of a teller immediately after signing the bank's signature card, but the check was still refused because the signatures were not totally identical. No kidding. The person immediately closed the bank account.

I learned not to bother writing checks in Mexico, because none that I had written were ever accepted by any of the banks for cashing. There appeared to be no place where a person holding a check drawn on a Mexican bank note could get it cashed.

Phone Service

Prepaid cell phones can be purchased in Mexico, but the service is very costly, and each phone has to be registered using the FMT, a temporary visa issued to all visitors. My experience is that monthly contracts for cell phones in Mexico require an FM3 or an FM2 visa. Rumor has it that this requirement is in place so that if a person does not fulfill the contract, the free or low-cost phone might be recovered. Nevertheless, one phone company in Guanajuato, U.S. CELL, refused to give us monthly phone service. They kept asking for more and more items: a rental contract, a bank account in Mexico, etc., until I finally contacted the president of the company and learned that "gringos" can no longer get a phone service from them. In Mexico, corporations can discriminate and not offer service to whomever they choose. Nextel refused to sell us phone service when we came to Mexico even though we had Nextel in the U.S. at the time. We had paid the bill without a hitch for four years and fulfilled two contracts to the very end. Don't be fooled into thinking that you are entering the same store in Mexico that you had entered in the U.S.—that is an illusion. Nextel Mexico is not Nextel U.S. in the same manner that Home Depot Mexico and Home Depot U.S. are not connected. You cannot use your established credit record or your store credit card from the U.S. in a Mexican establishment. Better pull out a Visa card and hope for the best. Many businesses will not take any credit cards, and if they do, there is a significant surcharge.

How the Visa System Works

The most amazing story of a business transaction procedure is that of an expatriate getting her first FM3 or FM2 visa. Someday a video camera is going to make its way into a Mexican Office of Immigration and the worldwide viewings will be off the scale, because no one will believe what typically occurs in that space.

First, a long—very long—list of items must be presented. These include one's contract for housing or title to land, recent power/water/phone bills with "paid" stamped across them, two or three recent color photographs of a specific size (without the subject wearing glasses or earrings), a birth certificate, a marriage license, the last three monthly bank statements for each bank account owned, and a letter explaining what "activities" the applicant is planning to participate in while in Mexico (tourism, studying, volunteering, engaging in business, etc.), since they might need to buy an additional work permit. Then there are numerous forms to fill out, and money must be paid at a specific branch of a specific bank. A visitor once had to buy a work permit for volunteer "work" for a nonprofit group. The person in command might also ask the applicant for other items, with all of them in multiple copies.

There will be a minimum of three trips required to the immigration office to get the paperwork completed, unless a university or a corporation applies for you in your name. It can take a year, but if the university or the corporation has the right connections or pays a bribe ("mordita"), then the visa will be issued.

This process can be quite time consuming if the immigration office is some distance away. The extremely loud sound of a rubber stamp usually provides a clue that the process of the first day may be coming to an end. The slamming of the rubber stamp by the initial inspector can be overwhelming and fast: "Boom! Boom!" will ring out all over the waiting area for up to 100 pages of paper. In the waiting room, one can find 20 or more people watching a DVD of a neutral subject while looking forward to the time when their paperwork will be slammed with such force and authority. The immigration process is so difficult that a large percentage of expatriates paid more to have a service complete the entire process for them than they paid for the FM3/FM2 visa itself.

Postal Service Challenges

Every expatriate handles mail differently; most of them use a courier service. Local rumor is that only 3% of the 75,000 expatriates in San Miquel de Allende are registered with the U.S. federal government. If that is true, some people here do not want to get mail.

We do not have a place near our home in Mexico to get mail. Our house is a place in a village that does not have a mailing address. We have received two pieces of mail here. Mail that is addressed to a name with the town name (no street or house number) will go to the town mayor, who will then give it to a local vendor. The vendor may ask someone to stop by the addressee's home to deliver the mail—maybe. It is very uncommon to get mail in the village.

We have a federal postal box about 35 minutes away in another town in Mexico. Letters take a long time to arrive there and are expensive for those who mail them from outside of Mexico. Some expatriates use the Mexican mail service and have reported having no problems other than the speed.

Our corporation is based in Arizona, so we have a legal address in Arizona where the corporate mail is delivered. Our corporate registered agent receives the mail and the UPS packages for us; this person is on all of our bank accounts as a signer and handles all of our corporate credit cards and U.S. phone calls. Direct mail, like magazines, is sent to Texas and forwarded to us using a courier service that has an office at a distance of a two-hour round-trip from our house. The courier service has an annual fee for letters; all packages have a handling fee per pound. There are services that do the same for people who are sailing on cruises or otherwise traveling out of their house country.

Summary: Let's Talk Business

In summary, doing business in Latin America is very difficult for those who have a history of doing business (1) where relationships are not of primary importance, (2) in less labor-intensive societies, (3) with more automation, and (4) with more of a focus on time and efficiency management as a means to reduce costs. Latin America has an excess of workers in every aspect of business: family, private, public, or government. Time or efficiency management is rarely applied at any level of business operatons in Latin America. People work hard, very hard, but in most cases using their backs and their relationships, not with an effective means of operating a business efficiently as the main priority. In the same manner that relationships with family, extended family, and friends take precedence over any career or employment situations, extensive social networks and class structure form the foundation of business operations in Latin America. Even for a "gringo," the first time any interaction takes place (such as when applying for an FM3 visa), there will be countless delays; the second time, however, usually goes much smoother and faster.

The best advice for doing business in Latin America is: Put an hour aside for any transaction that you would expect to take a maximum of 15 minutes in the U.S. (such as getting change at a bank). Additionally, do not to expect any form of customer service until you are at the front of the line. Prepare to stand in line for a very long time, expect no eye contact to occur during that wait time, and anticipate that much social interaction will take place behind the counter between employees on the phone or on the computer. You will probably be asked for some obscure piece of information that will take considerable time to obtain from some other source. If even one part of the above scenario does not occur, be relieved.

If you still want to do business in Latin America, be sure to read *Mexicans and Americans, Cracking the Cultural Code* by Ned Crouch (2004). The author does an outstanding job of explaining how to be successful, and how to avoid being as frustrated as most people from other countries become when they do business in Latin America.

The building with the flag, beyond the outdoor restaurant tables, is home to government offices. The traditional structure is impressive. The guards are well armed and visible at all times. Photographing of the offices is not encouraged.

10

The Hand of Government

We are imperfect. We cannot expect perfect government.

    —William Howard Taft

All Secondhand Information

This section is a record of what I was told by Mexicans about the relationship between people and the laws of Mexico.

As a religious leader, I have no ethical, legal, or moral right to state my opinion about politics in Mexico, the U.S., or anywhere else—and I do not care to do so.

My only interest is in how people react to political influences in their country. Specifically, I am interested in the laws of either the U.S. or Mexico as they might relate to the education of monolingual Spanish or disabled Mexicans.

The greatest resource in Latin America is the ability to survive today in joyful celebration of life in spite of promises of gloom on tomorrow's horizon.

Regardless of what political oppression rages in the cities, in rural Latin America, tortillas are still passed from hand to hand before they hit the fire, music plays loudly, and colorful cut-paper shapes sway in the breeze from nearly invisible fine cotton strings draped over trees or rooftops in a haphazard "Live for Today!" fashion.

129

Culturally unaware observers cannot help but be mystified at the resilient Latin Americanss exhibiting such unusual carefree behavior when so much in these Latin Americans' lives care-fraught.

Something mystical, magical, spiritual, or otherwise invisible to the naked eye and yet very real is going on in these rural communities.

My efforts to find answers led me to many excellent books on Latin American history and politics. Each one helped me to grasp the complexity of a country that has been oppressed by brutal violence, as conquests and repressive government actions raped both people and natural resources. What remained a mystery was how great cultural achievements had been accomplished in the midst of recurring political chaos.

As I observed life in the *campo*, it seemed as though while economic or political news told of cities figuratively *burning to the ground*, in rural Mexico music played, relationships were nurtured, bright colors further enhanced the richness of the landscape, and good food was relished among friends and families.

My own cultural history directed my thoughts. I asked: "Why was a fiesta taking place now? Why was nothing being done to save the cities?" I finally allowed my analysis to reveal the sociocultural framework of a rural Latin American living, where a once non-democratic society oppressed the poor so deeply that a *social infection,* a sore spot ready to fester once again, was still right below the surface. A place where unreasonableness, not logic, prevailed since social status dictated how much power and control could be exercised. But wait! By whose cultural standards are both *unreasonableness* and *logic* defined? I began to see more cross-cultural questions than answers.

The simple fact remained that *there was nothing socially powerless people could do or wanted to do to save the cities and their unpredictable politics.*

Rural Latin Americans seem to feel hopelessly lacking control. This non-executive function of domestic life is repeatedly observed: There are no physical caches of food, pencils, toilet paper, or anything else on hand in the homes. There isn't even a shopping list of what needs to be replaced, apparently because life is simply too unpredictable to make plans ahead of time.

One clear example of the lack of preplanning was partying preparation. Repeatedly, preparation began right at the time when the party was announced to start. Every time I arrived at the announced starting time of a rural-area party, the hosts were only beginning to gather tables and chairs, to put decorations together, and to gather food. At the same time, the children were sent to a local store ("tienda") with a few pesos to buy cold beer. "Why chill a beer or buy it before there is a need?" seemed to be the thought process.

I once arrived at a wedding of an expatriate male and his Latin American bride. Because it started on time, over half of the invited guests missed the actual ceremony. The most amazing part was that one of the bridesmaids walked in just before the bilingual, bicultural, 60-minute-long ceremony ended. She seemed totally comfortable walking into the middle of the program and taking her position next to the bride.

Social Service Hurdles

Strauss and Corbin remind the researcher "that different research projects are affected by changing conditions…because of bureaucratic regulations, costs, shortages of time, or language barriers."[1] All of these applied to my research. The first Internal Review Board (IRB) approval for my research arrived electronically days after I had arrived in Mexico in 2008. I immediately contacted the child care and preschool government-run organization (name withheld) where I had volunteered the previous two summers and had confirmed permission to continue as a volunteer researcher in 2008.

What I did not understand then was that within the hierarchic political structure of the Mexican government, in which a new president is elected every six years, is a system of overwhelming change based almost exclusively on the *relationship factor*.

The change of political power every six years affects even the lowest level of government employees. No social service protection is established for the low-level employment positions. Therefore, new people replace all positions in the government when the political power changes in Mexico. Commonly, the entire departmental organization, for better or for worse, changes with each political change. The replacement director of the (name withheld) school approved my continued observations and new research, but I was required to get approval from her new boss. For the next month, I attempted to gain that approval.

From the first day I had arrived at the school to do my research until the day before all university students under my adviser left the summer 2008 program, I was having two to five visits a week for five weeks with the person from whom I needed the approval. At that time, this naïve researcher did not realize that a "mordida" was expected within this society; the literal translation of "mordida" is "a little bite."

The actual meaning of "mordida" offered to a government official in the U.S. would be an illegal bribe. In Latin America, it is actually an anticipated service fee connected with doing business. This service fee applies to any Latin American citizen, in a government office or elsewhere.

Numerous research participants have explained that each employment position has a level of anticipated cash transactions connected with it.[2] Bureaucratic regulations offered me no options to contact anyone other than the sole administrator with whom I interacted. Additionally, I was ignorant of what was expected of me to gain that approval.

On the very last day of the University of Arizona summer 2008 program overseen by my adviser, I finally received permission to do my research. Only the administrator signed permission; the parents I was to interview were forbidden from signing anything, because by law, as Mexican nationals, they had given their authority over to the government.

My IRB required parental signatures; I needed to amend the IRB application with verbal consent from all of the parents to the paperwork read to them by my translator and witnessed by my translator.[3] That five-week period of frustration was only the first of many administrative hurdles within the social service legalities that I would face while doing research in Mexico, due to *bureaucratic regulations, costs, shortages of time, or language barriers.*[4]

The Government of Mexico Rules Social Variables

Mexico has a social division of about 14 castes, clearly defined lines of social status put in place by the Spanish.[5] The lines have become blurred over generations, but unlike the claim by Payne that only three social classes—poor, middle, and wealthy—exist,[6] Mexico has many more. Today, at least 14 levels are still in evidence. The current population of Mexico consists of 10% North European visitors, 30% Native Indians, and 70% mixed White, Indian, and/or Negro races.[7] Few people will admit to Native Indian (indigenous) status. However, the government makes that an easy distinction by identifying indigenous as falling into any one of five categories: (1) language, (2) rituals, (3) self-identification, (4) parental identification, and (5) birth place. As one of the classifications is based on the location of the family home, families who live beyond an urban city are classified as indigenous. In this case, where a person was born determines his sociocultural classification.[8]

There are clear reasons for the different classifications, since the rural lifestyle and native values modify the residents' way of thinking. If the family home is an agricultural community, the attitude of the people inside that home is probably *live for today because tomorrow is so uncertain*. Outside observers probably cannot imagine to what extent this attitude penetrates the lifestyle of rural people. These patient, stoic, Native Indian people use it as a way to cope.

Locals Remark that their Government Offers Few Helpful Alternatives

The local people will acknowledge few programs offered by the federal, state, or city governments as having valid benefits for citizens. When there are valuable programs—like "Oportunidades" ("Opportunities"), which supplies nutritional supplements to mothers and children—many of those who should be able to access these programs cannot do so, due to not being capable of filling out the paperwork or proving their need.[9] A rural mother frequently lacks literacy, cannot understand the question, or is unable to access required information (a receipt cannot be located, a husband's signature cannot be accessed because his location is unknown, etc.).

The laborer's protection program has the same intent as workman's compensation or disability insurance, but it is so mired in red tape and inefficiency that even those who pay into the program for years are aware that they will not be helped if they ever become unable to work. The same is true for social security: The worker and the employer pay into it, but the benefits do not make their way to the employees. Unemployment insurance does not exist. No central location to find employment is available. Few retirement programs exist, and those that do function poorly.

Interview with an Expert

The expert I was fortunate enough to interview was the director of educational programs in Mexico for seven years. Although he openly interviewed with me on January 26, 2010, I have chosen to keep his identity confidential, as politics can change dramatically in Mexico and economic harm to him or his family could result.

The *transcript* of our conversation follows:

QUESTION 1: "It is my understanding that the integration of students with disabilities into the public schools' classes in Mexico was your job for seven years. Is that correct?"

REPLY: *Yes. I was the director of the National Project of Educational Integration (dates withheld). It was not exactly the integration of students with disabilities but integration of students with special needs (with or without disabilities)."*

QUESTION 2: "Did you consider the program a success? Why or why not?"

REPLY: *It was really successful. It began in three Mexican states, working with 48 public elementary schools. It ended with 24 states, thousands of public (and some private) schools from pre-K to middle education. It integrated thousands of students with special needs. It was so successful that it was transformed into the current National Program for the Strengthening of Special Education and Educational Integration (PNFEEIE, in Spanish).*

QUESTION 3: "Todd Fletcher, Ph.D., stated: 'Entre el dicho y el hecho hay mucho trecho.' (Translation: 'There are a lot of distances between word and deed.') Does this occur because of a) inability to coordinate programs, b) lack of money, c) political infighting, d) shortage of technology or experts, or e) something else?"

REPLY: *In education, I would choose b) and e). The Mexican government states that it makes huge investments to education, and almost nobody sees that money. The government usually announces some impressive programs ("escuela segura" o "escuelas de calidad", even the PNFEEIE, safe schools and schools with quality, for example), and usually the programs do not have enough money to operate efficiently.*

REPLY: *The "something else" means that Mexican education has no academic leaders, but (the teacher's) union (is composed of) political leaders, whose interest is money and political power, not the (children's) education.*

QUESTION 4: "Are you saying that whereas the U.S. has President Obama demanding more funding for education, and that individuals in the private sector, such as Bill and Melinda Gates, are giving tens of millions amounts of money for education, Mexico lacks both public and private patrons focusing on education?"

REPLY: *Supposedly, Mexico spends a lot of money in education. And, it is true, the Mexican system of education is huge (more than a million teachers, 23 million students in basic education), but it is also true that a lot of people take a slice of the cake: the (teacher's) union, the governors, and the administrators. For example, there are thousands of teachers working for the teacher's union instead of teaching. So, my impression is that we need more money and, more importantly, we have to end the corruption in order to have the money in the schools.*

QUESTION 5: "Since childhood, my conversations about Mexico have always ended up with someone blaming corruption for causing a lack of efficiency. From where I sit, it seems that the U.S. is equally corrupt, especially in education. What is the difference in Mexico?"

REPLY: *Maybe that you should add impunity to corruption, impunity on many levels. If you have a political position in education, it is almost impossible that something bad will happen to you if you put some public money into your wallet. If you are a union teacher, the same (is true). Take into consideration that only 1% of criminal behavior is punished with jail in Mexico. And, of course, criminals are also poor people.*

QUESTION 6: "If you were the president of Mexico, what would you do to assure equal educational opportunities for a) children with disabilities, b) rural children, and c) those so poor that attending school is an economic hardship for their families?"

REPLY: *I would fight corruption and impunity to start with. I would invest more money in education, in order to guarantee that children at risk would really benefit from an education with quality. I would put the union leaders in their place, defending the rights of the teacher, not directing education. I would offer education with quality to adults.*

QUESTION 7: "My research found that nutritional problems the biggest reason that rural Mexican children do not excel academically. Do you agree that environmental shortages (including socioeconomic status), and not genetic issues, should be addressed in order to increase academic success within the public schools?"

REPLY: *Of course. I completely agree. I would like to add that rural Mexican children are provided with a poor education: not-well-prepared teachers, weak infrastructure in the buildings, scarce materials, and no access to technology, for example.*

QUESTION 8: "In my private school, which was funded with public money, on the Sonora/Arizona border, I served breakfast, mid-morning snack, lunch, and mid-afternoon snack. All meals were carefully developed for outstanding nutritional value—a full day's worth of nutritional value for a growing child. Do you think that the rural Mexican children need a nutritional program within the public schools to provide breakfast and mid-morning snack?"

> REPLY: *Yes, the rural (and many urban) Mexican children need a nutritional program within the public schools to provide breakfast and mid-morning snack. The problem is that schools do not have resources or the permission to carry a program like this; it has to be organized by the federal or local governments. On the other hand, other agencies try to do what you propose. They give some foods for the children, but the kids have to share them with the rest of the family. Or they give some breakfast to children at schools (called "desayuno escolar") with very good results. Nobody denies that this effort is not enough to reach all needed kids. So, your idea is very good!*

This interview was helpful in explaining cultural and administrative differences within public education practices between the U.S. and Latin America. Specifically, the seventh question addresses the lack of quality training for educators or instructors; this directly affects children in poor rural areas, where background diversity issues of indigenous heritage, poverty, domestic violence, incest, emotional disorders, and untreated disabilities are daily classroom challenges that the educators and instructors must face. Educators and instructors were not prepared to integrate people with disabilities or diversities into the public school classrooms,[10] nor were they prepared to deal with the problems researchers thought to be related to the indigenous heritage, including poverty, domestic violence, incest, and/or emotional disorders. [11]

Summary: The Hand of Government

The higher one's rank is in the social class system, the less stressful his or her interaction with government officials appears to be. People on the low end of the social class system try to avoid any interface with government administrators at all costs. Furthermore, it appears that at all levels of business, people try to avoid paying state and federal taxes whenever possible.

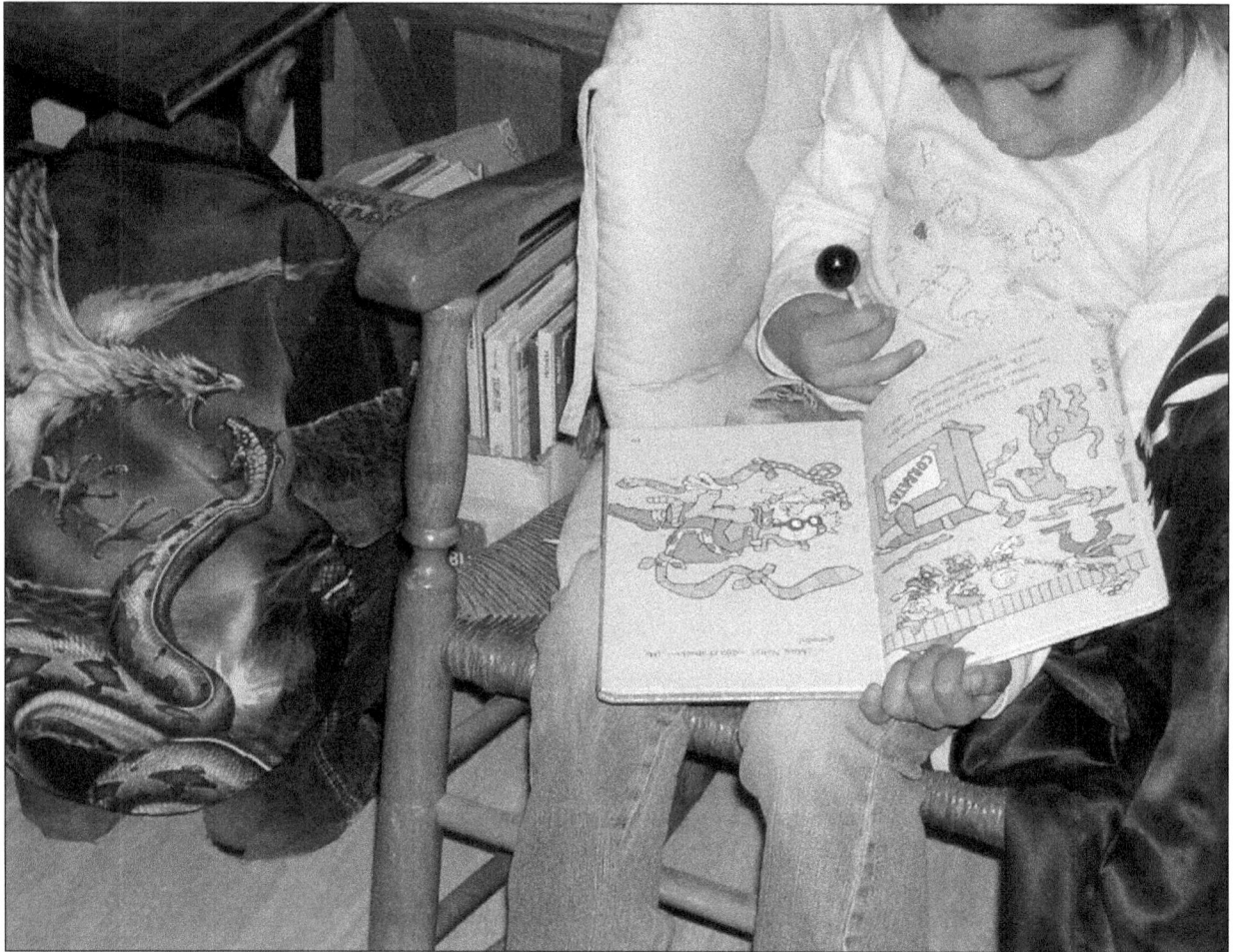

Almost immediately after arriving in our tiny community, we noticed that children would often ask to go inside and read books when they came over with their parents for a meal. The girl is reading in a chair, and the boy is looking through a new box of donated books. The children highly value books, because they know that getting an education means providing a better income for the family. Books are very expensive in Latin America. Children do not have books in their homes and cannot check them out from school "libraries," which usually consist of a single shelf in one classroom of the whole school.

11 The Value of Education to Latinos

The aim of education should be to teach us rather how to think, than what to think—rather to improve our minds, so as to enable us to think for ourselves, than to load the memory with thoughts of other men.

—BILL BEATTIE

Truth About Latino Attitudes Toward Education

All of the Latino parents I interviewed, including the over one-third of them who were unable to read, had a high regard for education.

Historically, Latinos have fought long and hard in the U.S. and in Latin America for educational reform for their children. They were very active in the Chicano Rights Movement of the 1960s and 1970s, but had less publicity than the Black Power Movement (1966–1975).[1]

Some battles have been won, but many still remain. When I interviewed 13 women in a focus group in 2007 regarding the question of access to education, only one mentioned that it was harder to gain an education in Latin America. Now that I have personally researched and taught within the Latino educational system, I am finally able to both understand her statement and thoroughly agree with her.

The Reality of an Education in Rural Latin America

Poor children in Latin America often have to leave school by the sixth grade. Those children with more financial resources stay in school until the eighth grade. Only wealthy children attend college. The women I interviewed emphasized that all Latino children, even those with minimal education, feel loved by their communities.[2] The women further stated that although Latino parents respect education, their children's behavior in school was the main concern for parents.[3] "Are they respectful?" the parents always asked the educators or instructors.[4] If the child was respectful, the parents were pleased.

Children's academic success was not necessary to have the love of their Latina mothers and their communities. Neither was worthwhile employment. This is not true in the U.S., where respect and love are often tied to academic success; that is why students are often paid a defined bonus in cash for each good report-card grade. A highly educated person may have problems finding employment in the U.S., but the academic success is still socially valued.

Universal acceptance by the Latina mothers of their children overshadowed any concerns about how able or how limited any child might be (physically, mentally, or emotionally); all children were loved and expected to be successful in contributing to the family unit—physically, mentally, and emotionally—by staying in Latin America and being involved in the family. The abilities of children to learn or to earn money do not have the same social value in Latin America as they do in the U.S. Nearly every child can choose to stay near the family home and participate, and making this choice is the definition of success.

Nonetheless, parents of disabled children are frequently motivated to travel to *el norte* for special educational services or for the opportunity to learn English in an English-speaking country. These parents see fame, money, power, and/or overcoming disabilities or other challenges as having a social value so high that the urge to stay close to family is given second place. Often the joy for these parents is short-lived, because although special educational services are legally available to any and all children in the U.S., recently school budgets have been cut to the point that such services can no longer be provided. This is also true of ESL programs, which have been so drastically shortened that they are often ineffective in helping immigrant students learn English. Additionally, immigration reform has all but eliminated the ability of undocumented students to attend a public school in the U.S.

An observer of educational systems realizes quickly that although the Western Model is the basic model of education in Latin America, this system differs significantly from the U.S. Western Model. One obvious example is that schooling continues nearly year round in Latin America. School days begin in the third week of August after only about six weeks

This young teenager attends school and does well because his physical disabilities do not prevent him from attaining academic success. He is about the size of a 6-year-old, but he has the self-confidence of a mature adult. His family is extremely supportive of him both at home and in school.

of summer vacation. The school year is heavily tied to the practice of faith, even more so than in the U.S. There are long Christmas and Easter breaks of at least two weeks each, allowing families to travel great distances to visit relatives. There are also many more days set aside for other religious holidays, in addition to days set aside for each individual community to celebrate the patron saint that protects that specific community. Break days for staff meetings or professional development are frequent, but are often poorly advertized to the educators, instructors, and parents.

Unscheduled closing of the entire school or individual classrooms are frequent. Because there is no funding or administrative policy allocating money for substitute teachers, there was often a lack of supervision and teaching in classes I visited if a teacher was absent.

Educators or instructors need to understand that little regard is given to maintaining published school schedules in rural Latin America This is also true of backup plans for substitute teachers that are needed to maintain the flow of learning when a teacher is absent. With that as the norm, how can a dedicated teacher in the U.S. or in Mexico expect in Latin Americas to comprehend the value of education? It is your job to educate the student not only with content (school curricula or corporate training), but also with appropriate procedures necessary to gain a quality education or a promotion. The student probably has never had a mentor to explain what it takes to be academically successful.

In one local school, one teacher never came to school on Thursdays; no explanation was ever given to those who inquired. The classroom remained unattended every Thursday; the students did their assignments on their own. That teacher was not rehired in the fall.

Health was such a big issue that parents usually kept children home if the weather was cold (close to 45 degrees Fahrenheit) or very wet. Once the homes and school classrooms cool down in the fall, they stay cold until spring because there is no heating or insulation. Whenever there were outbreaks of flu, colds, or other contagious diseases, there were few students attending school. There was no program in place to bring students into school or to make parents accountable if a child was absent.

The Style of Teaching

Although the textbooks in Latin American schools were colorful and appeared to be very modern, the actual model of teaching reflected the 1800s in the U.S.—when children were disciplined and exhibited respect and patience for the teacher, other classmates, and students. That was also a time when students did lots of repetition, just as they do today in Latin America. Numerous teachers told me that the lesson taught in a third-grade classroom in Northern Mexico on the second Tuesday in November was exactly the same as the lesson dictated to be taught in every third-grade classroom in all of Latin America on that same day. This had distinct advantages but also disadvantages. The same behavior that I observed in business, where peers were watching each other, was evident with students in the classroom. Also, the teachers had little room for creative expression in lesson plans. The method of teaching was typically rote memory.

Students were normally given copies of the tests that they would take later and given the answers to multiple-choice or other test questions ahead of the assessment. They then copied the information until they learned the answer to the specific question—*the exact question they would see on the test*. They also copied pages of text, seemingly endlessly, to absorb the correct information. The students always helped each other.

When this method of teaching is clearly understood, educators or instructors using a different style of teaching can easily understand why their Latino students may be confused about being expected to conceptualize information and to formulate their own answers. To these students, this is a totally unknown way of learning. Furthermore, since helping each other is the norm in Latin America, the concept of cheating is simply not comprehended by immigrant Mexican students.

The positive result of the teaching methods applied in Latin America was that *a high level of self-discipline was established* by the children. They *learned how to be patient*, to do as they are instructed in a respectful manner, to sit still, and to *encourage and help each other to get the job done.*

I have only seen one student exhibiting ADHD symptoms out of (1) 665 infants, children, and youth examined in Mexican health centers and (2) additional children observed while volunteering in public and private schools since 2005. I cannot help but wonder if this style of teaching, outdoor living, and/or cultural expectations might have something to do with this finding.

Self-discipline is certainly a valuable trait for students to acquire.

Mismatch Between Home and School

We must consider that the students were not typically taught in Latin American public schools how to be creative problem solvers; *they learned this at home* by observing their elders accomplish tasks and deal with challenges.

In more than one way, there was a clear mismatch between the home and the school environment; the two environments did not seem to reinforce each other.

The child was learning self-discipline, patience, and teamwork in both places. However, the subjects taught at school were about life outside of the community, while the lessons presented at home were related to home life, family business, extended family needs, and community affairs.

My research examined the mismatch that existed between the resources available to rural children and the resources that were simply out of reach. An additional mismatch existed between caregivers' aspirations for their children's education and those higher-social-class teachers who assisted children with learning, literacy, and language tasks.[5] Topics of learning and learning styles often differed considerably depending on the setting, whether it be at school or at home.[6] At home children learned by observing and imitating, while at school they needed to acquire advanced language and modern technical skills—something they could not likely practice at home. The rural students did not acquire technical computer skills they needed to "fulfill responsibilities in future employment,"[7] because the rural schools had few technical computer resources and there was no opportunity for students to practice.

There was a serious lack of qualified educators or instructors, resources, and instructional time needed to prepare for life. The teachers lacked both the academic preparation necessary to develop creative thinking skills to apply to academic lessons and permission to apply those techniques in the classroom.

All rural and urban public school classrooms I observed in Mexico lacked basic resources, including such simple amenities as adequate bathrooms.

Often there was no provision to flush a toilet, other than a 55-gallon drum filled with water and a bucket to manually pour water into a toilet. Some interviewees stated that posted signs about influenza reminded the public to wash their hands, because this activity was not a traditional part of the culture, especially in rural areas. Hand-washing sinks were often not available in schools, and they were typically not installed in rural homes. A local charity found children who did not know how to wash their hands. Statistics indicated that only 48% of homes throughout Mexico had functioning toilets.[8]

Access to Knowledge

The actual school days were short, with appropriate time management sorely lacking. Teachers arrived to rural schools by bus, so class start and end times were dependent on the teachers' bus schedules. If the bus was delayed or did not run, the teacher was late or absent. Teachers were not accessible to parents or students after school, since the end of their teaching day was determined by the local bus schedule. The average salary for a teacher was $10,465 (USD), which did not make vehicle ownership economically realistic. [9]

School usually began about 8:30 A.M. Local mothers broke up the day by bringing food, to be sold and consumed, to the playground from 10:30 A.M. to 11 A.M. Outdoor exercises occurred for another half hour thereafter. There were no school bells. Preschool for 3- to 5-year-olds lasted for three hours: from 9 A.M. to 12 P.M. High school functioned all day—from 8 A.M. to 3 P.M.—with breaks for eating; rural students spent another three to four hours on the bus home.

It was delightful, but unusual, for young boys to join us for after school classes.

A shockingly small percentage of the students who graduated from elementary school ("primeria") in July would move on to middle school ("secondaria") in August. Only 70% of the females enrolled in middle school; I could locate no statistics for how many of them graduated and made it to high school.[10]

Observers of the rural world learn firsthand just how hard the whole process of obtaining a quality education becomes for the children of subsistence farmers. Actual academic activities in school occurred for about three hours each day—not enough to give the children the quality education they deserve.

Statistics do not tell the whole story of high school ("preparatoria") graduates in Latin America. If there are 5,000 students who want to attend high school, only about 500 will pass the entrance examinations that would allow them to attend. Of those 500, fewer than 25% would typically graduate. The reported average length of schooling is 7.2 years, which is consistent with the findings from the interviews. Most rural people finish fifth or sixth grade and drop out to work full time. Less than 60% of the entire Mexican population enrolls in middle school; high school statistics were not available.[11] This is why fewer than 10% of adults in rural communities have a high school education.[12] Most rural adults have no access to reading materials to retain or enhance the reading skills they may have acquired in school. Contrast these figures to the USA where a truant officer arrives if a student misses school before age 16.

From June 2009 through May 2010, many volunteer teachers worked at our local community center as teachers in the after-school program; we transported them to and from town four evenings or more a week. Having a male teacher brought out the young men. When the male teacher left, male student attendance dropped to about 10%. Dogs normally attend public, private, and after-school programs.

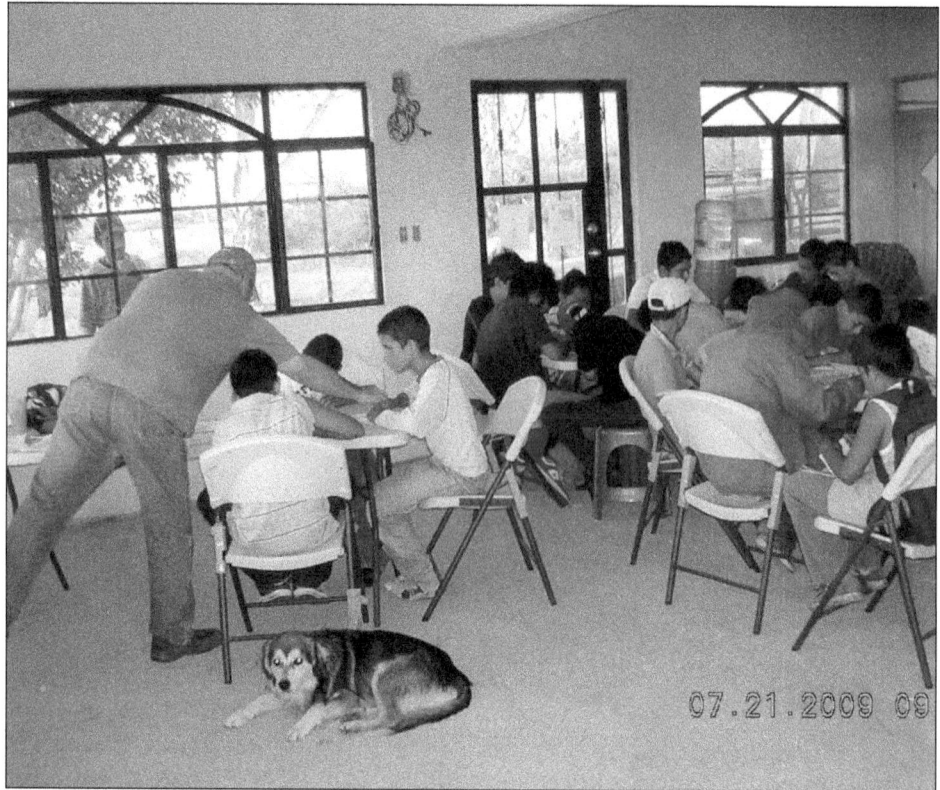

From June 2009 through May 2010, many volunteer teachers worked at our local community center as teachers in the after-school program; we transported them to and from town four evenings or more a week. Having a male teacher brought out the young men. When the male teacher left, male student attendance dropped to about 10%. Dogs normally attend public, private, and after-school programs.

Salsite's Story

I knew that Salsite's mom, Lupe, was not able to find steady employment, but she looked for and took any work she could find to have the money to pay for her daughter's school needs. Until I saw for myself, I had no idea what that task involved. Lupe was always a hard worker, even though she battled a ganglion cyst on her wrist for months. She had surgery a short time ago, and she either worked or got someone to fill in for her in order to keep her jobs while in recovery. Her fortitude impressed me. Nothing stopped her from fulfilling her position as a capable mother.

Her physical frame was very Native Indian: short and squarely shaped. Her movements were labored, like those of a heavy machine short on oil for its interlaced moving parts. Lupe probably lacked trace minerals all her life. Her chocolate-colored skin showed very little signs of the hard work she had accomplished because she protected her body with the right covering when exposed to the sun. She was a creative, self-preserving, and careful woman who had taught her children to be the same.

Salsite was her oldest child. Salsite had the same lovely warm-colored skin tones as her mother, but her frame was very different. Salsite was extremely thin, agile, and quick. She was a humble, bright, alert, and self-assured girl. When I first met her, I knew that she was a very special young lady. She jumped right up on Missy, our tallest horse, and rode her from the pasture to our house. Young girls growing up in rural Latin American farming communities do not jump up on horses, but Salsite did! Then she began to attend free English classes at the community center where I taught English as a volunteer. There I was able to experience firsthand how bright and ambitious she was. Young girls growing up in rural Latin American farming communities were not typically ambitious, but Salsite was certainly the exception. Knowing that knowledge could help to protect a girl from teenage pregnancy, I told Salsite last winter that if she graduated from elementary school and wanted to go to middle school, I would pay for her bus fare and buy her a uniform. She beamed with a grin mixed with humility and disbelief, which may have come from living with few resources and too many disappointments from unkept adult promises.

Salsite graduated in July, after I had already begun the search for a middle-school uniform. I worked with Cacy, the Caucasian adoptive mother of Karmen, a Latina girl who was the same size and age as Salsite. Weeks passed as Cacy looked in different stores to try to locate all the pieces of a middle-school uniform. Alice, Cacy's friend, was able to donate a skirt and a sweater, both too large for Salsite but of the right school colors and with lots of wear left in them. Finally, other pieces were found, tried on, and returned or altered in my living room to make Salsite ready for middle school.

Salsite's school uniform required a white blouse. I took out 8 inches from the back of the donated blouses, sewing in pleats in each one. She was also required to wear knee-high white socks. We found those in León, a town an hour's drive away from the community, on Salsite's birthday. Her pleated skirt was to be of a specific gray color and a very sturdy fabric. The sweater was a deep navy-blue, nearly black, with the name of the school embroidered on the front in mostly white and red. A sweat suit was required for certain days. The name of the school was embroidered on the front of the navy-blue pants, which were of a very heavy weight and had white stripes along the outside of the legs; the pants were accompanied by a navy-blue jacket, also with stripes, of the same a heavy-weight fabric. Under the jacket was a white heavy-knit shirt with a navy-and-white collar and the name of the school embroidered in the chest area.

The total cost for Salsite's school uniform was $120 (USD), which is equivalent to 240 hours of work for a parent in a minimum-wage job. Minimum wage in Mexico was 50 pesos a day, or about $0.50 an hour.

All children seem to know that if they are allowed to attend school, they are very fortunate. Each uniform piece for Salsite was located, evaluated, and handled with the utmost care.

There was also the seemingly endless list of materials required for attending school. Each child had to have four lined notebooks of specific styles—one double-lined for writing exercises, two graph-paper notebooks with different-sized blocks, a small blank notebook, and a small lined notebook—as well as pencils, highlighters, pens, erasers, pencil sharpeners, one legal-sized file folder, a package of plastic geometric shapes, colored pencils, a plastic pencil box, a calculator, a four-roll package of a specific brand of toilet paper, a bar of soap, a backpack or book-bag, and more. Jolene, my translator, spent $50.16 (USD) for these school supplies for Salsite, which is equivalent to over 100 minimum-wage work hours in Mexico.

Frida and Mary's Story

Jolene had one of the most joyful days of her life buying those school supplies for Salsite. She took along a former employee's 13-year-old daughter, Frida, after buying her a school-uniform skirt, blouse, and sweater in a small store near her school in a neighboring town. To get the school supplies, they went to the Mega, a department store located about 30 minutes away by car. Frida had *never* been to the Mega or any other store like it. Without missing a beat, she checked prices on each item and compared quantities and quality. She and Jolene shopped for a book-bag and got all of the things that Frida, her younger sister Mary, and Salsite needed for school.

Frida, Mary, and their mother, Lacy, were facing additional survival concerns. The girls' father, Javier, was bedridden with what might have been a ruptured disc. He had not worked for two weeks. This meant that not only were school supplies lacking, but so was food. Few staples are kept on hand in the rural communities, and most food is consumed on the day it is purchased. While Jolene was getting school supplies, my husband and I bought food staples and vegetables for the family. We have learned that family and extended family mean the same thing in these rural communities. The three of us have become extended grandparents to nine children living in three families.

These relationships have enabled us to gain more satisfaction and inner balance than we could give to any of the people on the receiving end. Many volunteers visiting Latino rural communities make similar statements.

Manuel's Story

When we delivered the school supplies, we found out that Salsite's little brother, Manuel, also had no uniform to wear to the elementary school on the following Monday. Therefore, we packed the family into our car and went shopping. Just $24 (USD) later he had navy-blue dress pants, a white shirt, and a V-neck navy-blue sweater—and the biggest crooked smile on the planet! Manuel had been bitten in the mouth by a dog in the early spring. He had already undergone two surgeries to correct the damage to his lips, gums, and teeth. His teeth were still crooked, but the initial horrid infection had healed. His confidence was returning as a result of learning to swim over the summer. Sending him to school without a uniform would not have been good for his self-esteem.

Preschool

A great deal of rural family pride went into sending a child to school. The emphasis was on appearance and behavior.

The preschool uniform was a colorful horseshoe-shaped smock that slipped over the child's head and hung from the shoulders. It looked like a typical painting smock but was made out of heavy-weight cotton, not plastic. These uniforms were usually trimmed in contrasting-colored bias tape, with two ties made out of the bias tape at the waistline on each side of the smock. The child usually wore a white blouse or shirt under the smock. Girls wore dresses or skirts, and boys wore pants.

Clothing was usually washed every day and hung on barbed wire to dry. I finally decided that Latina mothers practiced some magical techniques to keep holes out of drying clothing. Whatever it was that they did, it was a well-guarded secret. Each child was walked to school or escorted on a public bus. The parent and the child rarely talked during this trip, but somehow the child was very clear that his or her behavior was expected to be impeccable while in the classroom.

Behavior

My observation from 23-plus years of interacting with Latino parents—while living along the Arizona-Sonora border (1996–2008) and while visiting Central Mexico (since 2005)—was that the parents' first concern for school attendance was that their child appeared neat and clean. The second concern was respectful behavior. I have no clear understanding where gaining a solid education fit into that equation, because the parents all seemed to take the position that the teacher was responsible for providing an education and that as parents they should not interfere.

Latino parents did not consider themselves to be responsible at any level for the child's school performance or to be the primary teachers of the child.

My observations and those of other visitors over the last six years led me to conclude that the total responsibility for teaching a child in rural Latin America lay with the teacher. In the U.S., a person would state, "I missed the bus" or "I'm very concerned about my child's grades." A Latino would say, "The bus left me," "That teacher is not good," or "My child did poorly." Again, it appeared that as far as Latino parents were concerned, the sole responsibility for teaching students lay with the teacher.

The Teaching or Training Role

Latino parents valued education, but they did not know how to help their children to obtain a quality education, other than to ask for better teachers. Parents living in rural areas consistently did not consider teaching school subjects to be a parent's job; they thought that parents had only the job of teaching domestic subjects. Traditional rural parents whom I observed took no responsibility for the quality or quantity of education their children received, and there was never talk of moving to a better place to attend school. Wealthier parents, however, often drove their children to private or *better* schools as they defined them.

Teachers and visiting parents always welcomed me when I came into their public school classrooms. They often thanked me for bringing more access to knowledge for the children and for helping them in the classroom. I always thanked them, honored them, and praised them. The teacher's willingness to work as a team made working together very easy. When I offered free classes in a local community center, the classes were nearly always well attended, because teachers encouraged students to attend.

The line between teachers and parents was clearly defined by years of tradition. Rarely did parents ever help teachers in any way.

Parents who left rural communities for the U.S., who became good readers, and who acquired a broader world view were the opposite—they were actively involved in their children's education from all aspects, including literature, math, history, science, music, art, travel, and college planning. Upon emigrating out of Latin America in order to assure a quality education for each child, the whole family experienced major life changes. There was a shift from survival mode in the rural Latin American setting to numerous new challenges in an urban U.S. setting. The family had to leave the rural plot of land, locate a Latino community in an urban U.S. area, establish a residence in the U.S., attain U.S. citizenship, make retirement plans for both working parents, retain a relationship with other family members, and adapt to many other aspects of their new life. The transition was very complex for all members of the family.

Making an Education a Reality

After all that I have observed, I cannot imagine why U.S. citizens continue to say that Latino parents don't value education. Clearly massive amounts of time, energy, money, and family efforts are involved in making it possible for a child to attend school, especially middle school and higher, in Latin America. The confusion, I think, arises due to the difference between the Latino standards and the U.S. standards in defining the expected parent and teacher roles. The following interview with Maria demonstrates how she has adapted to the U.S. Her thought process expresses the "whatever it takes" mindset common in the U.S., while her focus, due to her Latina heritage, remains on a "good upbringing" for the children, which may or may not include a quality education.

And I would do whatever it takes! To do . . . to give them that good upbringing. Even if I had to get three jobs, I would do it!

An odd adaptation occurs for Latinos who either move to the U.S. or have relatives who have made that transition. There really is a sense among Latinos that anything is possible and not nearly as difficult to obtain in the U.S., including a quality education. Perhaps this outlook is due to wishful thinking, but it creates an obvious conflict. Any student of ethnography would be amazed and humbled by the optimism of Latino parents that their children would graduate from college if they lived in the U.S. Either the statistical evidence of how few Latinos complete high school or graduate from college is being ignored or the facts are simply not known. Additionally, Latino parents appear to accept the cultural bias problems being faced today and assume that their children will overcome those hurdles.[13] Social class differences continue to exist within each Latino family or community no matter what the current socioeconomic or social status of the family on either side of the border might be.[14] Students face many hurdles in getting a quality education in the U.S. or in Latin America.

Although student loans backed by the federal government are available in the U.S., the reality is that a student has to be motivated to be successful in high school before applying for and receiving a student loan. It appears that the reality of what it takes to make good enough grades to graduate from high school and to continue on to college is not clearly understood. I suspect that any parent who has given up so much to get to the U.S. cannot begin to imagine that anything will stop their children from showing the same determination to be academically successful. Unfortunately, graduation statistics tell another story.

Latino parents express quiet acceptance and deep joy when their children are respectful. The same praise does not occur when children accomplish high academic goals. Children know that they can easily learn or pretend to be respectful. The message from their community is that gaining their parents' love and appreciation is achievable no matter what other challenges may be faced.[15] The effort to achieve academic success is far greater than the ease of success resulting from appearing respectful. Therefore, the motivation necessary to achieve academic success is simply not present. Additionally, the sacrifice of cultural expectations, like spending time with family or friends, is usually too great.

Poor Health Affects Academic Performance

Most rural mothers have little nutritional knowledge and few options to gain more; they seem to lack the understanding that a child with a full stomach is not necessarily well nourished. Children who are not well nourished often find schoolwork difficult. Medical personnel explained to me that a seriously needed nutritional program designed by the Mexican

Department of Health was vastly under-utilized by rural mothers or other caregivers, because it was the norm to follow diet choices taught by relatives. Unfortunately, home gardens have become uncommon, depleted soil is less mineral-rich, and marketed foods are commonly viewed as status symbols. These variables make modern food choices less nutritionally rich.

When a child is living in an area where he drinks Coca-Cola in a baby bottle instead of drinking breast milk or formula, as I have observed since 2005, there are bound to be some nutritional problems. I have observed no rural homes with vegetable gardens, and few had fruit trees; most homes had just some herbs for medicinal use. Home gardens would be cheaper and healthier; typically, commercial vegetables grown on large farms in a nearby state were heavily sprayed with chemicals. Public water is not potable, and bottled drinking water is nearly as expensive as commercial soft drinks. Drinking homegrown veggie or fruit water that is high in nutritional value and low in calories would be an outstanding alternative to Coca-Cola; however, mothers need to comprehend this information if health and school performance are to improve.

Nutritional problems were very widespread in rural areas of Central and Western Mexico. Medical personnel confirmed that situation, and several referred to this endemic situation as an epidemic. Poor nutrition influenced school performance.

Emic Relationship with Research Participants Increased Cultural Understanding

I have previously explained that my interpretations can be validated though an examination of the effort involved in making certain that what I observed, investigated, and analyzed was regarded as culturally accurate. This section further elaborates on the effort put forth to assure that accuracy. A variety of people from at least 20 categories (Appendix A) were involved in helping me to gather information. These people assisted me by explaining cultural norms and clearing up misconceptions. I interviewed an extensive range of research participants in order to, as Maxwell states, "gain entry to the setting, or establish rapport with my research participants. I appreciate that Maxwell points out that this process is a complex and changing entity, not a one-time opening of a door. In qualitative studies, the researcher is the instrument of the research, and the research relationship is the means by which the research gets done."[16] The following field notes illustrate my team's position as learners.

As I drove down the dirt and rock roadway toward town at about 10 a.m., I noticed that Tio Pepi's store was closed; immediately I knew that someone had just died. The store was always open during the day unless there was a death. Many people have died here since I moved into this campo; I had learned the traditional signs. I wondered if it was someone I knew, someone I had given a ride to, or someone I had taught or bought services from in the past. It was not until the following morning that I learned it was a mother who had sold me vegetables out of her truck, with her challenging daughter always along. The young girl was about 5 years old. In my opinion she was a child with special needs related to Fetal Alcohol Syndrome. Mom agreed that she was a special-needs child who was very difficult for her to manage; the child's behavior was unpredictable. Mom said that caring for the girl was a lot of work, and there seemed to be no way to teach her to be polite and respectful. It took time on my part, but I was finally able to approach the girl and interact with her during visits to my house.

I had even been to their damp adobe house to give them a warm blanket last winter. It was necessary because the damp dirt house was on the riverbed with evidence that the river took parts of the house at will during the rainy season. No one here had heat in the winter, and certainly not that house. Living with dampness and no heat was not healthy, so I thought of them when I was asked to distribute 40 donated blankets late last cold season.

I had often wondered why the mother and daughter stopped coming by my house. The fall harvest was short this year due to the drought, but other vendors brought some produce here for sale. I thought that perhaps the father, a man who was continuously non-functional from alcohol excess night or day, might be keeping them home for some reason. I learned today that a far bigger evil had kept them away: The mother had been a victim of cancer. It was she who had died yesterday. The child was to be raised by my landlord's brother, my next-door neighbor, who already has a 2-year-old with epilepsy and a 9-year-old who was strong-willed to the point of stressing his normally high level of patience. Every day my neighbors taught me more about life in the campo and (showed me) what remarkable people they were to find ways to survive what this culture and living inside this campo asks of them.[17]

Though this culture's constant state of change aroused emotions of fear, interest, or politeness that may have affected the results of observations, the data indicated that for us to obtain reliable information, a valid study, it was necessary to use an emic approach. Time was required for us to become a trusted part of the community; we needed a total immersion in the culture.

We were able to achieve this to such an extent that I even reported in detail the exhibited behaviors of my own neighbors. Other researchers have had different approaches and outcomes. One report described researchers who had been forced to stop all observations of children over the age of 9 months, after being accused by someone in the community of having *the evil eye*.[18] Our experience did not reflect any such inference; perhaps this was due to the participants perceiving our genuine humility. Perhaps the community had also changed and adapted, which could have resulted in the acceptance of our presence among the *campesinos*.

The local medical personnel and the caregiver participants were very cooperative and seemed to welcome our presence. Admittedly, any observation was only a view of that community in that location at that point in time: what *they* were doing then within a sociocultural content, *not* what was done before or after. I believe that *qualitative research requires extensive time in establishing relationships in any culture*.[19] Within the Mexican culture, this factor was amplified due to the *relationship factor* having much more relevance, as the following example illustrates.

In Central Mexico, an entire department in the local Volkswagen dealership shuts down from 3 P.M. to 4 P.M. in order to allow all of the employees to eat their mid-day meal, "comida," together.

The willingness to lose money in order to accommodate the employees' need for a relationship was, for this researcher, a major social statement.

I have been told this arrangement is common in all but extremely large cities within Latin America.

Class Status Influences on the Abilities of Students

The cultural factors, sometimes referred to as environmental factors, that have influenced activities of the parents or other caregivers have been explained earlier. Influences appear to have resulted in the majority of the developmental delay *labels* identified within the study. Caregivers knew that exceptionalities existed when I identified them within my research, although several caregivers chose to ignore developmental delays or special needs—because, as they explained, options for special-needs services were inaccessible anyway.

On two occasions, a caregiver did not believe me and the medical doctor when we explained that a simple patch could cure a lazy eye. Qualitative data analysis appeared to imply that accumulated hopelessness might have been the reason behind that disbelief and, more notably, the reason for the occurrence of emotional breakdowns when caregivers were asked the final open-ended question.

Several mothers asked for suggested ways out of the demands required by their *campesino* lifestyle.

In many cases, a simple observation confirmed that a child had developmental delays, special needs, or other disadvantage. Some parents hid the facts from me, others asked for advice.

Qualitative data analysis implied that only a few reoccurring developmental delays (i.e. starting to talk very late and being unable to crawl) were directly related to cultural influences.

In general, *campesino* parents spoke very little and said even less to their children. There was little encouragement for children to speak, and not much need to do so—children mimicked what they observed instead of asking questions and did not expect to be verbally directed by a mentor. Hand signals were very effective and an expected/accepted form of communication between a mentor and a child.[19] Dirt floors, a common situation, soiled children's clothing. Mothers explained that holding the children avoided dirty garments and was also preferred due to the floors being covered with germs, rodents, or insects. Most indigenous infants did not learn the skill of crawling.

Caregivers stated that infants are rarely put down on the floor or in another place where there is an opportunity to learn to crawl.

Other developmental delays, such as not knowing how to count by the age of 4 years or not knowing the names of colors or animals, were shown by the data to be directly related to cultural influences. Caregivers explained that these skills were academic subjects to be taught (at least in the minds of the caregivers) by teachers, not by caregivers. Rural Central Mexican mothers explained to Jolene, the gatekeeper-translator, on several occasions that the role of the mother was that of a caregiver. The role of public school educators or instructors was teaching reading, writing, arithmetic, and other subjects not taught by the mother. The data implied that teaching roles did not overlap within the *campos*. Unfortunately, this eliminated the opportunity for children to practice school subjects in their home under the supervision of a caregiver.

Class Status Influences on Education

An individual in the U.S., in general, is able to access education and raise his personal social status significantly. Data gathered from a variety of people showed that education was not a significant aid in elevating class status in Latin America. The following journal entry explains why one research question, related to educational challenges, had such significance. *Campesino* children apparently were locked into their socioeconomic status for life. Their use of language revealed their socioeconomic status.[20]

Even if they (the parents) attained the highest of educational degrees and professorship positions in universities, it would be their children and grandchildren who would benefit from the eventual status change over three generations. That change will occur if, and only if, the parents continue to maintain a high level of education while giving birth to children and their children to their grandchildren: a total of three generations. Additionally, the parents must move into a higher social status residential location, as well as gain additional education for themselves and their children. If they remain in the campo, their social status will not change, nor will the social status of their children or grandchildren.[21]

The lack of opportunity to raise one's social status,[22] due to cultural influences and the socioeconomic class structure in Latin America, resulted in generational hopelessness. On several occasions, a youthful parent told me that education was of great value. It was believed that later generations would be helped by education, but the level of commitment required to obtain that education, caregivers explained, always seemed to take second place below family gatherings, rituals, or other family obligations.[23]

Compared to U.S. residents, Latin Americans are very far-sighted with regard to accepting fate or karma. Latin Americans will refuse to sell family land, believing that their fate is to protect this land. They will accept a loss of life, believing that the person's karma led him or her to die young. They do not exercise executive functions, such as planning ahead, well. It is hard for a Latino of faith to study for several years and spend lots of tuition money without first knowing his fate.

If a potential Latino student felt a sign from God, he might make an academic commitment—but God has already assured him that family comes first. He knows that it takes an average of three generations of educated people to raise social status.[24] Most Latin Americans would not put their family aside and their career or education first for that length of time.

Reading Abilities of Adults in Rural Mexico

Most rural residents of Central Mexico over the age of 50 were not taught to read as children.

In 24 months of living in the campo, I observed only one person over 50 reading a book at home. He was the town mayor and was reading the Bible.

I once saw a man of about 35 reading a book while standing outside and waiting for his bus to arrive; he was a youthful attorney. Sadly, even school children were not seen carrying or reading books. A conventional statement might refer to these non-readers as "illiterate," but that word is only refers to one's aptness for reading a language. As Luis Moll has reported, literacy has a much broader meaning.

Each multigenerational person is likely to have *community literacy* or *cultural literacy* stemming from the funds of knowledge gained by understanding the rituals and acceptable behaviors in his campo (community) and comprehending its norms.[25]

Of the younger adults under the age of 25, most stated that those in the *campo* usually only attended primary school until the fifth or sixth grade. Data indicated that the dreams of the children in the *campo* have more to do with an income for survival and less to do with careers, as the following journal entry points out:

> *The majority of young teenage boys of public school age stated that all they wanted was to go to the U.S. for work—work that was manual labor. More young teenage girls applied themselves to reading and classroom studies. The girls exhibited behaviors that made it clear (that) they understood education as a pathway out of life-long poverty and mandatory motherhood.[26]*

When asked, caregivers and students replied that they had no access to a library or the Internet for information.

Teacher Characteristics and Challenges

In the same manner that we traveled great distances by car to reach rural *campos*, most teachers traveled great distances by bus from their urban homes to reach a school in the *campos*.

We were informed that this could result in lack of consistent attendance by teachers, and that there were no substitute teachers available to take over the duties.

Children functioned alone in the classroom when the teacher was absent. The urban teacher was a person of status; the rural child was a *campesino*. We observed first hand that the children did not command much respect from their teachers.

Data confirmed that everyone knew the lines separating social class. Outsiders only had to hear the differences in language use.[24] After living in the *campo* for a while, the subtle body language differences also became evident. There does not seem to be awareness that those with an education have a higher level of sophistication, clearer speech, and a different body language—factors making it easier to obtain jobs in government offices or other professional positions.

Rural *campesino* mothers complained that the teachers did a poor job teaching; however, what is taught is not practiced outside of the classroom and, therefore, is not permanently learned.

At home in the campo, parents did not typically verbally correct the children to speak more clearly, nor did they correct subtle body language messages. In contrast to other cultures, rarely did an evening in the campo home include parents giving their children verbal lessons.[27]

Teachers complained that the mothers made students work so hard doing ranch chores, necessary for family survival, after school that assigning homework was useless. Further investigation revealed that teachers in public preschools worked only three hours a day; in the later grades they worked only four hours a day. At the end of each workday, the school employees made a mad dash to catch a public bus. Additional time to prepare lesson plans was unnecessary, as the federal standardized curriculum dictated for the same lesson to be taught on a given day to all students across the country.

Few teachers bothered to set aside time for parent-teacher conferences, because parents would not come and busses might not run later in the day.

Since there are no school busses, the bus schedules are planned around school schedules by expanding bus routes when school is in session. There are fewer busses to and from rural areas after school is over for the day. Missing a bus might cost a teacher an additional two hours, as he or she would have to wait for another opportunity to catch a bus home.

There was no after-school tutoring, as students were needed at home to help with the farming or other chores.

Adults and children alike appeared not to realize the value of learning lessons unrelated to *campo* life. Ultimately, even though parents wanted their children to find success in life, they also wanted children to remain in the *campo*. That conflict was a daily sociocultural struggle.[28]

Teachers in rural Mexican classrooms could not be expected to shoulder the entire blame for children who did not learn. Often, there were 40 pre-school students and only one adult teacher in the classroom. I have visited 16 local schools since 2005 and never saw or heard of teacher's aides.

Within the primary grades, having 40 or more students with one teacher in one classroom was common; having 80 or 90 students with one teacher occurred too frequently.

Teachers were frequently called away from the classroom and the children were left alone, due to a lack of additional staff available to assist and oversee the children. In some communities, an entire grade level was not taught for a whole school year or more, because there was no classroom available and/or no teacher hired. These factors explain the following statement, which a researcher should consider when examining people even within the same state or geographical area:

The difficulties experienced by immigrant students indicate that cross-cultural differences in cognition are most probably related to learning practices characteristic of different culture(s).... These differences can be observed not only between cultures but also within a given culture.[29]

Data confirmed that teachers were overwhelmed with the number of students, the lack of assistants or parental volunteers, the lack of training in how to work with students who have special needs, and the lack of teaching supplies or adequate reference materials. Additional complications occurred due to educators or instructors lacking familiarity with the local culture. Teachers normally resided in a higher-status community.[30]

Rushing to the Border for an Education

Thousands of Latino parents have risked their lives to give their children the opportunity to sit in public school classrooms in the U.S. However, few Latino children show the same determination with regard to academics after arriving in the U.S. The determination of the parents to find a means of making the best educational options possible for their children appears not to become an inherited family trait in the children.[31] Educators continue to ask why this situation is repeated.

This research data uncovered some answers for reducing parental heartache through alternative learning techniques that employ nothing more than tolerance and understanding of Mexican cultural norms, such as caring, support, advice, and respect for children.[32] The following journal entries elaborate how an understanding teacher can make a difference in a student's attitude toward education:

Suggestions are nothing more than practical ideas about how to initiate a positive trend in academic success, as researcher also acknowledged.[33]

Santamaria stated that Mexican students in one study *stayed in school because of strong ties to caring and understanding teachers* and suggested that *due to the high dropout rates in Mexican secondary schools, affectivity must not be overlooked as a means to retain students.*[34]

The data taught me that *in the Mexican culture, when a person is dressed poorly it means that poorly dressed person does not respect the other people with whom they are interacting.*[35 & 36]

This data helped me to understand why my attention to my overall dress and physical appearance inside my public school classroom had such a strong effect on my Latino students and their parents.

This information should be of value to educators or instructors of culturally diverse students, especially Latinos. Too frequently, educators or instructors assume that all social classes are the same inside a classroom, but nothing could be further from the truth. In Latin America, the teachers are in a higher social class. They are able to pay for a bus ride to the school to teach and they can afford the uniform they wear. Teachers live in the city where houses can protect written materials, books, and other items from damage by the weather; they expect their own children to attend high school. Rural children of a lower social status do not have the same opportunities, as the following journal entry explains:

Public schooling was available for all ages and all abilities in Latin America, but the data showed that it was not free and often physically or financially inaccessible. Parents are held responsible for covering the costs of daily transportation, meals, uniforms, and school supplies. These are costs that subsistence farmers are not able to meet, so children often stay home to work instead.[37]

Data repeatedly verified that a chronic shortage of financial support resulted in the oppression of rural females. Indigenous rural children in Latin America were kept financially oppressed, and their educational needs were ignored.[38 & 39] The result of not having access to education might have been what drove women of all ages to come to hear anything I had to say while assessing their children.

Data revealed that the women appeared to crave knowledge.

Any academic or practical means to offer knowledge would provide opportunity to assist marginalized females and to create self-sufficient female adult role models for other women in local Latino communities. Frequently females in rural Latin America lack the opportunity to achieve school success.[40] This situation occurs because they often get discouraged. As a result of getting discouraged, they may feel victimized about not having the correct social class. Their parents may be working so much that they do not have time to be involved in their daughters' education, and there are also no after school programs available for these girls. As a result, the future these females see for themselves does not require school success. A victim finds it hard to escape the system and become academically successful. The girls who have a mentor are the ones who take their education more seriously. In an ideal world, all of these girls would have a supportive mentor.

Summary: The Value of Education to Mexicans

In the spring of 2008, I had the honor of studying under a self-described "chicano," Dr. Rick Orozco. Those who knew him when he first came to campus told of "an angry young man." At the end of that class I was *an angry mature woman*—due to the power of the information coming out of the class, both on film and from my classmates.

The course included students from the College of Education, Mexican-American Studies, Anthropology, and others. Both graduate and undergraduate students participated in the class, which was called "The Teaching of Latinas/os." The room was filled to capacity; only three of us were not Latino—we were the only ones who had entered the class *not already deeply angry*.

Dr. Oroczo explained that we had to have knowledge of the sociohistorical and sociocultural schooling contexts from which Latinas/os emerged if we were to teach them. He was more right than I had realized at the time. He spoke of the education crisis levels that I was too familiar with, but he also showed films, news clips, documentaries, and home movies from the 1960s and the 1970s that made my blood boil. I had lived in that era; I had emotionally been on *simmer* for years until this class brought me back to a full boil!

We examined theories, policies, and practices that had shaped Mexican-American education; at the same time, we looked into the souls of a room filled with angry young people who became angrier as the semester progressed. Some evenings resembled an Alcoholics Anonymous Meeting, as students expressed their most inner feelings with total dedication to letting those feelings out. Somehow, using that interdisciplinary lens to view that time in the light of history, sociology, psychology, and anthropology awakened emotions in everyone to the point of raw nerves. We each became painfully aware of the social, cultural, economic, and institutional factors that contributed to the underachievement of Mexican-Americans and the continued oppression of all of those of Mexican heritage. Dr. Oroczo made each of us advocates for transforming a long-standing crisis into a passion to make positive changes. I headed to Central Mexico less than a week after his course ended, prepared to *make right years of wrongs*. The effect that one angry young man and his classroom of Latinos had on me will never allow me to even think about asking, "Do Mexicans value education?" Far too many have already given up everything to answer that question with an affirmative, "Yes!"

Most people who are street beggars are young women with infants and children. The older women often make the rounds of outdoor restaurants and approach people at their tables, asking for financial assistance. The lack of public social service programs for families and the elderly, and the level of poverty across all age groups are evident in this manner.

12 The Truth About Living In Poverty

You can't get rid of poverty by giving people money.

—P.J. O'Rourke, *A Parliament of Whores*

Hate Hurts!

Each Friday, along with teacher's aides and other trainers in Tucson, Arizona, I put on a white T-shirt that had big black letters across the front: **HATE HURTS!** That message was used as a means to reduce bullying in the public middle school where I was teaching. Nevertheless, in my last years of teaching in U.S. public schools, that same school district (as had the others before it) assigned me to take a Ruby Payne Professional Development course—a course that, to me, instructed how teachers could bully poor students. That was not the title, nor the intent, but that was the ultimate message.

Arizona was one of 38 states misguided into thinking that Dr. Payne[1] knew what she was taking about regarding the habits of Mexico's poor, who now include my neighbors. I can assure you that her broad derogatory statements related to generational poverty are founded on ignorance about poor subsistence-farming communities in Central and Western Mexico and along the Arizona-Sonora border.

Payne's[2] position is deficit thinking and reflects an embarrassing lack of solid research. Other researchers agree with my statements.[3] Bomer and co-authors explain that Payne "reveals the degree to which we use the education system to protect our own sense of entitlement to privilege."[4]

165

I cannot agree more. Unless I find out that Payne is living in a poor village, helping out the poor to the extent of her financial resources, giving her time as a volunteer teacher, and actually observing the behaviors she says exist, I cannot imagine what could have driven her to make the statements that she has made. Like me, others have taken the route of emic research to learn the truth. I wonder how Payne developed her biased conclusions.

Payne's words made me feel great sadness and horror that her misconceptions are being presented as factual information. Teachers need facts and appropriate tools and techniques. Payne's statements and other popular myths must become exposed through solid research, or harm will continue to come to poor students.

Poverty is about Stepping Back in Time

Living in a Central Mexican, low-socioeconomic-status, rural, farming community is much like living in the late 1700s, when trains had been invented but riding as a stowaway was the only option. Or imagine the late 1800s, when telephone and telegraph existed, but neither you nor your neighbors had access to them. The key word in this book is *access* for the poor. For example, it is common knowledge that public school is offered, free of tuition, to Latino children. However, parents in small farming communities lack *access* to these schools for all the reasons I have already described, including but not limited to cost of transportation, cost of uniforms, cost of meals, rigid testing with limited openings for additional students, and so on.

The same is true of other items. Marketing came into homes with the television in the 1950s, reminding women what *labor-saving devices* were available for consumers: a car, a carpet, and air conditioning. Women had already entered the workforce during World War II, so they already knew that they had the skills to work outside the home, and they liked earning their own money. The family structure changed. Children no longer walked home for lunch with their mothers, and not all mothers were home after school.

Even the U.S. lifestyle of the 1950s is too modern compared to the lifestyle in a *campo* in the 21st century. Few homes in rural Mexican communities have a television today, and most have one bicycle but no car. Most homes have dirt or bare-concrete floors with no carpet. The only air conditioning is available in a movie theatre in the main town, which is over an hour away by bus. For most things, living in today's *campo* is more comparable to living somewhere between the 1750s and the 1900s. The difference today is that MP3 players exist, as does the Internet, and cell phones are now affordable. Those who don't have these items within their reach feel deprived.

It isn't a problem when a Latino is unable to own an item not yet popular, but a commonly used item creates envy among those without it and brings status for those who own it. Lacking ownership of a popular item due to lack of financial resources is emotionally painful. The difference is in the self-esteem. A wise teacher knows this fact and finds another way to enhance self-esteem.

Review of *A Framework for Understanding Poverty*

Payne asserts that (1) people have choices about whether or not to remain in poverty and (2) there are "hidden rules" separating ways of thinking and behaviors of those in poverty from the middle or wealthy classes. Her position is that the poor are void of socially acceptable values related to work, economics, behavior, and relationships. Scientific research does not back up her position. Academic scholars, including me, are taking the position that not challenging her assertions harms school teachers through faulty information, harms marginalized people through slandering, and harms the public through misinformation.[5]

In my opinion, the greatest danger to education that Payne's statements reinforce is low expectations by educators or instructors of students who are *economically disadvantaged*—and these are the most vulnerable students in the education system.[6] Due to cultural bias, any student with a Latino surname is likely to be lumped into that category without being first appropriately qualified. I met a Latina woman who was a clinical psychologist; her income and social status were on par with upper middle class. This professional woman's 6-year-old daughter was bilingual and had attended kindergarten in the U.S. However, her surname alone placed her in an ESL classroom in grade one, perhaps because Payne's workshops and unsubstantiated theories are so widely promoted and accepted. Payne's one-woman-show is not likely to change statistics regarding the number of immigrant Latinos graduating from high school for the better. In general her statements are so extremely prejudiced and false that I can only join other academics in agreeing that Payne has **not** grounded them in **evidence-based** or **scientifically based data**. When valid research is ignored, taxpayer's dollars are wasted because education does not improve. Her defense is to use a deficit model for teachers, stating that *her book and workshops are for teachers, not researchers*. As a teacher, I resent teachers being stereotyped as having less academic sophistication than researchers. This falls into the same pattern as her books apply to the low-socioeconomic-status poor. Apparently she knows that historically policymakers at the federal administrative or school district levels have shown little regard for *evidence-based* or *scientifically based data*. The following direct quote makes that historical position clear:

> *High-quality empirical research can guide policy. Admittedly, due to the disconnect between the research base and policymaking, that potential is often squandered. The mere existence of careful, rigorous research makes little impact if policymakers remain oblivious or if lesser-quality work is more effectively communicated and advocated.*[7]

On page 47 of *A Framework for Understanding Poverty* Payne states, "Often the attitude in generational poverty is that society owes one a living." This statement is certainly false in my Mexican state! My first example is brief and from my field notes:

> *Other research participants (names withheld) included two different directors in 2006 and 2007 of a large school run by a Mexican state government. The second one (director) stated: "Mexican people are the most creative in the world. They have no social service programs so they must figure out how to earn an income."*[8]

What Traits My Research Uncovered

Since I first came to Mexico to volunteer in the schools and other organizations, my experiences have always shown Latinos to be honest, hardworking, relationship-oriented, self-reliant people with high moral values and profound ethical practices; these people were in a survival mode, but took extreme measures toward mutual cooperation among their families and extended families.

My second example involves evidence-based academic research. In 2009, my translator and I examined 665 children for developmental delays. In each case we visited local Mexican Department of Health facilities, community centers, or private homes. These infants, children, and youth came from 18 predominately indigenous, isolated, rural communities: Three were either within a mile or two of a major city, four were 3 to

8 miles from the border, two were within 15 miles of the border, and nine were more than 15 miles from the border. Some people in these communities had no access to employment, either because the bus route did not run through or near their town or because they did not have money for the bus fare. Several towns had only one or two old men living in them and no younger men, as all the young men had fled to others parts of Mexico or to *el norte*, the U.S., for employment. The following field notes from 2009 in the state of Guanajuato elaborate:

> *Air Plains (what I am calling the town) was an isolated mountain campo located at about a 90-minute ride from Creekside (what I am calling my home town) off tightly winding dirt roads that were seemingly endless. This was one of the campos that did not seem to have a natural resources attraction; the streambeds were not a year-round asset, since they were dry when we visited. The clinic was very hard to access by vehicle; it was at a steep uphill climb from the community below. There were few other campos near this agricultural site and no bus transportation in the vicinity. This site was visited once and scheduled by the health department for more visits, but (the site) cancelled twice through our scheduler without any explanations. We are assessing the children for health issues that will slow learning and teaching the mothers how to stimulate the babies. We are seeing the effects of hopeless financial situations (that have gone on) for many years. Most girls drop out of school after fifth or sixth grade and get married; 12 is the age of consent. A few years and many children later they are so very sad. (They have) no printed material and no ability to read. Many of the children suffer from malnutrition. The work is rewarding; the mothers are thrilled to have the attention and feedback on their kids as most are single because their men are working in the U.S. and have another family now (in el norte).*[9]

The Mexican nationals who lived on both sides of the Arizona-Sonora border and with whom my nonprofit has worked since 1996 had several predominant characteristics. The most consistent trait of rural Latino people was politeness: an expression of respect in public and private places. Their second most predominant characteristic was an unwavering obedience of the rules of their faith, *as they understood them*. The majority of rural and urban Latinos follow the Roman Catholic Church doctrines; in addition, many other religious practices are also honored in Latin America, and there may also be specific or general differences within each faith. In Latin America, there is an overall appearance, publically and privately, of deep faith.

What each teacher or trainer must understand is that the way any faith is practiced must be taken into consideration in order to best enable teaching techniques to be effective and compatible with the students' religious beliefs.

Oddly, some of the complaints most frequently heard about Latino nationals are directly related to following *the tenets of a particular faith in a different manner,* often a manner that is accepted in the culture but not necessarily definitively tied to the culture. When people follow their belief systems, the actions do not have to follow the beliefs or logic of others inside or outside of a culture.

Educators must understand that some of the following statements (1–9) may—or may not—be part of the belief system of a Latino student. Following these statements are naive comments frequently made by English speaking critics of Latinos. This example was designed to help the reader become more tolerant of cultural differences and more aware of how the effects of *interpretations of religious practice* may affect the views of their students and their families.

1. Doctrine, cultural norma, and/or social class dictates to accept each conception as a gift; therefore, no artificial birth control and/or no abortion are allowed. Naïve English speakers ask uninformed questions or make culturally inappropriate statements:
    *   *She denies that he beats her, rapes her daughters, and has other lovers!*
    *   *She's too poor to have another child; she cannot care for the ones she already has!*

2. Doctrine, cultural norms, and/or social class dictates total obedience by the female of her male spouse is required. Naïve English speakers ask uninformed questions or make culturally inappropriate statements:
    *   *She denies that he beats her, rapes her daughters, and has other lovers!*
    *   *Why doesn't she leave him or get a job to help support the family and the church?*

3. Doctrine, cultural norms, and/or social class dictates all men be held at the highest level of esteem as a representative of Jesus or an apostle. English speakers ask uninformed questions or make culturally inappropriate statements:
    *   *She denies that he beats her, rapes her daughters, and has other lovers!*
    *   *Why doesn't she leave him or get a job?*
    *   *Why doesn't she/he get an education and have a decent career?*

4. Doctrine, cultural norms, and/or social class dictates no divorce. English speakers ask uninformed questions or make culturally in-appropriate statements:
   - *Why doesn't she leave him or get a job to help support the family and the church?*
   - *Why doesn't she/he get an education and have a decent career?*
   - *Why aren't they motivated to get out of poverty to afford counseling?*

5. Doctrine, cultural norms, and/or social class dictates placing the life of a child above the life of the mother. English speakers ask uninformed questions or make culturally inappropriate statements:
   - *She's too poor to have another child; she cannot care for the ones she already has!*

6. Doctrine, cultural norms, and/or social class dictates not to complain about the social position held in life. English speakers ask uninformed questions or make culturally inappropriate statements:
   - *Why doesn't she/he get an education and have a decent career?*
   - *Why aren't they motivated to get out of poverty?*
   - *Why do they live in that crowded shack with other family members?*
   - *Why is she/he too lazy to work toward a better life?*

7. Doctrine, cultural norms, and/or social class dictates to care for the elderly of the family. English speakers ask uninformed questions or make culturally inappropriate statements:
   - *Why doesn't she leave him or get a job to help support the family and the church?*
   - *Why doesn't she/he get an education and have a decent career?*
   - *Why aren't they motivated to get out of poverty?*

8. Doctrine, cultural norms, and/or social class dictates to be accepting of the physical, mental, or emotional challenges they face. English speakers ask uninformed questions or make culturally inappropriate statements:
   - *Why doesn't she leave him or get a job to help support the family and the church?*
   - *Why doesn't she/he get an education and have a decent career?*
   - *Why aren't they motivated to get out of poverty?*
   - *Why do they live in that crowded shack with other family members?*
   - *Why is she/he too lazy to work toward a better life?*

9. Doctrine, cultural norms, and/or social class dictates practicing the faith to the best of their abilities. English speakers ask uninformed questions or make culturally inappropriate statements:
   - *Why doesn't she leave him or get a job to help support the family and the church?*
   - *Why doesn't she/he get an education and have a decent career?*
   - *Why aren't they motivated to get out of poverty to afford counseling?*
   - *Why do they live in that crowded shack with other family members?*
   - *Why is she/he too lazy to work toward a better life?*

Years ago an FBI agent explained to me that what people report they see may be a long way from what is actually going on within the visual area of the viewer. In many cases that is what is occurring in Latin America when someone from outside the culture views the activities. It takes an unbiased researcher a long time to identify what might be actually occurring, and even then there may be differing opinions among researchers.

What Requests Were Uncovered by My Research

Of those hundreds of mothers with whom I spoke, many asked for information on heath care, child care, employment, legal issues, education for themselves and their children, immigration issues, management of disabilities or old age, and management of other economic issues. They also asked for information on preventing drug use, preparing children to work, strengthening marriages, getting a mortgage, and other topics. They consistently asked for access to books, access to the Internet, and access to information; in an entire year, only *one* person simply asked me for money.

The people in generational poverty who are neighbors do not ask me for money either. They ask me to buy homemade cheese or farm-raised eggs from them. They ask me to teach them to speak English, to help their disabled children, and to teach their children to swim. They ask when the library will be built, but they do not ask for money. Even the people who have fallen into the lowest social class in society, such as men lying drunk in the streets, do not express a "society owes me a living" attitude in Central Mexico.

Summary: The Truth about Living in Poverty

While living on the Arizona-Sonora border, I was an active community member. I read the local newspaper and paid attention to what was reported in this area, which was defined by the U.S. government as one of the lowest socioeconomic regions in the U.S. Crime was very low, and drug trafficking was even less prevalent. My husband and I had checked the historical records at local law enforcement offices in 1996 before relocating to the area; these records also showed low crime and low drug-related activities. I volunteered at the local prison, worked with youth in crisis programs, was involved in many humanitarian efforts, and was in the first graduating class of the Douglas (Arizona) Leadership Council for nonprofit leaders. For three or four years, my group gathered donations of clothing and household items in Phoenix and Globe and redistributed them to northern Mexican barrios. We worked closely with the Chamber of Commerce, as well as with projects overseen by the Arizona Foundation, the Y, the public library, several local churches, and other nonprofits, including Just Coffee/Just Trade, the Business Incubator Center, and Arisewna, a HUD-funded sewing cooperative. Like Payne, I have stories to tell:

Once a "coyote" was caught for drug trafficking via humans.

1. While he was in jail, his wife and five kids were left in a lean-to structure attached to another's home. We made their lives a little easier. When he was released, he came to us to offer his labor as a way to thank us.

2. Many people stopped by our off-the-power-grid home about 12 miles north of the border. Undocumented aliens took water in jugs left with us by humanitarian volunteers. Those travelers had nothing but the clothing on their backs and yet *for 12 years not a single item was stolen from our unlocked dwellings by any Mexican nationals.* Volunteers once took our donation box. Other volunteers took welding tools, hand tools, clothing, gasoline, food, and many other items, but *in 12 years of our living along the border without locks on our buildings not a single undocumented alien took anything.* Some stopped by and asked for work or a ride back to the border, but not a single person took anything from our unlocked retreat.

3. From 1996 to 2006, people near death from overexposure to walking in the intense desert heat along the Arizona–Sonora border drank water from the well below our line of sight. They did not

leave trash, they did not cut our fences, they did not have drug paraphernalia; they were respectful unseen travelers.

4. I had 120 children enrolled in the school where I was the director. Only one child was not on supplemental meals. Not a single Mexican child was left at the school by an irresponsible parent.

It is my opinion that people living in generational poverty have finely tuned survival skills, or what scholars[10] call *funds of knowledge*. This represents a knowledge base gained through experience. This knowledge differs from Payne's "hidden rules" of those living in poverty.[11] I have found nothing to substantiate her opinion that the behavior of people in the middle and wealthy classes differs structurally from the behavior of people living in poverty.

Volunteer teacher Jolene Gailey is teaching English to students and adults who dream of becoming bilingual (Spanish/English) to improve their lives. The class is held in the early evening in a rural community where access to classes or books is commonly not available. Jolene helped with the construction of the room where she is teaching.

13 Language: One Roadblock to Dreams of a Better Future

A different language is a different vision of life.

—Federico Fellini

Children Become the Family Voice

Parents sit in Latin America and dream of a better future for their children. They rip children away from their familiar Spanish-speaking homeland and take them into the stark reality of life in a foreign environment, where frequently a young child moves into the role of language broker. The 2000 U.S. Census validated that 8.1% of the U.S. population is categorized as "linguistically isolated," a term that defines a lack of fluency in English among adults in the home. This means no member of the household older than 14 years of age speaks English with ease. Researchers state that these linguistically challenged families make frequent use of family members as language brokers.[1] This highly demanding position is forced on marginally bilingual children who have picked up some English at school or at the playground. Examination of the long-term consequences of language brokering is necessary, as these children's dream of a better future is overshadowed by the reality of life without the familiar support of the extended family that existed in Latin America.

I previously referred to this overbearing role as a nightmare because of the emotional toil, the gender differences, the situations where the child translator is compromised, and the positive or negative side effects of the adult-child role reversal. There are many facets of this complex problem of communication. The children had never asked to move out of their

177

cultural and linguistic home in Latin America; once on foreign soil, however, they are asked by adults to always be ready to help translate. Children are not used to being in adult conversations, nor are they normally expected to make decisions on their own. There are times when the child has to reply and is unable to accurately translate the family's needs. Children accomplish this extraordinary work. They may often feel like they are living in a dream, or in a nightmare, because so much has changed culturally and, at the same time, so much is demanded of them.

We still lack a clear understanding of the long-term consequences of using young children as translators—a survival tactic used to sustain and subsidize Mexican families in their transition into a different geographical environment with new cultural surroundings.[2] The public media focus on immigration issues, perchance motivated by an academic interest in researching the linguistic challenges facing Latino youth who have relocated out of their country of birth. Whatever the motivator, the results are important to evaluate for all American educators or instructors faced with the responsibilities of teaching Latino youth who live a bilingual environment and become, at an early age, the family's bridge into a new culture.[3]

Many adult immigrants speak exclusively Spanish at home; in school, however, their children's use of language other than English is restricted. A bilingual lifestyle can be confusing for a child. At school, English is mandated; English is the language used for teaching. Some schools even monitor playground communication, restricting the use of languages other than English during recreational breaks.

When I interviewed a focus group about Spanish-English linguistic concerns, the mothers had clear linguistic complaints regarding their children. When asked about what language their children used when spoken to in Spanish in the household, they all replied:

(The children) always answer in English. They can speak Spanish and I (the mother) speak it to them, but they continue to reply in English: Grrr!

The mothers were very clear about wanting their children to be bilingual for social and economic reasons, but at home they wanted them to be Spanish speakers and to demonstrate the values learned from their Latino culture.

Communication in the first language (L1) is vital to cultural identity.

In the publication *I Am My Language,* the reader learns how language is a lens that magnifies the various components that make up identity in children, in addition to the multiple facets of life in the borderlands.[4] The borderlands are a common place for language to erupt in a coordinated dance or a vicious fight. Often the language that develops is called "Spanglish," a slang term denoting the blending of English and Spanish. This blend is so common that it has its own structure, which is separate from the structure of either English or Spanish.

One researcher has stated that the communication customs and the attainment of an education by Latina-origin mothers set the tone for the language appreciation and adeptness of their children. This phenomenon, a strong maternal influence to appreciate the language and to become truly bilingual, according to this researcher, is influencing those children 11 years of age or younger.[5]

Implications of Language Brokering by Youth

This is a complex issue with concerns ranging from:

1. a lack of personal freedom to the interconnectedness typical in Latino homes,
2. the time demands to the emotional impact,
3. the age of the child to the sex of the child,
4. the level of acculturation to the lack of acculturation,
5. enhanced self-esteem and academic performance to blurred generational responsibilities; there are no easy summaries.[6]

Similar to a hearing child whose parents are deaf, the Latino child who performs translation services for the family is given the responsibilities of an adult and the power to act on those responsibilities.

Children as young as nine years of age often speak for anyone in the family who is not fluent in English and make life-changing and legally binding decisions.

The following True/False statement was used in a questionnaire for children with an average age of 12.58 years: "When my parents are talking, I am allowed to give my advice."[7] Other studies have used similar references to adult decision equality for the young language broker.[8] One researcher quoted a letter, written by a ten-year-old first-generation Latina female, which made clear her expressed joy at helping her mother. That letter *also served as an example of her writing skills.*[9] Further research on the quality of writing by student language brokers may or may not show that they develop more comprehensive, clearer, or earlier writing skills.

It is typical of the Mexican culture for children to handle adult-sized responsibilities at home. When language use forces the student into yet another adult role, keep in mind that if you as educators or instructors expect less of them at school or in the workplace, you lessen that adult level of respect toward them and their capabilities. Such an action reduces self-esteem. Don't be guilty of this social offence!

For decades national concern over the abysmal graduation rate of native Mexican students in the U.S. has been significant. The details regarding elements that contribute to this situation of an unacceptably low graduation rate are of interest to researchers seeking clarity about what influences academic performance. The researchers have mixed conclusions about the impact of language brokering that include (1) an anticipated substantial improvement, (2) having little or no positive change in academic outcomes, and (3) dropping out of high school before any research data was collected.[10] An examination of different opinions is listed in Table 1.

Note that *Positive relationship to GPA* (1 and 7) as well as *Positively contributes* (2 and 5) are identical. These identical outcomes in two separate research projects increase the likelihood that these are in fact the positive aspects of being a youthful language broker. These research results force parents, teachers, or trainers of Spanish speakers to weigh the benefits versus the drawbacks of language brokering by young Mexicans. This end result warrants further study, as it might also apply to brokering in other languages.

Adolescents learn to adapt to their environment. As a result, they become opportunists. This behavioral characteristic makes it possible that unless the strong cultural commitment to Mexican family interconnectedness is present, translators have the opportunity to take advantage of their power over the family when the situation affords them that opportunity. This could happen by allowing the broker to not relate a conversation with an English speaker accurately to his family, like manipulating the choice between two rental agreements in favor of the neighborhood the broker prefers. This would be accomplished by saying that the other rental agreement was not as favorable for the family. Researchers had

Table 1: Comparison of Academic Outcomes from Language Brokering

Findings by Five Different Scientific Studies: Each Study was Related to the Academic Outcomes Expected from Young Language Brokers

1. Positive relationship to GPA[12]
2. Positively contributes[13]
3. Positively related to academic performance[14]
4. An expanded opportunity to realize academic success and better scores on standardized reading tests and somewhat improved math scores[15]
5. Positively contributes[16]
6. Not a clear understanding of the relationship[17]
7. Positive relationship to GPA[18]

mixed outcomes regarding this phenomenon, often based on essential acculturation issues, the age of the child, the degree of harmony within the home, and the parent-child bonding already in place.[11]

Body Language Analysis

Children's body language in rural Latin America does not mimic the typical teenaged *eye-rolling, downward look and sighing,* or other exasperated signals frequently used by U.S. teenagers express frequently with adults, including educators or instructors. Teens in the U.S. live in a *cult of youth,* where little is demanded of them and marketing is directed toward them as a special group. They are generally isolated or relieved of family responsibility. Children are compartmentalized by age from birth through college. In rural Latin America, there exists a continuum of socialization within the family, the schools, the churches, and the communities. This shows up in all facets of the social structure, except among the extremely wealthy urbanites. This one difference in behavior of Latino infants, children, and youth with regard to the expectations of their families is of paramount importance in a learning environment, as well as in other contexts.

The rural Latino child readily connects emotionally with both younger and older children, as well as with adults; this is done on a sincere level, with full-faced smiles, hugs, and comforting gestures, and without the visual separation that their U.S. counterparts demonstrate specifically through exasperated body-language signals. It is my opinion that this willingness to connect with others occurs because Latino children have self-confidence as a result of a cultural expectation to be loved, adored, given respect, and honored as part of the family team, while not being isolated from family matters. They work alongside other family members in a store or a field, doing the same activities adults are doing and using *adult-sized tools*. They feel included in the family, not falsely *isolated or protected* from the issues of domestic life. They participate in birth, death, and all of life's intimate lessons alongside their parents (or at least with their mothers) in the local mini-church or the family bed. They grow up with a different, far more realistic adult world view. They also develop a healthy curiosity of the world outside their small community.

Emotional Costs and Benefits of Language Brokering

The emotional costs to an adolescent who has the continued obligation to help his or her parents regarding matters of daily living may be compared to caring for a disabled relative. Some caregiving is tolerated with ease, but being responsible for all translating for the family can become overwhelming and may impact self-esteem in a negative manner. First-generation translators, the children who had been born in Latin America and traveled to the U.S. where they learned English, tended to start the task later in life, while second-generation translators, children born in the U.S. to immigrant parents, tended to start earlier and were less well-equipped to take on the full-time responsibilities.[19, 20]

The results of several studies, both with adults and with young public school students, are briefly examined here. The results are insightful and yet leave the reader wanting even more answers. As additional research is published, hopefully more insight will surface. One study considered 40 emotions—13 positive emotions (e.g. helpful) and 27 negative emotions (e.g. worried)—with participants ranging from 19 to 54 years of age. The research rated emotions using a 1–5 Likert Scale with a resulting 0.70 alpha scale using Cronbach's method.[21] Some participants considered themselves gifted with a talent that was beneficial to their family.[22] The majority of the studies reported that the participants had unsubstantial depression, though not statistically significant levels of depression to be out of a normal range compared to their peers who were not asked to language broker for their families.[23] Those who had been in bilingual education classes were more at ease as brokers than those who had learned English informally.[24] Aspects of bilingualism without specific regard for translating were also examined.[25] Universally, participants reported that stresses resulted when someone other than their parents made the request for translation, especially if that request came from anyone coming unannounced to the door of their home.[26] In all research studies, the reported positive emotions were higher than the negative emotions.

Many adolescents reported feeling pride in being able to language broker for their parents.[27] Feelings of social self-efficacy, biculturalism, acculturation, and enhanced academic performance have also been reported.[28] When the students had a close relationship with their parents for whom they brokered, researchers reported diminished anti-social behavior and reduced risk-taking behavior.[29]

Gender Specific Role: Language Brokering

In keeping with the tradition of the Latina female's responsibilities for maintaining the home and the male's responsibilities for things outside the home, girls are more often chosen to be the language brokers.[30] When a young child is given responsibilities that are far outside of the traditional beliefs regarding children's autonomy, the results vary depending on the level of acculturation: The more acculturated, the more the child feels stressed.[31] Males were more stressed by translating requests than females. The older and more acculturated male children reported more stress.[32]

Researchers speculated that while Latina females may view translating as an extension of their household duties, the males may feel humiliated by being asked to perform that same job for their parents. The boys must have considered any household activities to negate brokering. Some females reported positive emotional outcomes that were more valuable to them than their own personal freedom.[33] A single researcher found no gender differences relating to the brokering; however, this researcher reported that the females felt more favorably about doing the task.[34]

Advantages for the females who are translators, mediators, or individuals who act as surrogate parents for their siblings may include increased freedom, status, and authority beyond that which they normally anticipate in a traditional Latino home. Admittedly, a dynamic social change of far-reaching proportions might accelerate acculturation and rob a female child of her childhood innocence; this is especially true when she is asked to translate legal documents and/or complex medical information.[35]

Communication Translated by Language Brokers

In the traditional Latino home, interdependence is the norm; therefore, all written communication, and much public communication, is a family matter.[36] A bilingual child will translate notes from school, bills, tax forms, phone calls, insurance, leases, and other legal documents, as well as medical information/forms.[37] Examples from this research have shown that educators or instructors and parents have a continuous flow of information between them because of the parents' high regard for education for their children. There are many other documents that must also be translated, but it is the notes from school that are mentioned with universal consistency.[38]

Parent-Child Relationship Stresses are Associated with Language Brokering

Family dynamics, the interaction between the adult and the child, habitually change in a positive or negative manner.[39] The majority of the researchers found family harmony to be the key for continuing positive family dynamics.[40] When a young person is a language broker for the parents, there is the danger of role-reversal overwhelming the child;[41] this was a more universal response from the 9- to 11-year-olds than from older children.[42] Parental loss of control is possible when the child has to make decisions about legal matters that the parent does not understand. Also, a young child is predisposed to be cognitively limited by both a lack of experience and a shortage of coping strategies.[43]

Many students, as they mature, report feeling more empathy for their parents as they become immersed in the daily demands placed on their parents for whom they must interpret.[44] Several researchers concluded that a clear understanding of help or harm to the parent-child relationship is not yet understood.[45]

Summary: Language—One Roadblock to Dreams of a Better Future

Ideally, every teacher or trainer will travel for about a month to a foreign country where a language other than his or her own is spoken. Such an experience is an opportunity to experience firsthand what it is like maneuvering around without having the means to communicate normally. Alternatively, since this ideal is rarely an option, visiting a local Chinatown or another ethnic area of a nearby city can help teachers or trainers better understand the classroom or workroom experience of their immigrant students.

Understanding the level of adult responsibility handed to a child is less easy to experience firsthand. What is of great value is for the teacher or trainer to appreciate the importance of treating a Spanish-speaking student with a high level of respect **and** expecting outstanding results in the classroom. Educators are all taught to help their students reach the highest potential, but myths about Spanish speakers may overshadow that expectation.

I assure you that not expecting your Spanish-speaking students to reach their highest potential is a disservice to them and to their community, as well as to your employer and to your country.

Educators or instructors must rise above the general population with every student and expect the student's best performance under culturally appropriate guidance.

Author Mackenzie is teaching English outdoors at a basketball court near her home. There are teenagers, mothers, and elders looking on as she is speaking. The eager students are laughing happily as they learn the sounds of another language. The setting is ideal for those who often learn outdoors.

14 A Culturally Appropriate Education

If you can speak three languages you're trilingual. If you can speak two languages you're bilingual. If you can speak only one language you're an American.

—Author Unknown

Cultural Capital Defined

Educational capital is a non-financial social asset people are normally able to acquire. Intellectual or educational achievements which increase social mobility or social status beyond economic improvements are educational capital. Pierre Bourdieu and Jean-Claude Passeron[1] addressed "Cultural Reproduction and Social Reproduction" in their written work on the outcomes of education in France in the 1960s. Later, more was written about how this form of capital, educational capital, works as *a system of exchange worthy of being sought after.*[2] Bourdieu and Passeron related acquisition of this asset in France to the expected social and economic benefits .

Cultural Heritage Increases Social Liabilities

Capital is an asset, something that adds value. Liabilities are debts, time, or effort owned to another.

Joseph's Story—Studying Latinos Clarified My Alien Roots

My Polish father, Joseph, raised me to believe that education was, in his words, *the way out of immigrant status*; he knew that firsthand. My grandfather, Rudolph, was a Polish immigrant, as were some of his children. His last-born, Joseph, was born in Connecticut and was, therefore, a first-generation American. Joseph followed his father, Rudolph, into a trade brought over from Poland; he became a butcher. Rudolph was a very successful businessman, but he drank, apparently because he missed Poland and his friends there.

Communists spread the same propaganda about the Polish[3] as is currently being spread about Latinos: *lazy, stupid, funny-talking*.

Rudolph became more and more stubborn about protecting his heritage and refusing to allow his children to become *too American*. Joseph saw endless opportunities in America. His primary concern was his low social status as a Polish immigrant. That fact caused him endless pain.

Rudolph could have easily sent Joseph to college—he had the savings, and Joseph would have easily passed the college entrance exams. However, Rudolph wanted Joseph to be a butcher, not an educated man of a higher social status. As a result, angry young Joseph eventually left. He enlisted in the Army Air Corps on the first day his age allowed, leaving the Polish community where he had grown up. He rejected his first language, his birth community, his birth religion, and his birth family because he wanted to leave what he saw as a low social status. Joseph was passionate about raising his social status. At that time, he had little regard for economic improvement—he was driven to raise his social status. He had that option with increased education. Later he also raised his economic status, but not any more than if he had remained a butcher. What was really a problem for him was his self-image as being from a low-status cultural background.

Joseph left his heritage even further behind when he met and married a woman of Scottish heritage outside of his Catholic faith. He turned his back on his family, and they did the same to him. What he did not give up was his physical appearance. He was short (5 feet, 6 inches), had a dark complexion with dark brown hair and eyes, and always wore a handlebar moustache. Although he never spoke Polish, he often spoke Spanish, so he gave up being thought of as Polish for being mistaken as Latino. He studied all the time he was not working in order to pass military achievement tests to raise his rank and social status. He had the option to raise his social status through education and hard work. He retired as a Warrant Officer even without a college education.

Cultural Capital of Rural Latinos

This concept of gathering non-financial assets to elevate social status occurs in France, the U.S., and many other Northern European countries, but *not in Latin America*. More than any other aspect of living in this culture—in which people demonstrate amazing talent, high levels of intellect and local knowledge, self-discipline, ability to adapt to social change or natural disasters, acceptance of life's path, ability to solve problems nontraditionally, humility, and respect for one another—this aspect is totally incomprehensible to me.

The list of positive attributes of Latino culture seems endless, and yet *not only do educational or intellectual achievements not increase social mobility or social status in Latin America, but such positive efforts just barely improve a person's economic position until at least three consecutive generations have reached the same levels of achievements.*

This is the strongest aspect of Latin America's social structure that ignites in me the relentless passion to create positive change.

This is the single reason why I am so driven to build libraries in rural Mexico. I abhor unfairness; being born into a low class status and not being able to make a change within a single lifetime is unfair. What often occurs is that these capable individuals leave for *el norte,* the U.S., and work at low-paying manual-labor positions while their wives and children stay behind and family relationships fracture. It is my belief that when Latinos of the lowest social status learn to read and write bilingually, they will be able to remain in Mexico with their families and their unenhanced social status while *stepping out* economically by working through the Internet.

Not all Latinos will become famous authors, Web engineers, or programmers, but most will find a way to earn a living that will financially outpace what they can currently earn in Latin America. More importantly, in a culture where the work of an ancestor is honored, their children will have the same opportunities to economically improve their lives in the very next generation.

What Colors Are Your Classrooms?

Educators in the new millennium may have noticed that children seem to lack

1. an identity with place (their community),
2. a play-space knowledge or environmental education (within their schools),
3. a familiarity with their own backyard (classic nature-deficit disorder) and
4. an overall environmental awareness.[4]

This has been a weakness of children in the U.S. and a strength of those living in rural Latin America, *if educators or instructors have been able to acknowledge and enhance these cultural capital assets* of rural Latino students.

Today most parents of urban children have not connected them to the natural world.[5] Observed day-to-day activities seemed to be far more focused inside the house than outside.[6] Parents appear to ignore the long-term psychological cost of excessive safety devices and electronic babysitters used in lieu of natural explorations outdoors. Perhaps they needed to ask themselves:

1. What is the total cost to our children for learning abstractly indoors?
2. What is the long-term cost to our community?
3. What is the cost to our cultural heritage?
4. What is the economic and environmental cost to our planet?
5. How do the answers to any of these questions help us understand the Latino learner?

Applying the formerly discussed "head in the sand" technique to this inquiry might result in a "no interest to my family" response to these five questions. Nevertheless, if we accept the statement that *all education is environmental education,*[7] because we all share the same planet, then we are failing ourselves, our future, and our children and their future. We should be far more aware of what is happening to our youth and doing something to facilitate positive change.[8]

All of life as we know it exists on planet Earth. If we treated our houses or our cars with the same disrespect that we often show for our planet, they would fail far sooner than either our children or our planet might.

Social Factors Highly Influence the Ability to Learn

The quiet, polite, indigenous person, who is living far from a city and normally travels by foot, is unlikely to have the capacity to relate words spoken by a visitor to actions taken within an indigenous home or immediate rural surroundings. Generally, things are still perceived through an inherited frame of reference. Data confirmed that respect for ancestors often triggers such behavior, as though a new idea insults the way it *has always been done.* Latino youth who are bicultural are far more able to accept new ideas into their private lives and social circles;[9] they are also far less likely to respect older ideas of ancestors, but they do not necessarily completely overcome the influence of the *campo.* Even those Mexican-American immigrants attending school in the U.S. were aware that their inability to learn was profoundly influenced by their culture and traditions.[10] U.S. educational services for Latino-American ESL students did not meet their needs. These students performed worse than their U.S. peers in math, mental health, and interpersonal functioning.[11]

Teaching Response to Intervention Helps Every Child

At my border school, we applied Response to Intervention (RTI) techniques[12] to all children. My processing within that RTI framework might be appropriate in Central Mexico. Whether or not a specific learning disability is identified, all children and their caregivers might benefit from such a broad approach, because it reaches every learning level without requiring a diagnosis of a problem. Unquestionably, because I was from outside of the culture, I had to identify/codify what I observed and determine the actual meaning of the activity. This is why the emic perspective was the most logical for this study. I had an opportunity to observe behaviors repeatedly and ask questions of many different people over a long period of time in order to discover the actual meaning of the activity.

Insight Gained From Recalling Historical Successes
With Latino children

I reached back into my past experiences for insight. In my U.S. classroom, filled with public middle-school students of Latino heritage with special needs, I used logic to promote communication and understanding. I spoke of simple mathematics. The students never seemed to tire of hearing me say the following:

Until the percentage of Hispanic leaders in positions of political power and financial influence equals the same percentage of Hispanic people living in the U.S., a mismatch exists; it is a wrong that is in dire need of correction.

Acknowledging that a wrong exists was not culturally inappropriate; it was instead the first step toward positive change. Positive change could be equality regarding basic human needs, which are often unfulfilled in the *campo*. This logic in service of change was my students' favorite story; yet, they accepted my proposal as a fantasy, having already become all too aware of their social status.

There is a Mismatch Between WSM Curriculum and the Campo
Lifestyle

My research examined the mismatch that existed between what resources were available to rural Latino children and what resources were simply out of reach. An additional mismatch exists between aspirations of caregivers for their children's education and those of higher-social-class educators or instructors who assist children with learning, literacy, and language tasks.[13] Topics of learning and learning styles often differed considerably depending on the setting, whether it was in school or at home.[14] At home children learned by observing and imitating, while at school they needed to acquire technical skills—something that they could not practice at home. Rural Mexican students do not acquire technical skills they need *to fulfill responsibilities in future employment*,[15] because the rural schools have few technical resources and there is no opportunity to practice. My research was conceived to define how to begin to correct some of these inequalities. The goal has been to suggest some means for empowering those indigenous residents and getting them the educators or instructors, resources, and instructional time that they need.

Mixed-Methods Data Describes "Consequences" of Rural Mexican Lifestyle

Observations, interviews, and analysis of data implied that there were several likely consequences of residing in rural *campo*. Malnutrition was the leading concern for the children and other family members. Data results indicated that many children were outside of the expected developmental ranges in other areas as well (Table 4.0).

The data showed no statistically significant difference in malnutrition between genders.[16] Behavioral standards taught and used in the U.S. universities and schools were used to access cultural influences or culturally based factors common to indigenous children as compared to those of children labeled as developmentally delayed or as having special needs. U.S. assessment standards were analyzed to see if the criteria might be inaccurate or inappropriate for identifying the special educational needs of Latino children.[17]

My research data implied that cultural influences or culturally based factors contributed to an incorrect assessment of indigenous children due to biased assessment standards, a lack of cultural-sensitivity training for the observers/evaluators, and/or rigid testing materials written in a foreign language. This is a considerable problem, because misunderstandings of cultural influences or other culturally based factors may reduce the likelihood of attaining academic success;[18] the opposite may be true if cultural influences and/or biases are comprehended.

Academic success is not the only consideration of this study. When a rural indigenous child is given a *label* of having developmental delays or special educational needs, the classification in and of itself is a considerable problem. The stigma of a *label* defining a child as having a disability may cause:

1. *disbelief and resistance*, especially by Latino fathers, in acknowledging having sired a child with disabilities, which often results in a refusal to advocate for the child,
2. *a lowered self-image* for the child, which may lessen social acceptance or diminish the opportunity to acquire a good education less likely, and
3. *increased emotional stress* for the family without access to special educational services, with or without an official diagnosis and/or label, and without the extra time and resources that would be necessary to care for the child.

My research sought to determine if rural children were frequently the victims of misunderstood sociocultural factors/environmental influences that are typically considered liabilities. These factors could instead be considered academically beneficial experiences and achievements that with appropriate interventions could enhance and speed up the learning process. If a rural Latino lifestyle was approached as a deficit, culturally appropriate academic enhancements or interventions might be overlooked. The goal should be to consider a rural Latino lifestyle as an asset to be enhanced in an academic setting.

The *campesino* infant was often in the care of a 3- to 5-year old; the infant was bound in fabric, wedged into a bed for safety, and staring at the ceiling, while the rest of the family was engaged in domestic or income-producing activities. The *campesino* child was observed seven days a week; he or she was awake and engaged before dawn and would work into dusk, completing activities that required quietly watching and mimicking adult income-producing or domestic activities within a multi-generational, non-competitive, and interdependent educational process with caregivers. Additional caregivers are typically parents of other children, uncles, aunts, or other members of the extended families.

Nearly every activity was a family activity *with little in the adult world hidden from small children....Night time does not involve segregation from social life.*[19]

For a brief period of the mid-morning/early afternoon, the child or youth might be sent to public school to copy endless streams of printed material or to fill in the blanks of various worksheets; this education sorely lacks creative expression or instructional activities needed to prepare the children for adult life.[20] When children are not able to work beside adults and accomplish something, they are *missing a valuable arrangement that can contribute both to children's learning and their satisfaction.*[21] The children I observed in rural schools were copying text for most of the school day, an activity lacking scaffolded[22] learning and a sense of personal accomplishment/satisfaction related to experience.[23]

Educators of *campesino* students would benefit from understanding life within the *campo*. They could emphasize what can be done to make it the most sustainable, most economically worthwhile, and the healthiest lifestyle in the world. The *campesino* child could be eagerly entering the adult world, prepared and informed as to how to live a sustainable lifestyle within the *campo*. *Campesino* children could be educated in the classroom and within the family in preparation for a lifestyle that is

Young "Chiclet" salesmen, like this young man, roam the streets during the day and at night as a way to help their mothers cover basic expenses.

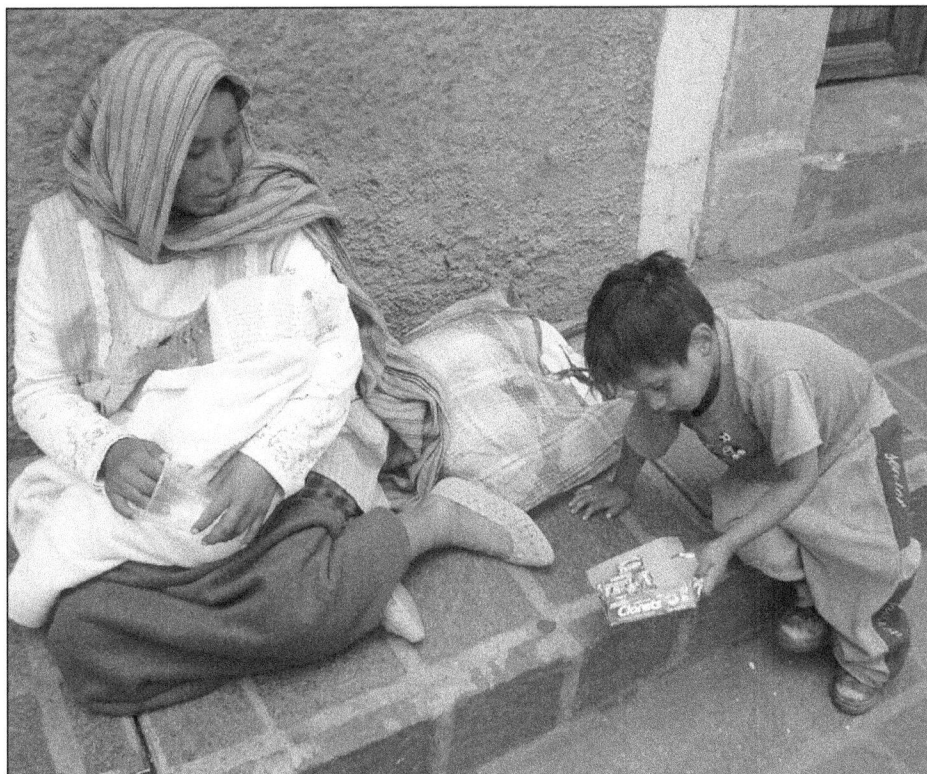

ecologically wholesome and spiritually, morally, ethically, and economically balanced. This, in turn, could become a model for the rest of the modern resource-depleted world to follow.

The *campesino* child could be *connecting hand, mind, and community (through) vocational education for social and environmental renewal.*[24]

That would be an alternative to copying text for countless hours or filling in the blanks on seemingly endless worksheets, although the latter activity does build individual discipline in students. Teaching is always a trade-off in making sure that time invested is time spent logically to afford the best options for the majority of the students.

Life-long malnutrition adds to the difficulties faced when an indigenous rural Latino child attends school to gain an education; fortunately, this can be overcome with an adequate diet.

Latino federal efforts to elevate and develop uniform educational standards across the nation have resulted in severe restrictions: The daily curriculum is rigid, and federal programs fail to provide or recognize the importance of food. Because of the rigid nationwide curriculum, no time/ space has been left for thematic activities related to local surroundings or adult income-producing activities, and provides almost no nutritional information related to *campesino*. Extensive and colorfully designed educational material has very little correlation to rural activities; it was provided without an *academic bridge* to assist educators or instructors in relating it to the life in the *campos* or to overcoming malnutrition in the communities. This unfortunate example shows that one academic curriculum program cannot span across the best academic interests of all students who reside within the enormous land mass known as Latin America. In such a deeply engrained and multileveled social class system as Latin America, ignoring the basic human needs for adequate nutrition is not an option if the goal is learning.

By ignoring the *deficit hypothesis*[25] approach and instead focusing attention *within each public-school classroom* on options available within rural Latin America for improving life, such as through gardening or other *campesino*-appropriate activities, the current nutritional shortages could be vastly reduced or perhaps totally eliminated.

Data implies that *campesino* children are educationally marginalized because of their cultural status; other researchers have obtained the same results. *There is ample evidence that children from these social class backgrounds are limited by their schooling, by the nature of the instruction that they receive.*[26]

As educators or instructors, we need to *accept different ways of knowing*[27] and apply that premise within our overall pedagogy. Immigrant Latino students in the U.S. public schools face the same mismatch between home and classroom when they spend the entire school day with educators or instructors who keep them rigidly seated while promoting *passivity of knowledge getting*.[28] This is further amplified by these students' experience of being spoken to in a language they do not understand, in a multicultural setting[29] that *devalues their background and knowledge*.[30] This system unrealistically expects these students to learn outside of their well-established learning pattern of observation and mimicking, a pattern that is acquired by Latino children in order to accomplish adult-like tasks within the rural Latino *campo*.

Summary: A Culturally Appropriate Education

Those who have read this far must realize that the techniques used to teach Spanish speakers in learning situations are not necessarily expensive or time-consuming; instead, a depth of understanding about the culture is required. Looking into the "souls" of the Spanish-speaking students is imperative to develop a clear appreciation of their depth of knowledge and style of learning in the rural arena. Once teachers or trainers grasp that concept, that lifestyle, that cultural uniqueness, they can appreciate the many ways to awaken students by initiating motivation. Once the students get engaged in learning the tasks at hand, the awakening process will become easier to initiate and to retain as a part of normal instruction methods.

PART THREE

Summary of Techniques, Solutions, Options, and Considerations

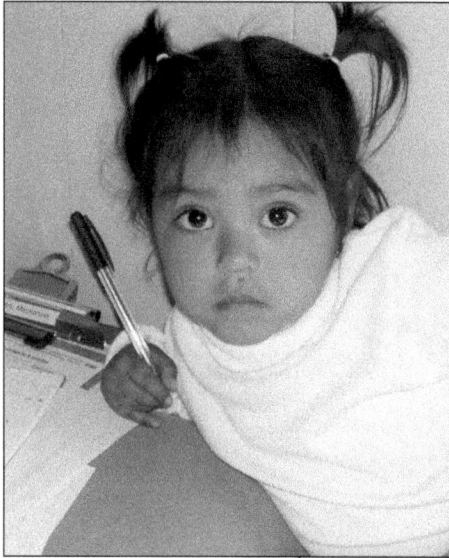

"Ready to Learn" original oil painting. It takes a sincere teacher who will "speak with your heart" to make the difference in every child's life.

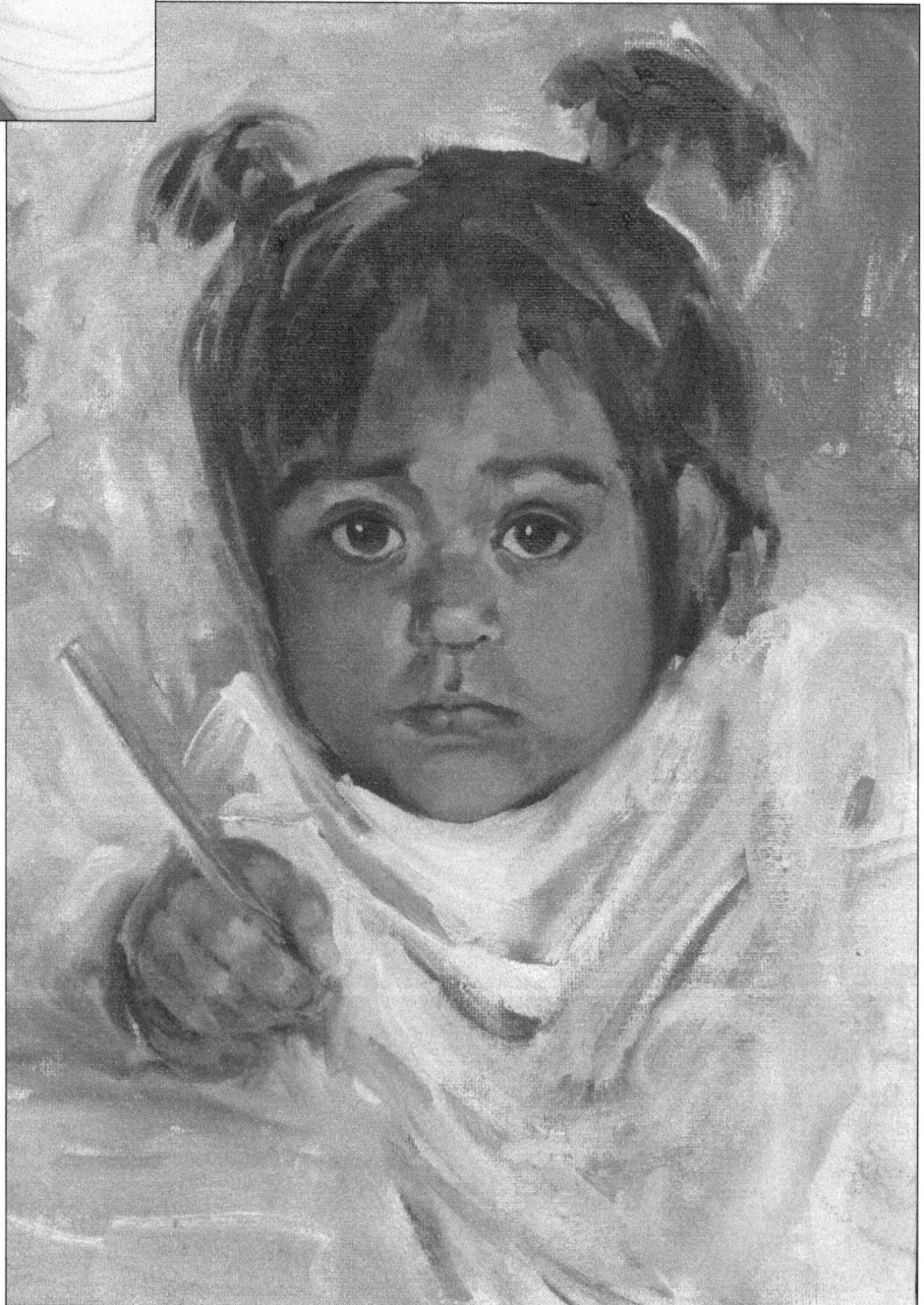

15 Answers for Educators, Business People, and Friends

No man who is occupied in doing a very difficult thing, and doing it very well, ever loses his self-respect.

—George Bernard Shaw

Questions from Chapter 1 with Summarized Answers

This chapter summarizes what has already been elaborated on with stories, research data, field notes, transcripts, quotes, references, and other comments. If you read this book in its entirety, then you can skip this chapter or use it as a quick reference. You can also use it to share thoughts with friends or to facilitate conversations with peers, but you already have the answers.

The basic "survival of the tribe" question placed before the elders has always been...

1. How do we best prepare and educate the next generation?

Offer Children Adult-Sized Tools and Problems

Play is the work of children. It's very serious stuff.[1] This certainly applies to the lifestyle of most American children, but rural Mexican children, like African children[2] work with adults' tools (not children's toys) from the time they can stand up alone and mimic adults' activities. They do not live a *sanitized* life.

Do Not Expect Latino Parents to Sanitize Their Environment

American children, for the most part, have numerous protections in place, which *sanitize* their environment by making it so safe, secure, clean, and unchallenging that the children grow into adulthood without having to apply the level of common sense that is demanded every day from rural Latino children. This level of mental, physical, and emotional demanded on agriculturally raised Latino children requires them to be capable of making quick, mature, adult decisions within a community of young learners and doers. This occurs even in life-and-death situations. They become both natural leaders and experienced team players, because their lives depend on making wise split-second decisions.

Economic shortfalls require the student to find fast temporary solutions; most things in the rancho resident's life are expected to need maintenance and repair. Therefore, if the teachers or trainer will expect the Spanish-speaking student to comprehend a sanitized environment, both will be confused. Expect the student to find the fastest, the cheapest, the easiest, and the most adult method for solving a problem and the student will be a winner.

If a safe, slow, high-quality method dependent on consumer materials is required, then the rural student is likely to be less confident. He or she is not well informed about marketable products and has less familiarity with consumer products, has fewer opportunities to practice without pressure to perform quickly, and has more pressure to adapt to available materials. There is a need for instructions to be given and a demonstration to be shown of how to accomplish such a task with consumer products and perhaps without as much speed, ease, cost-cutting, temporary-fix, and adult-like thinking being applied.

No OSHA Concept of Safety Concerns in Latin America

Children commonly ride in open pickup trucks while sitting on the narrow bed-rail—while these trucks hit bumpy rocks in the dirt roadways. Family businesses are frequently located along busy highways, on the small shoulder of the road; toddlers run from parents to other caregivers right alongside rapidly moving vehicles. Seatbelts are rarely used, and children are not strapped into infant seats in cars. Men in the construction trade do not normally use safety equipment. The balancing act that workers perform on a ladder placed on top of other unstable bases seems surreal to those who have lived with OSHA safety rules.

Teamwork is Typical

Cultural values strengthen the roles of all participants, both young and old, in the community. The blur that occurs in who is a leader and who is the follower shifts the title of *expert* from one person to another, as each skill is required in a *cooperative manner*. Traditional Western style of teaching pits students against each other in a *competitive manner*. The Spanish-speaking student is normally totally taken by surprise when he or she is accused of *cheating* after leaning over to help a classmate. Assisting each other in all aspects of living is the norm in Latin America.

Cooperative Social Networking

If the positions of teacher/student, researcher/learner, or professor/intern are allowed to shift in a *cooperative manner*, then the entire community benefits. That same method of honoring each other's experiences and looking at new challenges in the classroom as a team is effective, engages the soul of rural knowledge, and results in workable solutions both in the classroom and in the community.

2. Why aren't Latino students motivated to learn?

Interactive and Relevant Tasks Spark Motivation

Effective evidence-based practices results occur when conceptual and academic development is enhanced. Students must be engaged and interested enough to comprehend the information (including understanding the language being used by the instructor), and the information must be of relevant interest to the student. If the themes are boring, relating to nothing from which the student can scaffold to previous knowledge or experiences, then the student will lose interest. Interactive tasks that draw on gained wisdom or life experiences are fun because comprehension is there and some mastery has already occurred. The student can easily be mentally, emotionally, and physically overwhelmed when the subject is not understood and/or when there is no connection to past experiences or knowledge.

Effective teaching demands that the educators or instructors know the linguistic, cognitive, and academic challenges facing each student. Each skill must be practiced in order to reach the necessary proficiency to both obtain and retain the conceptual and educational information.

When wise educators or instructors explore the *funds of knowledge* that each student's background brings to the classroom, then second language learning and new content acquisition begins to be assimilated by the student with both ease and eagerness. Knowing something about a subject that is of interest to the student motivates the student's willingness to have a conversation about the subject. Abstract subjects in a foreign language create a state of exhaustion and avoidance in an already overwhelmed student of a second language or in students who may be functioning far outside of their acquired life experiences.

3. How do I teach English as a second language to Spanish-speaking Mexican students?

Cyclical Organization of Materials

Effective educators or instructors of Spanish-speaking students, especially of those from rural areas, should focus on cyclical organization of subject matter; this approach mimics the change of seasons common to the cycles of a farmer's life. When classroom presentations follow a simple cyclical pattern already known to the student, this approach leads to a natural growth in the understanding of ideas (one building or scaffolding upon the previous one). When a misunderstanding occurs, a gradual correction of misconceptions is easier to pinpoint early and modify quickly.

Contextualized Thematic Curriculum

Curricula, using the same approach, must be contextualized that is presented with a logical transition from one area of concentration to another. A classroom filled with gifted high school seniors might easily transition from quantum physics to ancient Greek philosophy, but few others would find such abstract concepts easy to follow, let alone to transition between them. Creating thematic cross-curricular units is worth the effort if the theme is a subject already familiar to the student. A week-long study of the breeding of dairy cows could easily include a range of subjects, including but not limited to a mathematical analysis, scientific study, historical research, nutritional needs review, and animal husbandry processes. The less abstract and dry the lesson, the more motivated the students will be to engage in the learning process. The use of "hands-on" manipulatives, photographs, student-generated drawings, and graphic illustrations that bring complex ideas within students' reach are very effective in contextualizing the curriculum into a worthwhile tool.

Modeling and Guidance of Acceptable Expressions

Effective educators or instructors guide and model for the students. They know when to let the student's own motivation *take over* and when successful understanding occurs. Even second language learners, who may spend a year in silence, will respond to effective modeling and guidance. They want to learn and be accepted as equals within a group of others. Making the student aware of acceptable expressions for writing, talking, and presenting academic material is helpful to the student socially and academically.

Multiple Opportunities to Demonstrate and Expand Knowledge

Applying trial and error often results in success, since the task has been *practiced to perfection.* If every new task does not build on acquired knowledge, the possibility of failure increases because no *practice* has occurred. When multiple learning opportunities in novel new situations are presented and acquired, *practiced knowledge* can be drawn into the activity and the opportunity for success increases. There is also a positive emotional response that increases permanent understanding of the topic of study. With this approach, more demanding tasks will be attempted; success also encourages generalization and standardization of the application, thereby relating the learning to more complex activities.

Relevant, Engaging Tasks

Evidence-based instruction is relevant, meaningful, varied, and engaging for students, especially for economically or socially marginalized or learning-disabled students. All students learn easier and retain more when they are presented with relevant, meaningful, varied, and engaging tasks. Endless problems unrelated to any goal or visible result are boring and nonproductive. Casual surveying of a group of people at a class reunion revealed that when the task of creating a rocket in a classroom lesson had been successful, the students were able to recall it full 55 years after completion. This lesson was not monotonous or teacher-directed; the students interacted with each other. Group activities for solving problems are a welcome and normal means to engage Spanish-speaking students; they are familiar with teamwork-based problem solving. Each student engages in his or her own constructive development of critical thinking while working in a group.

Collaboration

When collaboration is used as a means to solve complex problems, solutions seem reachable. Learners maximize opportunities to interact and reinforce each other without any threat of competition. Wise educators or instructors will make certain that students understand the assignment is a group project and not focused on any one leadership position.

Accurate, Authentic Assessment is Vital

Students crave accurate, authentic assessment of their work by their peers and their mentors. Educators or instructors must take the time to offer specific areas of guidance, praise, and constructive criticism. Learners need to be able to have options for self-directed learning through disciplined inquiry. Group projects encourage an analysis of problems; they enable students to share success and to learn without the stigma of personal failure.

4. What is going on globally that affects Mexican students?

To some degree, most residents of Earth are feeling the effects of

1. *overpopulation,*
2. *limited resources,*
3. *communication and marketing* through the use of the Internet, mobile devices (iPhone, BlackBerry), and the like, and
4. the pressing need for nurturing the *natural survival instinct* present in all living beings.

It does not matter if you have been raised by a stone mason, a computer programmer, a politician, or an adult who was laid off; nearly all of us are trying to figure out how to move forward in our careers in a changing world. Violence, anger, frustration, and other vast swings in emotional responses often occur when an individual engages his or her natural survival instinct; in extreme cases, this may result in a shooting rampage in a former place of employment or in a school. At this time, this situation has reached a global scale; solutions are evasive.

In the past, our elders guided us toward a goal of self-reliance with relative confidence, something I will refer to as *the rules of life.* More than likely, three or four generations back someone in the family was a subsistence farmer able to grow enough to keep the family healthy, even in times of Great Depression (1930s) or World War II (1940s). That family relative may have learned *the rules of life* from his father or grandfather.

After this relative passed away and the family land was divided, the individual chunk of land that he had worked on with some success grew smaller, and it may have also become less productive as the Korean War (1950s) raged. Then the Vietnam War came into our living rooms every night for nearly two decades (November 1955 to May 1975). We began to accept a global view of life, with at least one divorce within the family or the extended family, another war (1990–1991) or two (2003–present), and a dot-com crisis sandwiched in between (1995–2000). Then the biggest blow to financial security since the Great Depression occurred, and the world economy changed even further from *the rules of life* handed down by the ancestors (2007–present). Options for employment and the means to support a family changed dramatically in the past 100 years from what had been *the rules of life* since 10,000 B.C. or earlier.

Predominately indigenous rural Latinos, who are at the bottom of a 14-level social class scale, continue to make every effort to be self-sustaining as subsistence farmers in agricultural Latin America. These hardworking, sincere, respectful people continue to do all that they can to follow in the footsteps of their ancestors. Predominately indigenous rural Latinos continue to apply *the rules of life* they learned from their ancestors, and yet their lives get less productive with every year that passes. Even the "good years" (when the rain falls) do not increase their quality of life, because there is too much need with too few resources available.

5. How might our shrinking access to land and nature affect education?

Kaplan's Attention Restoration Theory[3] (1995) states that attentional functioning may be enhanced by time spent in nature. Additional evidence indicates that adults who function within normal attentional ranges utilize nature to support that attentional functioning.[4] According to Kaplan,[5] children who have been diagnosed with Attention Deficit Disorder (ADD) may appear symptom-free when in natural environments and even for some time after coming indoors. "For children with ADD and their parents, these findings have a clear and inexpensive implication: Children with ADD can support their attention functioning and minimize their symptoms simply by spending time in green settings."[6] I take the position that attentional functioning, feelings of self worth, motivation to learn, and other emotional and cognitive developments expressed as behaviors may be negatively affected by emotional stresses, and that symptoms may be positively affected by exposure to nature.[7]

Two researchers were concerned with gaining knowledge about where children of this generation play, indoors or outdoors, compared to where their parents played when they were about the same age. The concept was to compare childhood activities of family members who were a generation apart: The researchers compared what the parents did when they were about the same age as their children to what their children were doing now.[8] They interviewed children between 5 years to 12 years of age; most of the parents were between 31 and 40 years of age. In each case, one questionnaire was allocated to the parents and another was given to the child. The child's questionnaire examined (1) many aspects of play outdoors, (2) use of technology indoors, and (3) questions designed to determine the socioeconomic status of the family. The parents' survey was much the same, except it relied a great deal on memory of their own childhoods. Both questionnaires also had a section for free expression.[9]

The reader is challenged to look at his or her family's lifestyle today and compare that to what probably occurred 50 years beforehand, based on family stories. Across the U.S., most families have moved away from the *spare the rod, spoil the child* mindset of aggressive, physical punishment for the infraction of speaking out of turn at home or at school to positive behavioral management practiced even in the public schools. Fifty years ago, society demanded that children entertain themselves— with their peers and in the neighborhood streets, backyards, or parks— by using their imaginations.[10] The child of today is often kept indoors; neighborhoods are transient and parks are not safe, which terrifies today's parents.[11] Many parents prefer to use electronic babysitters and keep the children inside the home.[12]

Parent's own fear is keeping kids indoors with far more restrictions than the parents experienced when they were children themselves. It is important to note that in the outdoor time study previously mentioned, 91.4 percent of the children had bicycles—they could be mobile. The parental controls were the issue: 50.7 percent of the females and 67.2 percent of the males were permitted to ride on the road.[13] The play area for children near their homes shrunk between 1970 and 1990 to one-ninth of what it had been.[14] What children are doing in this generation is staying indoors: 63.4 percent of the children aged 5 to 12 spent more than three hours a day watching television, and 55 percent indicated that game-playing devices were used in their home for more than one hour every day. Although 85 percent of the parents of these children owned a television, the parents watched only a few specific shows each week.[15]

6. What else might our shrinking access to land and nature affect?

Children fear what they do not know. Lack of experiences around a different-speaking and a different-acting person creates fear. This fear makes it difficult for the ESL person to be accepted in the classroom or the workplace. The same is true for experiences with nature. If people are not taught to love and respect nature when young, they will fear it and not protect it. If all people had a healthy respect for nature, Latino people raised in rural areas would be more respected for their vast knowledge of nature. The wise teacher or trainer should make certain that lessons involving nature are entwined in other lessons, so that Latino participants can exhibit their *funds of knowledge* to the other participants; this will help Latinos to stay engaged longer and to retain more information on other subjects, as well as to assist the non-latino participants to expand their knowledge for global good.

Eco-literacy, defined as knowing enough about the outdoor environment to love and respect it, has a multi-faceted benefit that parents need to appreciate.[16] Prior to the mid–1950s, children naturally spent a great deal of time alone outdoors as a part of growing up. That commonality no longer exists,[17] however, often due to parents' fear of the harm that may come to a child left alone outdoors.[18] Today the challenge for parents is to find the time to be outdoors with their children.[19] Fortunately, taking the time to get their children outdoors to *improve health and well-being* may have become a mainstream concept; it was recently added to the list of good parenting guidelines.[20] The November 16–18, 2007, Parade Magazine front-page headline read, "Special Report: Raising Healthier Kids." The subtitle stated, "Learn about the exciting new theory experts believe may solve many of your child's ills." On the cover, a woman and a child, who appeared to be mother and daughter, were both dressed in green sweat suits; they were hugging while standing on a computer-enlarged pair of leaves.[21] In the same month, Instructor Magazine's cover had a picture of two students, an Asian girl and an African-American boy, painting what appeared to be their white, blonde, European-descent teacher with green paint; the wall, the desk, the floor, and the blackboards were also partially covered in green paint. The lead story was titled, "How Green Classrooms are Reconnecting Kids with Nature,"[22] and the issue was titled, "Be a Hero for the Planet."[23] This positive trend is likely due to increased awareness of the pressing need to teach eco-literacy; most developing countries have surpassed us in being informed about nature (Forest Stewardship Council, 2007).

I have examined findings regarding research and other public reports on the need for eco-literacy, especially involving the education of adolescents on this vital subject,[24] which has great importance for the planet and for the child's overall health.[25] Appropriate eco-literacy models may have a positive effect on the future stewards of the planet.[26] Evidence exists about the effect of the lack of eco-literacy; ignoring signs of Earth's climate change is an international problem.[27] Being detached about climate change has had the same effect on Earth as ignoring predominantly sedentary indoor activities of children has had on overall child health;[28] situations related to health and climate have deteriorated. For example, when the only body parts exercised are the child's fingers and eyes, the frequent result is childhood obesity.[29] Obesity and the health complications[30] of that sedentary trend reduce a child's well-being; on a broader scale, detachment from Earth's needs might hurt the children and the planet.[31]

Regardless of how often parents promise themselves to allow for some relaxed time in nature time with their children, the fast-paced life of the 21st century interferes with time needed for the outdoors and time needed to teach children eco-literacy.[32] If public schools offered more courses about nature, to help the students to develop a deep love of nature, parents could have the luxury of being less concerned. I take a very hard stand that eco-literacy must be taught by parents, or others, as an investment in tomorrow's leaders. According to Vygotzky's theory of scaffolding (Zone of Proximal Development),[33] by building on what the child knows and following that knowledge acquisition with more specific information as the child develops, a well-rounded individual is raised. By the time an adult is cultivated, an appreciation for nature will be deeply engrained.[34] That adult will honor, respect, and protect nature,[35] using whatever means is at hand. That adult will be mentally, physically, and emotionally healthier from having acquired the love for, the knowledge of, and the exposure to nature,[36] as well as an understanding of ecological or environmental literacy (eco-literacy). Even cognitive functioning improves with exposure to nature,[37] as does the behavior.[38]

"It (eco-literacy) provides a capacity to analyze for the interpretive models upon which phenomena of concern are based and with these models in mind to propose strategies for acting "metaresponsibly" in environment. The intellectual basis of this approach is developed and then applied to a range of current issues. An unusual and liberating set of responses is generated." (Steps to an Ecology of Mind *by Frank Fisher, 2005)*

Especially after living in rural Latin America, I am in favor of parents investing time to teach eco-literacy to their children, preferably in the outdoors; the results might be surprising on many levels. *A Sense of Wonder* by David Orr can be used as a tool to assist those parents who are asking about the value of instilling eco-literacy in their children. They want to understand what eco-literacy is and how teaching it to their children could be a benefit.

Researchers show repeatedly that eco-literacy needs to be taught early in life and broadly through different means, because children learn differently.[39] Yet, ask adolescents what they are most concerned about regarding their future, and if they do not first say *Earth changes*, then they are lacking in educational models that embed concern for the natural environment—they are lacking eco-literacy. The fast-paced life of modern obligations interferes with time in nature;[40] sadly, there always seems to be time to explore the Internet together,[41] where Earth's challenges and wonders are presented only as icons. Reaction time has been severely lacking. Nevertheless, some researchers have regarded eco-literacy as a vital topic to study.

The phrase *a contagious attitude of attentiveness* was used by one researcher to describe a world in which a child explores the outdoors in a primarily self-motivated experience that he or she finds engaging. This means of learning usually results in the child becoming an adult with a passion for nature. A passion for the world of consumerism results in a *wasteland* mentality toward nature.[42] This situation is often developed by children who are self-preoccupied due to fear and anxiety when in nature.[43]

The opposite of a wasteland mentality—a lack of awareness—is an adult who

1. learned how to care for the land as a child with a concerned caregiver,
2. has developed a disapproval of actions that destroy nature,
3. can find joy in the simplest exposure to nature, and
4. is engaged with the details of nature's earth and sky. The children who live near my house have these qualities, which could be built on empirically without having any awareness of their *funds of knowledge*.[44]

7. What can we as educators do to make school fun, to keep students engaged, and to help children form a life-long habit of learning?

Children, like adults, are happy and engaged when they feel appreciated, loved, admired, respected, and comfortable. Positive emotions make learning easier; a desire to repeat the activity is then more likely (creating a habit). If those feelings occur in the classroom, the emotion of happiness[45] will override opportunities for nonproductive emotions. Conversely, as long as the classroom is a place where fear, humiliation, disregard, confusion, misunderstanding, and prejudice prevail, anything associated with that classroom will be considered negative: Information will not be retained, learning will be ineffective, and resistance to forming a habit will be firmly put into place.

8. Do Latina mothers care if their children are educated?

Latino parents with social normalcy want the best for their children, including education (the focus of Chapter 11), health, wealth, and happiness.[46] Parents rarely allocate time for outdoor explorations with their children;[47] therefore educating parents is advisable.[48]

Parents and educators need to read the following line before deciding that time in nature is not worth the investment in their children: *The quality of life isn't measured only by what we gain, but also (by) what we trade for it.*[49] Children are suffering from cultural autism[50] by living with tunnel vision. Cultural autism means we are emotionally detached from nature.

9. How do Latina mothers see their children's futures in the U.S. or in Latin America?

My spring 2007 research project, referenced several times in Part II, focused on 13 Mexican women who were interviewed while working in a preschool and in an after-school program on the Arizona-Sonora border. The original research task was simple: examine the attitudes of Latino parents toward their children's future. The study took quite a surprising turn when Maria was interviewed. She was very clear that asking male parents was a waste of time. Her suggestion was to ask the mothers, the grandmothers, the sisters, and the aunts, who care for the children[51] and know the children. She advised us not to bother asking the fathers about how they see their children's future, because it is not their responsibility to think about it, do anything about it, or take any credit or blame for how it turns out.

Maria explained that a Latina female has one job: caregiver. The female rates her success by how her children turn out. Maria was emphatic that asking male Latino parents about their dreams for their children was a waste of time. She went on to explain that, "Latino men have only one job, to earn a living; some do [earn a living], other's don't [earn a living], but that is their only job."[53] For Latina women, the role is far more complex, truly multi-faceted. The Latino male may or may not play the father role, or even the husband role, and very little stigma is attached either way. But the Latina female is expected to be *the* head of the household, *the provider for anyone in the immediate or the extended family, an outstanding mother* to anyone who is in her home, *a cool-headed leader* regardless of what might occur in her home or in the community, *the teacher of all* cultural or religious activities in the home, the one to *shoulder any responsibility* that might be asked of her, *a giver of advice* and labor to anyone who asks that of her, and the one who is *always in control.* There is no significant stigma if a girl is pregnant and unmarried,[52] as long as she is a good mother, but not caring for her children is unthinkable. Maria's interview stated: *Mexican women do not leave their children.*

Maria's interview included the following exchange:

QUESTION (BY AUTHOR): I know that you have gone through some transitions (life changes) this past year and yet you are feeling really good about where your children are?

REPLY (BY MARIA): *Hmmmmmm…*

QUESTION: So, could I say that you feel like you've really succeeded in your life, that you feel really good about your life?

REPLY: *I have succeeded, but I have not accomplished yet what I want for them (her children)—but I think I have succeeded.*

QUESTION: It is (through) them (i.e. how they, the children, are doing in life)—that's how you rate yourself. It's (through) them, is that right?

REPLY: *That is how I rate myself. I knew that since they were small, a reflection of me was going to be in them. I know that each one of them has to be them (an individual), and that is the way I want it.*

Maria went on to explain that the way a child looks and behaves is a direct reflection on the mother of that child. I had suspected this, because in all the years I had taught Latino children I noticed that mothers questioned me about classroom behavior but not academic performance. I thought then that education was taking a back seat; now I realize that the mother was verifying her success or failure as a mother, not ignoring educational efforts by her children. This is an area where it is easy to make an incorrect assumption or to be unintentionally biased due to cultural influences.

Mothers are also evaluated by how clean their children appear, because the dress of the young person speaking to an elder directly reflects the respect that youth has for the older person. I immediately noticed the cleanliness of children when they arrived at school and how well their clothing fit them (although often visibly altered). Even the children with "thread-bare" clothing were physically spotless; their clothing was always washed and fit well. There is no teenage *baggy-pants* look in the *campo*. This fact explains why Mexicans cannot comprehend *casual dress days* that often occur on Fridays in the U.S. For them, it is important to look good and act with respect every day. It may also be that with 14 levels of social classes, the observer is expected to assume that the person being observed is of a higher status; the culture may necessitate that every effort is made to convey this impression.

The question, "Why on earth would anyone dress down?" must be on the mind of Mexicans when they hear or see this practice in the U.S.

This is another example of cultural differences. Typically, citizens of the U.S. cannot imagine why women would wear four-inch heels, massive makeup, and sequined shoes, sweaters, and/or belts to work in an office environment. Work attire in Latin America often includes excessive eye makeup, with shaved off eyebrows that are penciled in much larger and darker than natural eyebrows. Additionally, skirts both very short and too tight to sit down are common. A woman may be heard complaining that "Jose (her husband) is so jealous! I don't know why!" Educators need to be aware that the correlation between dress and sexual flirting is apparently less obvious in Latino culture or at least there is less of a direct link compared to the U.S.

10. If a child had special needs, would that child's challenge(s) change your expectations for that child's adult future?

This question was asked of all women in my 2007 research project. The following is the final summary statement of this research:

No. Universal acceptance of all children overshadows any concerns about how able or how limited the child might be (physically, mentally, or emotionally); all children are loved and expected to be successful.[53]

11. Why is it so difficult for a rural Latino child to acquire a decent education through high school in Latin America?

It is difficult to gain a decent education in a rural area in Latin America because (1) the cost of attending school is prohibitive for a subsistence-farming family, (2) universal coursework is related to urban educational needs, (3) students are rarely able to show their knowledge of outdoor lifestyles in an indoor learning environment, (4) teachers are of a higher social status and may not relate as well to lower class students, (5) travel to middle and high schools takes excessive time away from family chores, (6) homework takes too much of the time needed for family obligations, and (7) it is very hard to get accepted into urban high schools.

12. Why is it so difficult for an immigrant Latino child to acquire a decent education through high school in the U.S.?

As shown in Part II, it is difficult to gain a decent education in a rural area because (1) the costs associated with attending school may be economically stressful, (2) much of the coursework is related to technical skills that the student may need to acquire, (3) students are rarely able to show their knowledge of their outdoor lifestyles in an indoor learning environment, (4) teachers are normally speaking only English, and the student is likely not fluent in English, (5) no one in the family can assist with homework due to a lack of English proficiency and possibly lower educational attainment levels of the older family members, (6) homework takes too much time that needs to be allocated to family obligations, including language brokering, (7) it is very hard for immigrant students to get accepted as equals in high school, and there may be no one with whom they can study as a team, and (8) nearly all schooling relates to a modern urban upbringing, not to outdoor living and rural lifestyles.

The surveys in several studies showed that the preferred place to play in the U.S. is "at home" (in contrast to a park or a planned playground).

The big difference is that yesterday's children were allowed to explore, investigate, and experience to a much higher degree than today's children. Of today's children, 61.3 percent must stay in their own back yard or play under adult surveillance; of yesterday's children, only 39.9 percent had those restrictions. Keep in mind that the researchers also had to factor in the fast-food play parks; yesterday's children did not have those.[54]

Teach Bilingually and Change the Economics of Mexico

I am especially familiar with infants and toddlers of Latino heritage within an educational setting. I was the director of a preschool and a day care facility on the Arizona-Sonora border, where I lived for 12 years. I also worked along the border as a teacher or trainer of children with special needs. Therefore, I knew that the more I understood within my research about cultural influences that might mask my understanding of what was actually occurring, the more likely I could offer some culturally appropriate solutions or ways to overcome consequences. One option was to provide bilingual Spanish/English instruction for children and adults in both public and private schools or other institutions. The Spanish-speaking caregivers must want such services, since they frequently ask Jolene and me for English classes for themselves and for their children. While out in the field, I wanted to find a means to ease the burden of developmental delays or special needs for indigenous caregivers. Even though I had a school-director background, I lacked information specific to Central Mexico. This was an area far different from the border regions with which I was familiar. So, I looked at lifestyle factors that could have a bearing on my observation of children or on my interviews with their caregivers.

Indigenous Caregivers Evaluate Education in Unexpected Ways

Caregivers did not have the same outlook on educational priorities and school administrations as might be expected by someone with my background. Caregivers were not active within the schools and did not enhance their children's education for many reasons. The following journal entry explains some of those reasons:

Last Friday I was also able to reconnect with "Chico" (not real name), the head teacher at the school (name withheld), and with Dr. Lidia Rios Villalpando (her real name by request) from the Health Department in the city (name withheld). I am working on opening the doors to students volunteering at both of those schools. Dr. Lidia Rios and I met at the preschool (school name withheld) where I have stopped several times. Again, this is another excellent school for visiting students, teachers, or others to use as a volunteer experience.

Chico again bemoaned to me the fact that there is such a short supply of teaching tools. Often there is no Internet access, the Smart Board imitations from China are only used as a wall decoration, and parents are too intimidated to be involved at the school at any level other than bringing food to the kids. When parents cannot read, they stay away from the schools, Chico explained.

Caregivers simply trust that the teachers will make sure the children are taught what they need to know, but with so little to use for teaching, it's a nearly impossible task. His comments mirror those of "Jose" (not real name), the 34-year veteran teacher at the school (name withheld) just 8 miles away. Jose also explained that feeding the kids is the main goal, so having the child work to earn money to buy food has real value; school takes a back seat.[55]

This journal entry shows that some factors existing in rural Mexico contribute to the perpetuating myth that children's education is not of interest to subsistence farmers. These parents' priority is feeding the children. According to data, parents and other caregivers lacked the training and understanding of how to enhance their children's educational experiences. They also appear to be easily intimidated by educators or instructors, especially those who exhibit a higher class status. Researchers in other Latin American countries have found the same results.[56]

Reading to Children Was Limited

Many parents could not read, and others lacked the time to read. Books were not present in the homes, and they were not considered as tools toward the development of literacy. In general, researchers found what I found: poor literacy rates among Latin American children and a lack of interest in written code.[57] Most caregivers were giving directives to children (*Watch the goats*) or requesting items in a question-answer format (*Where is the tortilla press?*). Rarely did caregivers request more detail, like how long the child had watched the goats, where he or she had gone for pasture access, or how much grass had been consumed by the goats. Children infrequently asked parents to explain something to them. Researchers found that parents appeared to lack an understanding about assisting children with school tasks;[58] the same findings were noted within this study. There was no notable activity that I observed in any classrooms or homes related to the education of rural Latino children that was unique to this part of Latin America, other than what has already been discussed or what has been noted by other researchers.

Lack of Reading Skills, Expression, and Ease by Latino Adults Makes Reading and Listening Boring

As explained throughout Part II, I found limited verbal acuity in the parents or other relatives, which was often coupled with a lack of reading materials. While reading, Latino adults sometimes displayed flat expressionless faces. When reading without expression or intonation is offered to infants, there is a minimal enticement toward learning to socialize. Additionally, infants were offered very little sound or movement to mimic while being read to, because reading was such a labored and unnatural act for the Latino adult.

Researchers have studied the meal-time conversations of middle-class Caucasian families outside of Latin America and found that their table conversation had a very exacting *school-style way of speaking*, which allowed children to practice public speaking.[59]

Researchers have discovered that children hearing a language or style of speaking repeat that style with more ease.[60] The rural Latino children's vocabulary development is presumably reduced due to their parents' limited academic vocabulary and habitual resistance to excessive speaking. My research found that 23% of children aged 18 months to 5 years had acquired no audible speech or developed other speech problems.[61] The incidence of speech problems among the children aged 3 years to 17 years in the U.S. is 2.3% for girls and 4.6% for boys.[62]

Mothers Lacked Time to Teach Their Children Non-Domestic Subjects

For extensive information related to this topic, refer to Part II.

There were little or no printed materials in the rural Latinos' homes. After the age of about 12, most teens or adults had no access to books.

The school libraries I examined usually had one 4- to 5-foot-long shelf that had accrued books over many years. Not only were books not in the home, but the caregivers' reading skills were limited and mothers had little time for teaching academics. The lack of a public library system meant that there was no access to books or other forms of knowledge. Although some older siblings were able to read, the majority of the caregivers had marginal reading skills, because they rarely had the opportunity to practice reading since secondary school. Data indicated that they were intimidated by schoolwork. Most marginalized, ingenious, rural Latina mothers accepted no responsibility for the job of teaching children anything other than domestic tasks and obedience. Mothers told me in different clinics, often in a defensive manner, that in the *campo* caregivers expected educators or instructors to do the entire job of teaching academic subjects to children. This fact was further hampered by other factors related to living in the *campo*.

Malnutrition and sociocultural disadvantages have been found to increase the clinical characteristics of learning disabilities or other special needs in socioeconomically disadvantaged Latino children.

Latino researchers working with economically marginalized Latino children found that undiagnosed learning disabilities were being faced by many of the children, and especially by those in rural areas. Caregivers are at a big disadvantage when attempting to teach those children. Other researchers have found a high correlation between poverty, low nutritional levels, and a lack of academic success.[63]

Summary: Answers

Many techniques, solutions, options, and considerations have been discussed in this chapter with references back to Part II. Consider taking what relates best to your style of teaching first and then expanding to include other choices as needed. The results will be worth everyone's efforts.

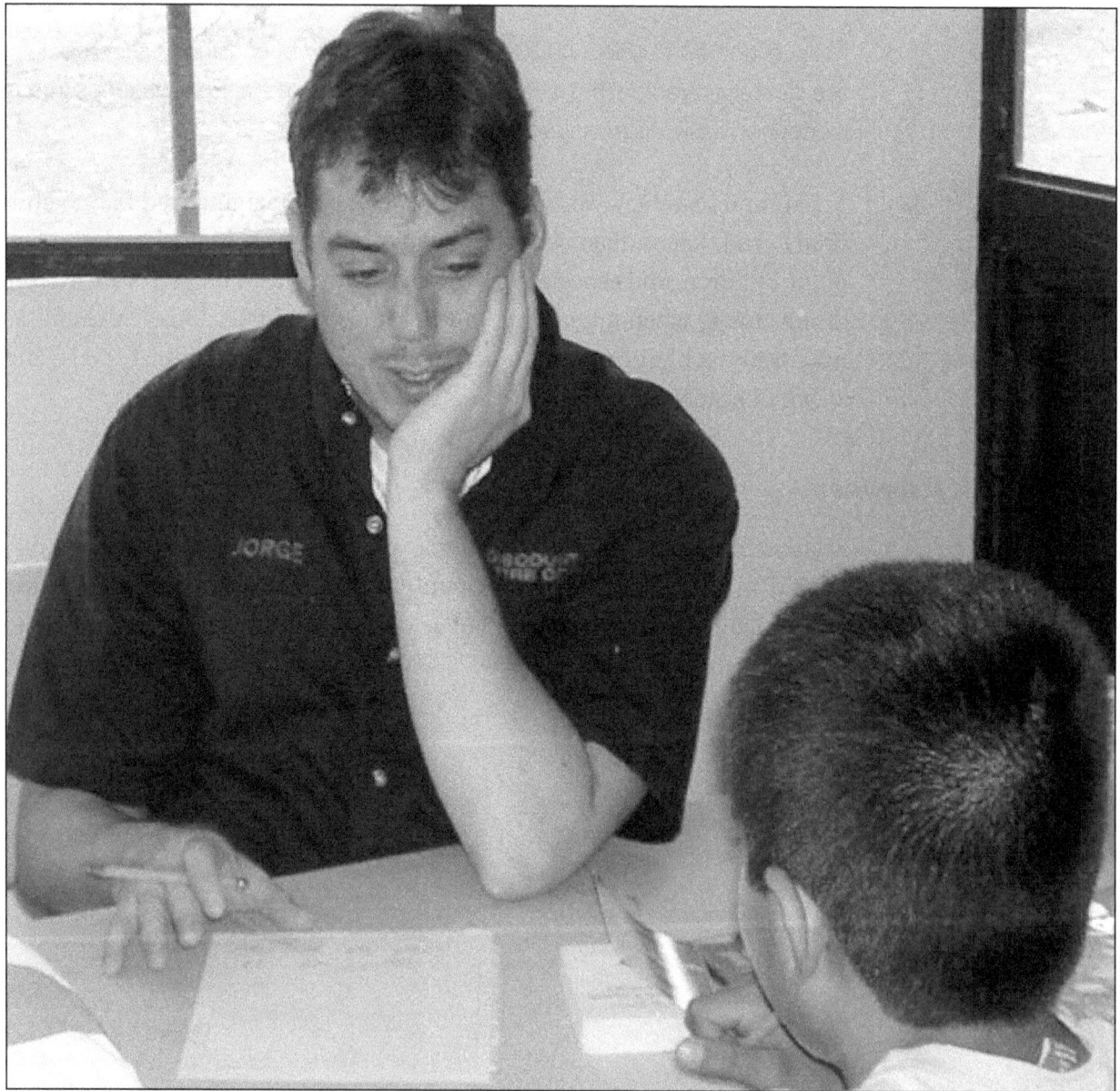

Volunteer teacher Matt Hogel tutors a rural Latino student in an after-school program in a small subsistence farmers' community in Central Mexico. Volunteer teachers from the U.S., Canada, Germany, France, and Japan have given their time, skills, and kindness to the children in this program.

16 Closing Words

If we plant seeds of failure from the first day of school, the crop will certainly not be satisfactory at harvest time.

—GERALD HAWKINS, 2010

Research-Based Summary: Culturally Sensitive Educators are the Key to Academic Success for Latinos

My research has made me an advocate for positive change relating to the way Spanish speakers, especially immigrants who lived in other parts of Latin America, are treated in schools, corporations, and social settings. I am not alone in my opinion that most of the change must come from you—the school teacher, professor, or corporate trainer has the power to create positive outcomes on a national level. You as an educator, a business owner, a peer, a friend, or a neighbor must **make a commitment to develop and implement programs that are sensitive to the needs of Mexican-American people.** The following U.S. ERIC preserved abstract reached the same conclusion. The power to make a difference lies in the attitudes of those who are communicating with Spanish speakers:

This literature review examines the effect of teacher expectations on minority students, and especially on Mexican-American students. The review focuses on four areas: (1) teachers' attitudes and expectations toward Mexican-American children; (2) teachers' attitudes and expectations toward minority children; (3) teachers' performance expectations of students; and (4) other expectations which determine teacher behavior. The research indicates that teachers do not expect Mexican-American children or minority

221

children as a group to excel in school; that Mexican-American children lead double lives—family atmosphere and values are in conflict with the school environment and Caucasian values; and that school districts appear to lack a commitment to the Mexican-American student, thereby allowing institutional racism and racial bias to flourish. In order to develop insight and awareness to counteract the negative expectations of teachers, it is recommended that boards of education, community groups, district administrators, and government agencies make a commitment to develop and implement programs that are sensitive to the needs of Mexican-American children; and that teachers be trained and made more aware of the vast influence that their attitudes and prejudices have on pupils.[1]

You opened this book because the cover said,

- "Develop any age Latino student into leaders"
- You wanted to know how to effectively communicate with Spanish speakers.
- You now have the knowledge you were seeking.
- You now have the knowledge to make positive changes.
- A better tomorrow is possible for Latinos because of your acquired knowledge.
- Your peers will now look to you for the answers—enlighten them.
- With cultural sensitivity toward Latinos you can improve your school, workplace, and neighborhood.

The outcome related to your ability to reach Spanish speakers in your classroom or corporate training room, to sell your product to Spanish speakers, and to have rewarding relationships with your Spanish-speaking peers, neighbors, or social contacts is now up to you.

Attitude is Everything

Every society has people who mean others harm. In general, however, immigrants, expatriates, or visitors in Mexico who are having a positive experience came to Mexico with a positive attitude. They are open-minded, rational people who have taken the time to understand the culture and develop tolerance and understanding. The opposite is true for those who arrived and have remained biased. Among the emotionally alert people, attitude is everything. Those who show a willingness to understand, who attempt to learn the language, and who are sincere have a vastly better experience. The same will be true in your classroom or corporate training room when Mexican learners are present. If the teacher or trainer has a bright attitude, the Mexican student is more likely to have a positive learning experience.

When we moved into a rural area of Mexico, I was one of only three adult gringos ("gren-gos": a light-skinned foreigner, an English-speaker) there, and I was doing my best to adapt to life as a *campesino*. I was different from the locals, however, in that I was a deeply dedicated professional with little Spanish and even less time to study the language due to the specific demands of my academic pursuits.

During daylight and evening hours, the rural air rings with an amazing variety of sounds. Sound comes from every direction: from high-volume radios, from poorly coordinated human drummers, or from honking or loudspeaker systems announcing public buses. Then there are tortilla vendors, propane peddlers, baked-goods salesmen, and green grocers with pick-up trucks on the local dirt roads, seeking clients who are unable to read the printed flyers. The means to communicate is auditory. In addition, one can hear screeching by distant tractors or burros or mules pulling machines that grind the rocky soil—the scream of metal against rock could pierce the eardrums of anyone nearby. Normally there are also exuberant fiestas. Most fiestas are of a religious nature and combine the Native Indian culture and social activities with Catholic or Jehovah's Witness expressions. These frequently include fireworks, which often ring out from dawn to dawn, all through the night, and commonly for days on end. The sounds of this country literally vibrate within me from December 12 until January 16, as the locals celebrate the year-end holidays and mark the beginning of the new year.

Now that I have learned what to expect and have a better understanding of the heritage, I have come to enjoy the cultural activities going on all around me. I often join in, because polite Mexicans always welcome us like family members.

Time to Evaluate Your Harvest

If I have done a good job compiling my research into a format that is helpful, then you should have the confidence to walk into a school classroom or a corporate training room armed with the tools you need to reach Spanish-speaking individuals who require training in some area they have yet to master.

I will continue to research other parts of Mexico and pass on what I learn. I hope that you will feel free to write to me with any questions or needed clarifications. I welcome you to visit my workplace and see these fine Spanish speakers for yourself.

Jacqueline Z. Mackenzie, Ph.D.
220 N. Zapata Hwy., Suite 11
PMB 512-A
Laredo, TX 78043-4464 (a US mail forwarding service)
jzm@email.arizona.edu

Cajones, Guanajuato, is where you will find me: close to a Latino, in the campo and probably eating, talking, or both. Come and see for yourself what rural Latin America is like. We might also enjoy a phone conversation with each other.

Adios!

PART FOUR

Research, References, and Other Information

Appendix A

Those Observed for Original Research

Our connections in Mexico included but were not limited to the following:

- Established Mexican family connections;
- University affiliates, friends, and colleagues;
- City administrators, offices, and organizations;
- Former governor and his wife;
- Nonprofit organizations;
- Office of Social Services;
- Child care and preschool government organization;
- Severe and profound disability school;
- Language therapy facility;
- Department of Health Services;
- Bilingual women's organization;
- Visiting university students;
- Rural administrators and organizations;
- Rural health clinics and community centers;
- A Women's Cooperative;
- Our local rural Mexican family;
- Local rural community members;
- Rural teachers;
- Local rural community center.

Appendix B

Developmental Delays identified as Nutritional Problems

#	Age in Days	Nutrition Pro	Total Percent
51	60 days or less	10	19.6%
138	2–6 mo	31	22.5%
127	6–12 mo	45	35.4%
67	12–18 mo	24	35.8%
47	18–24 mo	18	38.3%
49	24–36 mo	19	38.8%
42	36–48 mo	14	33.3%
44	48–60 mo	11	25.0%
71	60+ mo	30	43.7%
636		200	31.4%

(Mackenzie, 2010)

Appendix C

Frequencies by Gender of Children Identified Outside Expected Normal Developmental Ranges in all Categories

Observed	Frequency		Total Percent	
	Male	Female	Male	Female
Nutrition Problems	98	105	31.1%	30.9%
Physical Disabilities	82	74	25.9%	21.9%
Emotional Behavioral	62	76	19.6%	22.5%
Language Problems	47	48	14.8%	14.2%
Severe and Profound	9	15	2.8%	4.4%
Cognitive Disorders	21	28	6.6%	8.3%
Gifted or Talented	4	12	1.3%	3.6%
Total	636	658*		

Individuals with one or more Developmental Delays 56.5%#
*Numerous multiple disabilities in a single child were recorded.
#Percentages based on a value of "one" for each child, even those with multiple exceptionalities.

A total of 636 campesino children between the ages of 2 days and 21 years and 9 months were observed. The data presented in this table came from patient history, open-ended comments from caregivers, and caregiver interviews.

Works Cited

AIR, (2005). *Effects of Outdoor Education Programs for Children in California*. Sacraments, AC: The California Department of Education.

Acoach, C., & Webb, L. (2004). The influence of language brokering on Hispanic teenagers acculturation, academic performance, and nonverbal decoding skills: A preliminary study. *Howard Journal of Communication, 15(1), 1–19*.

Amrein, A. & Pena, R. (2000). Asymmetry in dual language practice. *Education Policy Analysis Archives, 8(2000)*.

Arenas, A. (2008). Connecting hand, mind, and community: Vocational education for social and environmental renewal. *Teacher's College Record, 110(2)*, 377–404.

Artiles, A. J., & Trent, S. C. (1994). Overrepresentation of minority students in special education: A continuing debate. *Journal of Special Education, 27(4)*, 410–437.

Associated Press. (2010). 7 women in miscarriage cases freed in Mexico. Retrieved September 18, 2010, from http://www.mysanantonio.com.

Baez, B. (2002). Learning to forget: Reflections on identity and language. *Journal of Latinos and Education, 1(2)*, 123–132.

Baker, B.D., & Welner, K.G. (2011). School finance and courts: Does reform matter, and how can we tell? *Teachers College Record, 113(11)*, p. 1. Retrieved from http://www.tcrecord.org.

Banji, M. R., & Greenwald, A. G. (1994). *Implicit stereotyping and prejudice: The psychology of prejudice*. Paper presented at the Ontario Symposium, Hillsdale, NJ.

Bardeen, T. (2007). Be a hero for the planet. *Instructor, 6*, 26–31.

Behar, R. (2003). Ethnography and the book that was lost. *Ethnography, 4(1), 15–39*.

Bell, M.A., & Fox, N.A. (1998). *Crawling experience is related to changes in cortical organization during infancy: Evidence from EEG coherence*. USA: John Wiley & Sons. Retrieved September 17, 2010, from http:onlinelibrary.wiley.com.

Bernhart, M. (2008). Opportunities on the other side of the language barrier, *Employee Benefit Advisor: EBA Benefit News*.

Biesanz, O., Madigan Ruiz, O., Sanders, A., & Sommers, M. *(1994). Rich land, poor people*.

Bomer, R., Dworin, J. E., May, L., & Semingson, P. (2009, June 3). What's wrong with a deficit perspective? *Teachers College Record*. Retrieved September 21, 2010, from http://www.tcrecord.org.

Bomer, R., Dworin, J.E., May, L., & Semingson, P., (2008). Miseducating Teachers about the Poor: A Critical Analysis of Ruby Payne's Claims about Poverty. *Teachers College Record, 110*(12), 2497–2531.

Bonetati, D. (1994). The Effect of Teachers' Expectations on Mexican-American Students. ERIC, Internet retrieved www.eric.ed.gov.

Borrie, W. T., & Roggenbuck, J. W. (2001). The dynamic, emergent, and multi-phasic nature of on-site wilderness experiences. *Journal of Leisure Research, 33*, 202–229.

Broda, H.W. (2007). Schoolyard-enhanced learning: Using the outdoors as an instructional tool, K–8. Portland, Maine: Stenhouse Publishers.

Buriel, R., Perez, W., DeMent, T., Chavez. D., & Moran, V. (1998). The relationship of language brokering to academic performance, biculturalism, and self-efficacy among Latino adolescents. *Hispanic Journal of Behavioral Science, 20*(3), 283–96.

Cardona, P. G., Nicholson, B. C., & Fox, R. A. (2000). Parenting among Hispanic and Anglo-American mothers with young children. *The Journal of Social Psychology, 40*(3), 357–365.

Carnegie Mellon University (1998, September 1). Carnegie Mellon study reveals negative potential of heavy Internet use on emotional well-being. *Science Daily*. Retrieved March 1, 2011, from http://www.sciencedaily.com /releases/1998/09/980901024936.htm

Casper, L. M. (1996). *Who's Minding our Preschoolers?* : ERIC.

Cattey, M. (1980). Cultural differences in processing information. *Journal of American Indian Education, 20*(1).

Chapman, M., & Perreira, K. (2005). The Well-being of immigrant youth: A Model to inform practice. *Families in Society, 86*(1), 104–111.

Chawla, L. (2006). Learning to love the natural world enough to protect it. *Barn nr. (Norsk senter for barneforsking (NOSEB)), 2*(57–78).

Childstats. (2009). *America's children: Key national indicators of well-being.* (13045). Washington, D.C.: Office of Management and Budget, Retrieved from http://www.childstats.gov/americaschildren/.

Chu, L. (2004, November 9). Is Mexican Coke the real thing? *San Diego Union-Tribune*. Retrieved September 17, 2010 from http://www.signonsandiego.com.

Cleaver, S. (2007, November/December 2007). How green classrooms are going green. *Instructor,* 20–28.

Clements, R. (2004). An investigation of the status of outdoor play. *Contemporary Issues in Early Childhood 5*(1), 68–80.

Coffey, A. (1999). *The ethnographic self*. London: Sage Publications.

Cornell, J.B. (1998). *Sharing nature with children* (20th anniversary edition). California: Dawn Publications.

Crosnoe, R. (2005). Double disadvantage or signs of resilience? the elementary school contexts of infants, children and youth from Mexican immigrant families. *American Educational Research Journal, 42*(2), 269–303.

Dasha, L. N., & Ziviani, J. M. (2007). Use of time in childhood and adolescence: A literature review on the nature of activity participation and depression. *Australian Occupational Therapy Journal, 54*(1), 4–10.

Delgado-Gaitan, C. (1990). *Literacy for empowerment: The role of parents in children's education.* New York: Falmar.

Delgado-Gaitan, C. (1993). Parenting in two generations of modern Mexican-American families. *International Journals of Behavioral Development, 16*(3), 403–427.

Doidge, N. (2007). *The brain that changes itself.* USA: Penguin Books.

Dorner, L. M., Orellana, M. F., & Li-Grinning, C. (2007). "I helped my mom," and it helped me: Translating the skills of language brokers into improved standardized test scores. *American Journal of Education, 113*(3), 451–478.

Eckerd Youth Alternatives, (n.d.) A national leader in helping youth succeed. Retrieved October 19, 2010, from http://www.eckerd.org.

Ewert, A., Place, G., & Sibthorp, J. (2005). Early-life outdoor experiences and an individual's environmental attitudes. *Leisure Sciences, 27*(3), 225–239.

Fehrenbach, T.R. (1995). *Fire & Blood—A History of Mexico,* pgs 238–239. USA, Da Capo Press.

Fletcher, T. V., & Artiles, A. J. (2005). *"Inclusive education and equity in Latin America": Evaluating old and new international perspectives.* London: Routledge.

Fletcher, T. V., Bos, C. S., & Johnson, L. M. (1999). Accommodating English language learners with language and learning disabilities in bilingual education classrooms. *Learning Disabilities Research and Practice, 14*(2), 80–91.

Fletcher, T. V., Klingler, C., Lopez-Mariscal, I., & Dejud, C. (2003). The changing paradigm of special education in Mexico: Voices from the field. *Bilingual Research Journal, 27*(3), 409–430.

Fletcher, T. V., & Martinez de Ramos, M. (2005). *From Mexico to Chile: Assessing the advancement of inclusive education practices in two Latin American republics.* Paper presented at the International Special Education Conference. Retrieved from http:www.isec2005.org.uk.

Fletcher, T. V. (1999). *Helping individuals with disabilities and their families: Mexican and U.S. perspectives.* Tempe, AZ: Bilingual Review.

Flores, L. Y., Navarro, R. L., & DeWitz, S. J. (2008). Mexican-American high school students' postsecondary educational goals: Applying social cognitive career theory. *Journal of Career Assessment, 16*(4), 489–501.

Foster-Riley, M. H., J. C. (1999, 1998, October 24–29). *Wilderness vision quest clients: Motivations and reported benefits from an urban-based program 1988 to 1997.* Paper presented at the Personal, Societal, and Ecological Values of Wilderness: Sixth World Wilderness Congress Proceedings on Research, Management, and Allocation, Bangalore, India, Vol. II., Proc. RMRS-P-000.

Forgas, J. P. (2000). *Handbook of effect and social cognition* (Chapter 14, pp. 410–428). Mahwah, New Jersey: Lawrence Erlbaum and Associates.

Forlin, C., Cedillo, I. G., Romero-Contreras, S., Fletcher, T. V., & Rodriguez, H. (2009). *Inclusion in Mexico: Ensuring supportive attitudes by newly graduated teachers.* Mexico: San Luis Poitisi University Press.

Frazier, L. J. (1993). *Genre, methodology and feminist practice: Gladys Reichard's ethnographic voice* ("Critique of Anthropology," p. 394). London: Sage Publications.

Freire, P. (1970/1993). *Pedagogy of the oppressed* (20th-Anniversary ed.). New York: Continuum.

Fried, R. (1995). *The passionate teacher.* USA: Beacon Press.

Frumkin, H. S. (2001). Beyond toxicity: Human health and the natural environment. *American Journal of Preventive Medicine, 20*(3), 234–242.

Fry, R. (2009). *The changing pathways of Hispanic youth into adulthood.* Retrieved December 1, 2009, from http://pewhispanic.org.

Gallagher, M. R., Gill, S., & Reifsnider, E. (2008). Child health promotion and protection among Mexican mothers. *Western Journal of Nursing Research, 30*(5), 588–605.

Gardner, H. (2000). *Intelligence reframed: Multiple intelligences for the 21st century* (4th ed.). New York: Basic Books.

Garger, S., & Guild, P. (1984). Learning styles: The critical differences. *Curriculum Review, 23*(1), 9–12.

Giangreco, M., Edelman, S. W., Luiselli, T. E., & Macfarland, S. (1997). Helping or hovering? Effects of instructional assistant proximity on students with disabilities. *Exceptional Children, 64*(1), 7–18.

Gober, P. (2007). Pasteur's quadrant and the education of an applied geographer. *Research in Geographic Education, 9*(1), 36–43.

Golden, J. Meckel, R. A., & Prescott, H. (2004). *Children and youth: History and culture.* USA: Greenwood Press.

Goleman, D. (2007). *Social intelligence: The new science of human relationships.* Bantam Books.

González, N. (2001). *I am my language: Discourses of women & children in the borderlands.* Tucson: University of Arizona Press.

González, N., Moll, L. C., & Amanti, C. (2005). *Funds of knowledge: Theorizing practices in households, communities and classrooms.* New York: Lawrence Erlbaum Associates.

Gorski, P. (2006a, February 9). The classist underpinnings of Ruby Payne's framework. *Teachers College Record.* Retrieved September 21, 2010, from http://www.tcrecord.org.

Gorski, P. (2006b, July 19). Responding to Payne's response. *Teachers College Record.* Retrieved September 23, 2010, from http://www.tcrecord.org

Grant, T. (1998, fall). Why environmental education is GOOD education. *Global Environmental, & Outdoor Education Council, 56.*

Greenwald, A. G., & Banji, M. R. (1995). Implicit social cognition: Attitudes, self-esteem, and stereotypes. *Psychological Review, 102*(1), 4–27.

Gulwadi, G. B. (2006, July 1). Seeking restorative experiences: Elementary school teachers. *Environment and Behavior,* 38(4), 503–520.

Hale, J. B. (2008). Response to intervention: Guidelines for parents and practitioners. Retrieved February 15, 2010, from http://www.wrightslaw.com.

Hargreaves, A. (1998). The emotional practice of teaching. *Teaching and Teacher Education,* 14 (8), 835–854.

Harker, R., Mahar, C., & Wilkes, C. (Eds.). (1990). "Education and Cultural Capital" in *An introduction to the work of Pierre Bourdieu: The practice of theory.* Macmillan Press: London.

Hartig, T. (1991). Restorative effects of natural environment experiences. *Environment and Behavior,* 23(1), 3–26.

Harvard University. (2002). *The Harvard civil rights project at Harvard University.* Harvard Graduate School. Cambridge: Harvard Press.

Hayes, K. (1992). Attitudes toward education: Voluntary and involuntary immigrants from the same families. *Anthropology & Education Quarterly,* 23(3), 250–267.

Headland, T., Pike. K., & Harris, M. (Eds.). (1990). *Emics and etics: The insider/outsider debate.* USA: Sage Publications.

Heft, H., & Kytta, M. (2006, December). A psychologically meaningful description of environments requires a relational approach. *Housing, Theory, and Society,* 23(4), 210–213.

Hofferth, S. L., & Sandberg, J. F. (2000). How American children spend their time: Changes in America's children's time, 1981–1997. *Journal of Marriage and Family,* 63(2), 295.

Holleran, L. K. (2003). Mexican-American youth of the Southwest borderlands: Perceptions of ethnicity, acculturation, and race. *Hispanic Journal of Behavioral Sciences,* 25(3), 352–369.

hooks, B. (1994). *Teaching to transgress: Education as the practice of freedom.* New York: Routledge.

Hoover, D. (2008). Infants, children and youth + nature. *Parks & Recreation,* 43(3), 68–69.

Horne, M., (1985). *Attitudes toward handicapped students: Professional, peer, and parent reactions.* Mahwah: Erlbaum.

Human Rights Watch, (n.d.). Biography: Verónica Cruz Sanchez.

Retrieved July 4, 2009, from http://clacs.aas.duke.edu/program//VeronicaCruzbio.pdf.

Jiménez, R. T. (2003). "The interaction of language, literacy, and identity in the lives of Latina/o students." In R. L. McCormack & J. Parratore (Eds.). *After early intervention, then what? Teaching struggling readers in grade three and beyond* (pp. 25–38). Newark: International Reading Association.

Jimenez, R. T. (2000). Literacy and the identity development of Latina/o students. *American Educational Research Journal,* 37(4), 971–1000.

Jimenez, R., Moll, L., Rodriguez-Brown, F., & Barrera, R. (1999). Latina and Latino researchers interact on issues related to literacy learning. *Reading Research Quarterly,* 34(2), 217–231.

Kagitcibasi, C. (1982). The Changing value of infants, children and youth in Turkey. *East-West Population Institute Publication,* No. 60-E.

Kagitcibasi, C. (1990). *Family and socialization in cross-cultural perspective: A model of change.* Paper presented at the Cross-Cultural Perspectives: Nebraska Symposium on Motivation, 1989, Lincoln, NE.

Kagitcibasi, C. (1996). *Family and development across cultures: A view from the other side.* Mahwah: Lawrence Erlbaum Associates.

Kahn, P. H., & Kellert, S. R. (Eds.). (2002). *Children and nature: Psychological, socio-cultural, and evolutionary investigations.* Cambridge: The Massachusetts Institute of Technology Press.

Kalman, J. (2000). Learning to write in the street. *Qualitative Studies in Education, 13*(3), 187–203.

Kaplan, S. (1995). The restorative benefits of nature: Toward an integrative framework. *Journal of Environmental Psychology,* 15, 169–182

Karsten, L. (2005). It all used to be better? Different generations and change in urban infants, children and youth's daily use of space. *Infants, Children and Youth's Geographies, 3*(2), 275–290.

Kellert, S. R., & Wilson, E. O. (1993). *The biophilia hypothesis.* Washington, D.C.: Island Press.

Kelly, Y., Panico, L., Bartley, M., Marmot, M., Nazroo, J., & Sacker, A. (2009). Why does birth weight vary among ethnic groups in the UK? Findings from the Millennium Cohort Study. *Journal of Public Health-Oxford University Press, 31*(1).

Kelly, Y., Sacker, A., Schoon, I., & Nazroo, J. (2006). Ethnic differences in achievement of developmental milestones by 9 months of age: The Millennium Cohort Study. *Developmental Medicine & Child Neurology.* 48(10), 825–830.

Kelly, Y. Watt, R., & Nazroo, J. (2006b). Racial/ethnic differences in breastfeeding initiation and continuation in the United Kingdom and comparison with findings in the United States. *Pediatrics,* 118(5), e1428–e1435.

Kemper, R. V., & Royce, A. P. E. (Eds.). (2002). *Chronicling cultures: Long-term field research in anthropology.* Walnut Creek: Altamira Press.

Knight, G. (1994). Socialization and family correlates of mental health outcomes among Hispanic and Anglo-American children: Considerations of cross-ethnic scalar equivalence. *Child Development,* 65(1).

Koplan, J., Liverman, C., Kraak, V., & Wisham, S. E. (Eds.). (2007). *Progress in childhood obesity: How do we measure up?* Washington, D.C.: Institute of Medicine of the National Academies.

Kottak, C. P. (2008). *Cultural anthropology* (12th ed.). New York: The McGraw-Hill Companies.

Kozulin, A. (1998). Mediated Learning Experience and cultural diversity. ICELP conference paper, Jerusalem, Israel. Retrieved October 20, 2008, from www.umanitoba.ca.

Lara-Alecio, R., Irby, B., & Ebener, R. (1997). Developing academically supportive behaviors among Hispanic parents: What elementary teachers and administrators can do. *Preventing School Failure, 42*(1).

Lareau, A. (1987, April). Social class differences in family-school relationships: The importance of cultural capital. *Sociology of Education, 60, 73–85.*

Larson, B. A. (2007). Adventure camp programs, self-concept, and their effects on behavior problem adolescents. *Journal of Experimental Education, 29*(3), 313–330.

Lawson, D. W. (2004). *The healing qualities of nature, a newsletter for the survivors of suicide.* Tallahassee: Alachua County Government.

Lichter, D., & Jensen, L. (2002). "Rural dimensions of welfare reform" (pp. 77–110). In *Rural America in Transition: Poverty and Welfare and the Turn of the Twenty-first Century.* Kalamazoo: W.E. UpJohn Institute for Employment Research.

Lohr, V. P.-M., C. H. (2006, September 1). Responses to scenes with spreading, rounded, and conical tree forms. *Environment and Behavior, 38*(5), 667–688.

Lopez, M. H. (2009). *Latinos and Education: Explaining the Attainment Gap.* Retrieved from http://pewhispanic.org.

Love, J. A. and Buriel, R. (2007). Language brokering, autonomy, parent-child bonding, biculturalism, and depression: A Study of Mexican-American adolescents from immigrant families. *Hispanic Journal of Behavioural Sciences, 29*(4), 472–491.

Lovu, R. (2005). *Last child in the woods.* Chapel Hill: Algonquin Books.

Maccarelli, S. (2006). *Vygotsky's theory of cognitive development, the socio-cultural perspective.* Williamstown, NJ. Retrieved February 1, 2010, from http://www.associated-content.com.

Mackenzie, J. Z. (2007). *Strong women: High standards, conversations with rural border resident Mexican women.* University of Arizona College of Education, Tucson, AZ.

Mackenzie, J. Z. (2008). *An ethnographic pilot study: Understanding how Mexican infants, children, and youth with disabilities learn outdoors.* University of Arizona College of Education, Tucson, AZ.

Mackenzie, J. Z. (2009). Personal Journal. Cajones, Guanajuato, Mexico.

Mackenzie, J. Z. (2010). *Sociocultural influences: Evaluations of indigenous children for special needs in rural Central Mexico.* Doctoral dissertation, University of Arizona, Tucson, AZ.

Maller, C., Townsend, M., Pryor, A., Brown, P., & St Leger, L. (2006, March 1). Healthy nature, healthy people: 'Contact with nature' as an upstream health promotion intervention for populations. *Health Promot. Int., 21*(1), 45–54.

Mary, N. L. (1990). Reactions of Black, Hispanic, and White Mothers to having a child with handicaps. *Mental Retardation, 28*(1), 1–5.

Mather, N., & Goldstein, S. (2001). *Learning disabilities and challenging behaviors: A Guide to intervention and classroom management.* Baltimore: Brookes Publishing.

Maxwell, J. A. (1996). *Qualitative research design: An interactive approach* (Vol. 41). Thousand Oaks: Sage Publications.

McCafferty, D. (2007, November 16–18). Raising healthier kids: Learn about exciting new theory experts believe may solve many of your child's ills. "USA Weekend" in *Arizona Daily Star*, pp. 8–10.

McHatton, P. A. (2007). *Creating welcoming schools: A practical guide to home-school partnerships with diverse families*. New York: Teachers College Press.

McMunn, A., Kelly, Y., Bartley, M. (2008). Lone parenthood, material deprivation and child emotional development in the Millennium Cohort Study. *Meeting of the Society for Social Medicine*, Southampton, England.

Medina, C. (2004). The construction of drama worlds as literary interpretation of Latina feminist Literature. *Research in Drama Education*, 9(2), 145–160.

Meyer, M. C., & Beezley, W. H. (2000). *The Oxford History of Mexico*, New York: The Oxford University Press.

Middlemiss, W., & McGuigan, W. (2005). Ethnicity and adolescent mothers' benefit from participation in home-visitation services. *Family Relations*, 54(1), 212–224.

Moll, L. C., Amanti, C., Neff, D., & Gonzalez, N. (1992). Funds of knowledge for teaching: Using a qualitative approach to connect homes and classrooms. *Theory into Practice*, 31(2), 132–141.

Monzó, L. D., & Rueda, R. S. (2001). Professional roles, caring, and scaffolds: Latino teachers' and paraeducators' interactions with Latino students. *American Journal of Education*, 109(4), 438–471.

Moore, R.C., & Wong, H. H. (1997). *Natural learning: The life history of an environmental schoolyard*. Berkley: MIG Communications.

Morales, A., & Hanson, W. Language brokering: An integrative review of the literature. *Hispanic Journal of Behavioral Science*. 27(4), 471–503.

Morse, W. (2006). *Americans in waiting: The lost story of immigration and citizenship in the United States*. New York: The Oxford University Press.

Nash, R. F. (2001). *Wilderness & the American mind* (4th ed.). New Haven: Yale University Press.

NationMaster. (2010). Health Statistics: Obesity by country. Retrieved April 11, 2010, from www.nationmaster.com.

Nazario, S. (2007). *Enrique's journey*. New York: Random House Trade Paperbacks.

NCES, N. C. f. E. S. (2001). *Dropout rates in the United States: 2000*. Washington, D.C.: U.S. Department of Education.

NCLB. (2002, January 8). Public Law 107–110. Retrieved June 3, 2010, from www2. ed.gov.

Ng, J. C., & Rury, J. L. (2006a, July 18). Poverty and education: A critical analysis of the Ruby Payne phenomenon. *Teachers College Record*. Retrieved September 21, 2010, from http://www.tcrecord.org.

Ng, J. C., & Rury, J. L. (2006b, July 20). Responding to Payne's Response. *Teachers College Record*. Retrieved September 23, 2010, from http://www.tcrecord.org.

NLCC Educational Media. (1996). *Chicano! History of the Mexican-American civil rights movement.* Video, University of Kansas. Retrieved September 20, 2010, from www.albany.edu.

Noddings, N. (1984). *Caring: A feminine approach to ethics & moral education.* Berkley, Los Angeles, London: University of California Press.

Noddings, N. (1992). *The challenge to care in schools: An alternative approach to education.* New York: Teacher's College Press.

Noddings, N. (2003). *Happiness and education.* Cambridge: Cambridge University Press.

Norton, N. E. J., & Bentley, C. (2006). Making the connection: Extending culturally responsible teaching through home(land) pedagogies. *Feminist Teacher: A Journal of the Practices, Theories, and Scholarship of Feminist Teaching,* 17(1), 52–70.

Ogbu, J. U. (1990). Minority status and literacy in comparative perspective. *Daedalus,* 119(2), 141–168.

Ogbu, J. U. (1992a). Adaption to minority status and impact on school success. *Theory into Practice,* 31(4), 288–295.

Ogbu, J. U. (1992b). Understanding cultural diversity and learning. *Educational Researcher,* 21(8), 5–14+24.

Ordonez, F. (2009, July 20). Coke Friends, Soda cultists seek out "hecho en Mexico." *San Diego Union-Tribune.* Retrieved September 17, 2010, from http://www.signon-sandiego.com.

Orellana, M. (2003). Responsibilities of children in Latino immigrant homes. *New Directions for Youth Development: Understanding the Social Worlds of Immigrant Youth, Winter,* (100), 25–39.

Orr, D. (1992). *Ecology literacy: Education and the transition to a postmodern world:* Albany: State University of New York Press

Outward Bound. (n.d.). *About Outward Bound.* Retrieved October 19, 2910, from http://www.outwardbound.org.

Payne, R. K. (2003). *A framework for understanding poverty.* Aha! Process Inc., Highlands, Texas.

Pergams, O., & Zaradic, P. (2006). Is love of nature in the US becoming love of electronic media? 16-year downtrend in national park visits explained by watching movies, playing video games, internet use, and oil prices. *Journal of Environmental Management,* 80(4), 387–393.

PEW. (2009). Graphic: Latino youths optimistic but beset by problems. Retrieved December 17, 2009, from http://pewhispanic.org.

Poblano, A., Borja, S., Elias, Y., Garcia-Pedroza, F., & Arias, M. (2002). Characteristics of specific reading disability in infants, children and youth from a neuropsychological clinic in Mexico City. *Salud Publica de Mexico,* 44(4), 323–327.

Poblano, A., Marquez, A., & Hernandez, G. (2006). Apnea in infants. *Indian Journal of Pediatrics,* 73(12), 1085–1088.

Ponzanesi, S. (2007). Feminist theory and multiculturalism. *Feminist Theory,* 8(1), 91–103.

Portes, P. R. (1999). Social and psychological factors in the academic achievement of children of immigrants: A cultural history puzzle. *American Educational Research Journal,* 36(3), 489–507.

Post, D. (2001). Region, poverty, sibship, and gender inequality in Mexican education : Will targeted welfare policy make a difference for girls? *Gender & Society,* 15(3), 468–489.

Prins, E., & Schafft, K. A. (2009). Individual and structural attributions for poverty and persistence in family literacy programs: The resurgence of the culture of poverty. *Teachers College Record,* 111(9), 2280–2310. Retrieved September 23, 2010, from http://www.tcrecord.org.

Puhl, R., & Latner, J. (2007). Stigma, obesity, and the health of the nation's infants, children and youth. *Psychological Bulletin,* 133(4), 557.

Ream. (2005). Toward understanding how social capital medicates the impact of mobility on Mexican-American achievement. *Social Forces,* 82(1), 201–224.

Ruiz, R. E. (1992). *Triumphs and tragedy: A history of the Mexican people.* New York: W.W. Norton & Co.

Rogoff, B. (2003). *The cultural nature of human development.* Oxford: The Oxford University Press.

Rogoff, B., Mistry, J., Goncu, A., & Mosier, C. (1993). Guided participation in cultural activity by toddlers and caregivers. *Monographs of the Society for Research in Child Development,* 58(8).

Romero-Contreras, S. (2006). *Measuring language- and literacy-related practices in low-SES Costa Rican families: Research instruments and results.* Doctoral dissertation, Harvard University, Cambridge, MA.

Roszkowski, W. (2003). *Najnowsza historia Polski 1914–1945* (pp. 236–240, 678–680, 700–701). Warszawa: wiat Ksi   ki.

Sanchez, J. (2007). *A Sociotechnical Analysis of Second Life in an Undergraduate English course.* Proceedings of World Conference on Educational Multimedia, Hypermedia and Telecommunications 2007. Chesapeake, VA: AACE.

San Diego Union-Tribune. (2008, March 24). *Mexico is second-fattest nation after U.S.: Where hunger once prevailed, diabetes is leading cause of death.* . Retrieved September 17, 2010, from http://www.signonsandiego.com.

Santamaria, C. C. (2009). *Mexican-origin parents with special needs children: Using a critical compassion intellectualism model to support and foster their participation in U.S. Schools through a Participatory Action Research Project.* Doctoral dissertation, University of Arizona, Tucson, AZ.

Saracho, O. N., & Martinez-Hancock, F. (2004). The culture of Mexican Americans: Its importance for early educators. *Journal of Hispanic Higher Education,* 3(3), 254–269.

Saracho, O. N. (2007). Hispanic families as facilitators of their children's literacy development . *Journal of Hispanic Higher Education,* 6(2), 103–117.

Schmal, J. P. (n.d.). Los Antepasados Indigenas de los Guanajuatenses: A look into Guanajuato's past. *History of Mexico.* Huston: Huston Institute for Culture.

Sheard, M., & Golby, J. (2006). The efficacy of an outdoor adventure education curriculum on selected aspects of positive psychological development. *Journal of Experimental Education, 29*(2), 187–209.

Shin, H. B., & Bruno, R. (2003). *Language use and English-speaking ability: 2000.* Washington, D.C.: U.S. Census Bureau.

Sizer, T. F., & Sizer, N.F. (1999). *The students are watching: Schools and the moral contract.* Boston: Beacon Press.

Spence, S.H., Najman, J.M., Bor, W., O'Callaghan, J., & Williams, G. (2002). Maternal anxiety and depression, poverty and marital relationship factors during early childhood as predictors of anxiety and depressive symptoms in adolescence. *Journal of Child Psychology and Psychiatry, 43*(4), May 2002, 457–469.

Strauss, A., & Corbin, J. (2007). *Basics of qualitative research: Techniques and procedures for developing grounded theory.* Los Angeles: Sage Publications.

Subedi, B. S. (2006). Cultural factors and beliefs influencing transfer of training. *International Journal of Training and Development, 10*(2), 88–97.

Tai, L., Haque, M., McLellan, G., & Knight (2006). *Designing outdoor environments for children: Landscaping school yards, gardens and playgrounds.* USA: McGraw-Hill Companies.

Tandy, C. A. (1999). Diminishing play space: A study of intergenerational change in infants, children and youth's use of their neighborhoods. *Australian Geographical Studies, 37*(2), 154–164.

Tapia, J. (1998). The schooling of Puerto Ricans: Philadelphia's most impoverished community. *Anthropology & Education Quarterly, 29*(3), 297–323.

Taylor, A. F., Kuo, F. E., & Sullivan, W. C. (2001). Coping with ADD: The surprising connection to green play settings. *Environment and Behavior, 33*(1), 54–77.

Taylor, T., Serrano, E., Anderson, J., & Kendall, P. (2000). Knowledge, skills, and behavior improvements on peer educators and low-income Hispanic participants after a stage of change-based bilingual nutrition program. *Journal of Community Health, 25*(3), 241–262.

Teachman, J., & Paasch, K. (1994). Financial impact of divorce on children and their families. *The Future of Children, 4*(1), 63–83.

Todd, H. (2005). *Cognition, development, and learning in low socioeconomic families.* Paper presented at the Verano en Mexico, Guanajuato, Mexico.

Tull, M. (2009). The fight or flight response: Our body's response to stress. Retrieved September 15, 2010, from http://ptsd.about.com.

Turner, H. A. (2007). The significance of employment for chronic stress and psychological distress among rural single mothers. *American Journal of Community Psychology, 40,* 181–193.

Ulrich, R., Simons, R. F., & Miles M. A. (2003, spring). Effects of environmental simulations and television on blood donor stress. *Journal of Architectural and Planning Research, 20*(1), 38–47.

Urba, T. C., & Maehr, M. L. (1995). Beyond a two-goal theory of motivation and achievement: A case for social goals. *Review of Educational Research*, 65(3), 213–243.

Urrea, L., & Lueders-Booth, J. (1996). *By the lake of sleeping children*. Garden City: Anchor Books.

UNESCO. (2010). *Mexican education statistics*. UNESCO Institute for Statistics. Retrieved September 20, 2010, from NationMaster.com.

UNICEF. (2010). *Percent of population using improved sanitation facilities; rural*. Mexico Health, UNICEF. Retrieved September 20, 2010, from www.unicef.org.

Valdés, G. (1996). *Con Respecto*. New York: Teachers College Press.

Valentine, G., & McKendrick, J. (1997). Children's outdoor play: Exploring parental concerns about children's safety and the changing nature of childhood. *Geoform*, 28(2), 219–235.

Valencia, R. R. (2009, June 25). A response to Ruby Payne's claim that the deficit thinking model has no scholarly utility. *Teachers College Record*. Retrieved September 21, 2010, from http://www.tcrecord.org.

Valencia, R. E (2002). *Chicano school failure and success: Past, present and future,* 2nd Edition: Routledge/Falmer.

Valencia, R. R. & Black, M.S. (2002). "'Mexican Americans Don't Value Education!' On the Basis of the Myth, Mythmaking, and Debunking." *Journal of Latinos and Education* 1, no. 2 (2002): 81–103.

Valenzuela, A. (1999). *Subtractive schooling: U.S.-Mexican youth and the politics of caring*. Albany: State University of New York Pres.

Van Matre, S. (1990). *Earth education, a new beginning*. Greenville, West Virginia: The Institute for Earth Education.

Vasquez, O., Pease-Alvarez, L., & Shannon, S. (1994). *Pushing boundaries, language and culture in a Mexicano community*. New York: University of Cambridge.

Velez-Ibanez, C. G., & Greenburg, J. B. (1992). Formation and transformation of funds of knowledge among U.S. Mexican households. *Anthropology & Education Quarterly*, 23(4), 313–335.

Villenas, S. (2001). Latina mothers and small-town racisms: Creating narratives of dignity and moral education in North Carolina. *Anthropology & Education Quarterly*, 32(1), 3–28.

Vygotsky, L. S. (n.d.). *Cognitive development: Vygotsky's sociocultural theory*. Retrieved December 13, 2009 from http://social.jrank.org.

Walker, D., Greenwood, C., Hart, B., & Carta, J. (1994). Prediction of school outcomes based on early language production and socioeconomic factors. *Child Development*, 65(2), 606–621.

Ward, J., Ghahremani, S., & Louv, R. (2008). *I love dirt! 52 activities to help you and your kids discover the wonders of nature*. USA: Trumpeter Press.

Weisskirch, R. S., & Alva, S. A. (2002). Language brokering and the acculturation of Latino children. *Hispanic Journal of Behavioral Sciences*, 24(3), 369.

Weisskirch, R. S. (2006). Emotional aspects of language brokering among

Mexican-American adults. *Journal of Multilingual and Multicultural Development, 27*(4), 332–412.

Wells, N. M. (2000). At home with nature: Effects of "greenness" on infants, children and youth's cognitive functioning. *Environment and Behavior, 32*(6).

Whitner, L. A., Weber, B. A., & Duncan, G. J. (2002). As the dust settles: Welfare reform and rural America. *Rural Dimensions of Welfare Reform.*

Wiltz, T. (2010, June). The most dangerous women in the world: Veronica Cruz Sanchez, *National Geographic*, U.S. edition.

Wissman, K. (2006). "Writing will keep you free?": Allusions to and recreations of the fairy tale heroine in *The House on Mango Street. Children's Literature in Education, 38,* 17–34.

Worby, P. A., & Organista, K. C. (2007). Alcohol use and problem drinking among male Mexican and Central American immigrant laborers: A review of the literature. *Hispanic Journal of Behavioral Sciences, 29*(4), 413–455.

WHO. (1996). Culturally appropriate measures for monitoring child development at family and community level: A WHO collaborative study. *Bulletin of the World Health Organization, 74*(8), 283–288.

Zentella, A. (1997). *Growing up bilingual.* Cambridge: Blackwell Publishers.

Glossary

Campesino a country person, country dweller, peasant, rural farmer or rancher; frequently the resident is also of indigenous heritage. A Latin American Indian farmer; *campo* is Spanish for *field or country* (Merriam-Webster). All definitions applied to the word *campesino* were used within this research report with the highest degree of respect.

Campo A *campo* is a field, a non-incorporated rural village, pueblo, community, rural residential grouping of people and animals.

Indigenous A person of Native Indian heritage is referred to as of an indigenous culture. Research sites included the following indigenous groups: Guamares, Chichimecas, Guachichile, Otomíes, Purépecha/ Tarascan: Celaya, Acámbaro, and Yurirapúndaro. Only the Chichimeca-Jonaz language is still used (Schmal, n.d.).

Developmental Delay A diagnosis of developmental delay typically occurs when a child has failed to meet a predictable milestone or more than one milestone relative to their cultural standards. Identifying if this failure might have a long-term affect on a child's speech and language, fine and gross motor skills, and/or personal and social skills an intervention is normally advised (ERIC, 1999).

The Relationship Factor This phrase is used in scholarly papers to explain personal interactions between people (Spence et al., 2002). This book uses this phrase to explain the primary force observed to be of the utmost importance in Mexican communities: caring for and personal histories with others, including family, extended family, and friends. In Mexico, relationships are held of higher importance than money, employment, status, power, position, or any other distraction requiring time, energy, or other resources (Ogbu, 1992b; Rogoff, 2003; Valdés, 1996; Valenzuela, 1999). The Mexican culture deifies ancestors (Mackenzie, 2008); all domestic duties, income-producing responsibilities, and other roles must be referred to with great caution and extreme cultural sensitivity (Saracho & Martinez-Hancock, 2004), because saving face and

247

preserving pride are of paramount value (Mackenzie, 2009; Valdés, 1996). Passing a person on the street or in a public bathroom requires asking permission of the other person: *"Con permiso"* (with your permission). Entering a doctor's office or another public space requires everyone in the room to receive a general greeting and eye contact: *"Buenos dias"/"Buenos tardes"/"Buenos noches"* (good day/good afternoon/good night) (Valdés, 1996). People of all ages will respond automatically when greeted in this manner using the same greeting. A greeting is initiated anytime a person enters a room or comes within a distance of 20 feet, even outdoors in undefined spaces. There is often a shortage of economic resources in Mexico, but there is no shortage of respect and an acknowledgement of respect for interdependence and its sociocultural influence (Ogbu, 1992b; Rogoff, 2003; Valdés, 1996; Valenzuela, 1999; Velez-Ibanez, 1992; Zembylas, 2002).

Other Books by the Author

Sociocultural Influences: Evaluations of Indigenous Children for Special Needs in Rural Central Mexico

Victoria's Crown

Thank You—Gracias

Net proceeds from the sale of this book help to support our non-profit programs.

This book earns money support teaching English, providing equine therapy and water therapy to disabled people, making swimming opportunities available for rural children, to build libraries in rural Mexico and to preserve their lifestyle through written records while increasing their opportunities to grow mentally and economically. These Native Indians have always been oppressed. Statistics tell us that they are the most likely to run to the north border. With access to knowledge they can remain in Mexico, remain with their families, and keep their indigenous roots. Thank you for helping to reduce emigration.

Afterword

Writing this book was a physical representation of my faith, a religious outgrowth in the form of an academic presentation that chronicles how my sacred vow of living my lifetime in Divine service to God by physical service others developed. Elder ministers within my faith normally take a vow of accomplishing a "Great Work." This book is a physical record of my "Great Work." Additionally, in 1996, I took a legal *vow of poverty*, to not personally own anything from my past, present or future. That vow, by design, spiritually guided me to the task of living this lifestyle of service because of my religion, but not to promote my faith.

Within my faith, the promotion of my faith, any form of proselytizing, is strictly forbidden. There is no collection of tithes, offerings, or other cash transactions. Assuredly, public service as an expression of faith is highly encouraged. Fundraising is only done to pay for the overhead expenses involved in offering services to others. Therefore, I carefully and thoroughly recorded what I learned during my residence in or visits to Mexico because I must make a physical record of my "Great Work" to show my mentor, my peer elders and to encourage salutations necessary to continue this service to others and so that the work is put into service to those I serve. I choose to focus on helping those of rural, predominately indigenous, Mexican heritage because they lack educational opportunities both in Mexico and in the USA. Solely due to my religious beliefs, I as a public school teacher in the USA was no longer able to enforce what I felt were emotionally abusive rules and culturally inappropriate demands on Mexican children often guided by directives that were not evidence-based and had no basis in solid research.

I wrote this book within a religious order where I am a volunteer member and the presiding elder. As a religious order, by definition, members are monks. Monks, by definition dedicate themselves to service of the Divine in whatever form is the mission of the monastery. Our monastic mission is education, the reinforcement of school subjects, ecology and improvement of self-esteem, plus the care of any age person with disabilities. Our corporate mission is education and our spiritual mission is selfless service. That reoccurring message has defined by us to serve any who are the "children of The Virgin of Guadalupe."

My mentor has always made it clear to me that "All Paths Lead to the Center" so it matters not the faith of the off-spring (the children) of The Virgin of Guadalupe, but what does matter to my "Great Work" is that they are from Mexico heritage, those who generally who worship The Virgin of Guadalupe. Therefore, the mission of this monastery is care for anyone of Mexico heritage needing knowledge, because our mission is education.

I can walk into any church, synagogue, temple or mosque without hesitation because within my faith, the Divine dual aspect of both God and Goddess are represented there. I am so completely at home within my self regarding where my faith resides that I have no need to broadcast my beliefs in public or to put down any belief system or the lack of belief either. I simply serve in all the Divine names of God, every day. The practice of my faith is quite simple. I don't necessarily dash off on Sunday mornings to attend a religious service, sit by a fire praying all night on sacred days or meditate for endless hours, weeks or days, but I might do **any** of those things. *What I do accomplish is to serve rural Mexican people every day to the best of my abilities; that is the main practice of my faith.*

This book was inspired by the forces of my faith that have ignited my passion to serve Mexicans with rural heritages for as many years as my own memory serves me. At this time, when those Mexican mothers who helped me survive my own childhood now need my services, I am certain that a Divine feminine force outside myself is both driving and guiding me.

Endnotes

Chapter 1

1. Fehrenbach, 1995, chart 238–239
2. Vygotsky. Cognitive Development—Vygotsky's Sociocultural Theory
3. Bright, William, Ethnologue, 2009; Immigration Information Source
4. Pew Hispanic Center, 2009
5. NCES, 2001
6. Kagitcibasi, 1982, 1990, 1996, p. 1
7. Mackenzie, 2010
8. NCES, 2001
9. Mackenzie, 2010
10. Frazier, 1993, p. 364

Chapter 2

1. NCLB, 2002
2. PEW Hispanic Center
3. Payne, 2003
4. Tull, 2009
5. Vygotsky, n.d.
6. Noddings, 1984, 1992, 2003
7. Payne, 2003
8. Mackenzie, 2010
9. Noddings, 1984, 1992, 2003
10. NCLB, 2002
11. Mackenzie, personal interview, September 26, 2010
12. NCLB, 2002
13. American Textbook Council, 1989
14. Fried, 1995
15. Hargreaves, 1998, p. 835
16. Coffey, 1999
17. Kozulin, 1998 - Feuerstein's Mediated Learning Experience (MLE)

18. Kozulin & Presseisen, 1998
19. Rogoff, 2003
20. González, Moll, & Amanti, 2005, p. 327
21. González, et. al, 2005, p. 325
22. González, et. al, 2005, p. 326

Chapter 3

1. Mackenzie, 2010
2. Poblano, Borja, Elias, Garcia-Pedroza, & Arias, 2002; Poblano, Marquez, & Hernandez, 2006
3. Mackenzie, 2010, personal journal, January 5, 2009
4. Mackenzie, 2010, reference interview, Chapter 10
5. Mackenzie, 2010
6. Mackenzie, 2009
7. Mackenzie, 2010, personal journal, May 18, 2009
8. Mackenzie, 2008, personal interview
9. Baez, 2002; Cattey, 1980; Kelly, Sacker, Schoon, & Nazroo, 2006; Ogbu, 1992b; Rogoff, 2003
10. Fletcher, 1999; Forlin, Cedillo, Romero-Contreras, Fletcher, & Rodriguez, 2009
11. Headland, Pike & Harris, 1990
12. Moll, Amanti, Neff, & Gonzalez, 1992
13. Rogoff, 2003
14. Forlin et al., 2009
15. Harvard University, 2002
16. Forlin et al., 2009; Fry, 2009; Lopez, 2009; NCES, 2001; Ogbu, 1990, 1992a, 1992b; Portes, 1999; Rogoff, 2003; Tapia, 1998
17. NCES, 2001; Ogbu, 1990, 1992a; Ream, 2005; Tapia, 1998
18. Flores, Navarro, & DeWitz, 2008; Lopez, 2009; Urba & Maehr, 1995
19. Schmal, n.d., p. 2
20. Forlin et al., 2009
21. Freire, 1970/1993
22. Maccarelli, 2006
23. Kottak, 2008; Ruiz, 1992
24. Kelly, Watt, & Nazroo, 2006b
25. Mather & Goldstein, 2001; Poblano, et. al, 2002
26. Kelly, Sacker, Schoon, & Nazroo 2006; WHO, 1996
27. Kelly, Panico, Bartley, Marmot, Nazroo, & Sacker, 2009; Poblano, et al., 2002
28. Cattey, 1980; Garger & Guild, 1984; Kozulin, 1998; Ogbu, 1992b; Rogoff, 2003
29. Flores, et. al, 2008; Forlin et al., 2009; Ogbu, 1992a
30. Baez, 2002; Biesanz, Madigan Ruiz, Sanders, & Sommers, 1994; Crosnoe, 2005; Freire, 1970/1993; Rogoff, 2003
31. McHatton, 2007; McMunn, Kelly, & Bartley, 2008; Middlemiss & Mc-Guigan, 2005; Spence, Najman, Bor, O'Callaghan, & Williams, 2002
32. Arenas, 2008; Fry, 2009
33. Arenas, 2008; Giangreco, Edelman, Luiselli, & Macfarland, 1997; Moll, 1992b; Monzó & Rueda, 2001; Walker, Greenwood, Hart, & Carta, 1994
34. Jimenez, 2000, 2003; Ogbu, 1990; Romero-Contreras, 2006; Saracho, 2007
35. González, 2001; González, et. al, 2005; Greenwald & Banji, 1995
36. Worby & Organista, 2007
37. Dorner, Orellana, & Li-Grinning, 2007
38. Worby & Organista, 2007
39. McHatton, 2007
40. Forlin et al., 2009, p. 4
41. Freire, 1970/1993
42. Frumkin, 2001
43. Saracho & Martinez-Hancock, 2004
44. Kagitcibasi, 2002
45. Delgado-Gaitan, 1993; Valdés, 1996

Chapter 4

1. Meyer & Beezley, 2000
2. Meyer & Beezley, 2000
3. Mackenzie, 2007
4. Mackenzie, 2010
5. Mackenzie, personal journal, August 24, 2009
6. Knight, 1994; Turner, 2007; Villenas, 2001; Zentella, 1997
7. Norton & Bentley, 2006
8. Mackenzie, 2010
9. Nazario, 2007; Urrea & Lueders-Booth, 1996
10. Mackenzie, 2010
11. Nazario, 2007
12. Morse, 2006
13. Lichter & Jensen, 2002

Chapter 5

1. Behar, 2003
2. Mary, 1990; Cardona, Nicholson, & Fox, 2000; Middlemiss & McGuigan, 2005
3. Horne, 1985; Todd, 2002
4. Dorner, et. al, 2007; Valdes, 1996
5. Casper, 1996; Middlemiss & McGuigan, 2005; Taylor, Serrano, Anderson, & Kendall, 2000
6. Lara-Alecio, Irby, & Ebener, 1997; Saracho, 2007
7. The Economist, September 24, 2010 (correction to earlier OECD report)
8. Koplan, Liverman, Kraak, & Wisham, (Eds.) 2007; Puhl, & Latner, 2007
9. Golden, Meckel, & Prescott, 2004
10. Lawson, 2004; Louv, 2005, pp. 34, 98-111; Taylor, Kuo, & Sullivan, 2001 - ADHD symptom free in nature
11. Louv, 2005, pg. 101
12. Doidge, 2007, pg. 287–311, Appendix 1 "The Culturally Modified Brain"
13. Louv, 2005, p. 56
14. Louv, 2005, p. 66, Nancy Dress, an American Psychological Association scientist
15. Sizer & Sizer, 1999
16. Maller, Townsend, Pryor, Brown, & St. Leger, 2006
17. Valentine & McKendrick, 1997
18. Pergams & Zaradic, 2006
19. Frumkin, 2001; Louv, 2005; Maller, et. al, 2006; Ulrich, Simmons, & Miles, 2003; Valentine & McKendrick, 1997
20. Louv, 2005, p. 65
21. Carnegie Mellon University, 1998
22. Gardner, 2000; Louv, 2005, pp. 70-84
23. McCafferty, 2007
24. Cleaver, 2007
25. Bardeen, 2007
26. Forest Stewardship Council, 2007, www.fscus.org
27. Subedi, 2006
28. Rogoff, 2003, pg. 106
29. Kagitcibasi, 2002; Ogbu, 1992b; Rogoff, 2003
30. Ogbu, 1992b; Rogoff, 2003
31. Mackenzie, 2007

Chapter 6

1. Mackenzie, 2010
2. Mackenzie, 2009
3. Wiltz, 2010
4. Mackenzie, 2007
5. Mackenzie, 2007
6. Mackenzie, 2007, 2009, 2010
7. Casper, 1996; Saracho, 2007; Taylor, et. al., 2000
8. Mackenzie, 2007
9. Bonetati, 1994

10. Valenzuela, 1999, pp. 144-147
11. Ogbu, 1992b; Rogoff, 2003
12. Greenwald & Banaji, 1995
13. Banji & Greenwald, 1994; Greenwald & Banji, 1995
14. Ewert, Place & Sibthorp, 2005
15. Chawla, 2006; Ewert, et. al, 2005
16. Kellert, 1993; Lovu, 2005; Orr, 1992; Van Matre, 1990
17. Mackenzie, 2009
18. Post, 2001
19. Post, 2001; Rogoff, 2003
20. Mackenzie, personal journal, December 12, 2008
21. Mackenzie, personal journal, December 13, 2008
22. Mackenzie, field notes, August 1, 2010
23. Wiltz, 2010

Chapter 7

1. Gallagher, Gill, & Reifsnider, 2008
2. Kottack, 2008; Ogbu, 1992b; Rogoff, 2003
3. Fletcher, 2005; Fletcher & Artiles, 2005; Fletcher, Kingler, Lopez-Mariscal, & Dejud, 2003; Fletcher & Ramos, 1999
4. Middlemiss & McGuigan, 2005
5. Mackenzie, 2009
6. Behar, 2003; Wissman, 2006
7. Mackenzie, 2007
8. Behar, 2003; Wissman, 2006
9. Behar, 2003; Medina, 2004
10. Turner, 2007
11. Teachman & Paasch, 1994; Whitner, Weber, & Duncan, 2002
12. Turner, 2007
13. Behar, 2003
14. Behar, 2003
15. Behar, 2003
16. Mary, 1990
17. Casper, 1996; Taylor, et. al., 2000
18. Middlemiss & McGuigan, 2005
19. Behar, 2003
20. Payne, 1997
21. Chu, 2004; San Diego Union-Tribune, 2008
22. Ordonez, 2008
23. Todd, 2002

Chapter 8

1. Rogoff, 2003, p. 103
2. Rogoff, 2003
3. Bell & Fox, 1998
4. Mary, 2003; Nazario, 2006; Valdes, 2001
5. Goleman, 1995
6. Forgas, 2000
7. Gardner, 2000
8. Louv, 2006; Walker, Greenwood, Hart, & Carta, 1994; Wells, 2000
9. AIR, 2005; Foster-Riley & Hendee, 1999; Kahn & Kellert, 2002
10. Outward Bound (http://www.outwardbound.org)
11. Tough Love (http://www.child.net/toughlove.htm)
12. Eckerd Youth Alternatives (http://www.eckerd.org)
13. Hoover, 2008
14. Dasha & Ziviani, 2007; Karsten, 2005; Tandy, 1999
15. Louv, 2005, p. 19
16. Louv, 2005, p. 3
17. Louv, 2005, pp. 39-53
18. Louv, 2005, p. 3

19. This long list is included to show the stark contrast with very limited resources just five years ago: Borrie & Roggenbuck, 2001; Broda, 2007; Chawla, 2006; Cornell, 1998; Dasha & Ziviani, 2007; Ewert, et. al, 2005; Foster-Riley, 1999; Frumkin, 2001; Gulwadi, 2006; Hartig, 1991; Kahn & Kellert, 2002; Larson, 2007; Lohr & Pearson-Mims, 2006; Mackenzie, 2008; Maller, Townsend, et.al, 2006; Moore & Wong, 1997; Nash, 2001; Orr, 2004; Sheard & Golby, 2006; Tai, Haque, McLellan, & Knight, 2006; Taylor, Kuo & Sullivan, 2001; Ulrich, Simons, & Miles, 2003; Ward, Ghahremani, & Louv, 2008; Wells, 2000

20. Artiles & Trent, 1994; Todd, 2005; Mackenzie, 2008

21. Poblano, Borja, Elias, Garcia-Pedroza, & Arias, 2002

22. Mackenzie, 2010

23. Rogoff, 2003, p. 132

24. Mackenzie, personal journal, December 4, 2009

25. Nader, Speech at Harvard Law School, Feb. 26, 1972

26. Post, 2001

27. Los Libres (http://clas.aas.duke.edu/program//VeronicaCrizbio.pdf)

28. Los Libres (http://clas.aas.duke.edu/program//VeronicaCrizbio.pdf)

29. Associated Press, 2010

30. González, et. al, 2005; Velez-Ibanez & Greenberg, 1992

31. Coffey, 1999

32. González, et. al, 2005

33. González, et. al, 2005, p. 327

34. González, et. al, 2005, p. 325

35. González, et. al, 2005, p. 326

36. Behar, 2003, p. 27

Chapter 9

1. Mackenzie, 2007, 2009, 2010
2. Meyer & Beezley, 2000
3. Mackenzie, 2009
4. Todd, 2002

Chapter 10

1. Strauss & Corbin, 1998, p. 62
2. Mackenzie, 2007, 2009, 2010
3. Mackenzie, 2009
4. Stauss & Corbin, 1998, p. 6
5. Meyer & Beezley, 2000
6. Payne, 1997, 3, 42-43
7. Meyer & Beezley, 2000
8. Mackenzie, 2009
9. Mackenzie, 2009
10. Mackenzie, 2009
11. Poblano, et al., 2002, Payne, 1997

Chapter 11

1. NLCC Educational Media, 1996
2. Nazario, 2006; Valdes, 2001
3. Lara-Alecio, et. al.,1997
4. Nazario, 2006
5. Romero-Contreras, 2006
6. Jimenez, 2000; Ogbu, 1992a; Portes, 1999; Rogff, 2003; Romero-Contreras, S., 2006; Tapia, 1998
7. Arenas, 2008
8. UNICEF, 2010
9. NationMaster, 2010
10. UNICEF, 2010
11. NationMaster, 2010
12. Mackenzie, personal interview August 13, 2010
13. Sanchez, 2007

14. Villenas, 2001
15. Middlemiss & McGuigan, 2005
16. Maxwell, 1996, p. 66
17. Mackenzie, personal journal, January 9, 2010
18. Rogoff, 2003
19. Maxwell, 1996; Rogoff, 2003
20. Vasquez, Pease-Alvarez & Shannon, 1994
21. Vasquez, et. al, 1994
22. Crosnoe, 2005; Saracho & Martinez-Hancock, 2004
23. Delgado-Gaitan, 1993; Mackenzie, 2008, field notes; Valdés, 1996
24. Mackenzie, 2007, 2009, 2010
25. Moll, 1992
26. Vasquez, et. al, 1994
27. Mackenzie, personal journal, August 15, 2008
28. Mackenzie, 2007, 2009, 2010
29. Ogbu, 1992b; Rogoff, 2003
30. Saracho & Martinez-Hancock, 2004
31. Kozulin, 1998
32. Valencia, 2002
33. Delgado-Gaitan, 1993; Monzo & Rueda, 2001
34. Santamaria, 2009
35. Mackenzie, 2008 field notes
36. Mackenzie, personal journal, December 5, 2009
37. Mackenzie, personal journal, June 13, 2009
38. Santamaria, 2009, p. 114
39. Poblano, et al., 2002
40. Post, 2001

Chapter 12

1. Payne, 1997
2. Payne, 1997
3. Bomer, Dworin, May & Semingson 2008
4. Bomer, et. al, 2008
5. Bomer, Dworin, May & Semingson, 2009; Bomer, Dworin, May & Semingson, 2008; Gorski, 2006a, 2006b; Ng & Rury, 2006a, 2006b; Prins & Schafft, 2009; Valencia, 2009
6. NCLB, 2002
7. Baker & Welner, 2011
8. Mackenzie, personal journal, June 2007
9. Mackenzie, personal journal, March 18, 2009
10. González, et. al, 2005
11. Payne, 1997

Chapter 13

1. Shin & Bruno, 2003, p. 5
2. Morales & Hanson, 2005
3. Vasquez, Pease-Alverez, Shannon, 1994
4. Gonzalez, 2001
5. Todd, 2005
6. Love & Buriel, 2007; Weisskirch, 2006
7. Love & Buriel, 2007
8. Buriel, Perez, DeMent, Chavez & Moran, 1998
9. Dorner, et. al, 2007
10. Love & Buriel, 2007
11. Love & Buriel, 2007; Buriel, et. al, 1998, Dorner, et. al, 2007; Weisskirch, 2006
12. Acoach & Webb, 2004
13. Amrein & Pena, 2000
14. Buriel, et. al, 1998
15. Dorner, et. al, 2007
16. Love & Buriel, 2007
17. Morales & Hanson, 2005

18. Weisskirch & Alva, 2002
19. Weisskirch, 2006
20. Bernhart, 2008; Kalman, 2000
21. Weisskirch, 2006
22. Dorner, et. al, 2007; Weisskirch, 2006
23. Love & Buriel, 2007
24. Dorner, et. al, 2007
25. Amrein & Pena, 2000
26. Dorner, et. al, 2007; Love 2007; Weisskirch & Alva, 2002;Weisskirch, 2006
27. Love & Buriel, 2007
28. Acoach & Webb, 2004; Dorner, et. al, 2007; Love & Buriel, 2007
29. Love & Buriel, 2007
30. Buriel, et. al, 1998; Dorner, et. al, 2007; Weisskirch, 2006
31. Love & Buriel, 2007
32. Weisskirch & Alva, 2002
33. Love & Buriel, 2007
34. Love & Buriel, 2007; Weisskirch, 2007
35. Love & Buriel, 2007
36. Love & Buriel, 2007
37. Acoach & Webb, 2004; Love & Buriel, 2007; Orellana, 2003
38. Valencia & Black, 2002
39. Weisskirch, 2006
40. Dorner, et. al, 2007; Weisskirch & Alva, 2002; Weisskirch, 2006
41. Weisskirch, 2006
42. Love & Buriel, 2008
43. Weisskirch, 2006
44. Love & Buriel, 2007
45. Morales & Hanson, 2005

Chapter 14

1. Lareau, 1987
2. Harker, 1990, p. 13
3. Roszkowski, 2003
4. Louv, 2005
5. Pergams & Zaradic, 2006; Tandy, 1999
6. Pergams & Zaradic, 2006
7. Orr, 1992
8. Louv, 2006
9. Holleran, 2003
10. Saracho & Martinez-Hancock, 2004
11. Crosnoe, 2005
12. Hale, 2008
13. Romero-Contreras, 2006
14. Jimenez, 2000; Ogbu, 1992a; Portes, 1999; Rogoff, 2003; Romero-Contreras, 2006; Tapia, 1998
15. Arenas, 2008
16. Mackenzie, 2010
17. Artiles & Trent, 1994; Fletcher, et. al., 1999
18. Cattey, 1980; Lopez, 2009; Ogbu, 1992a; Ream, 2005; Rogoff, 2003; Tapia, 1998
19. Rogoff, 2003, p. 133
20. Mackenzie, 2009; Rogoff, 2003; Mackenzie, personal journal, September 13, 2008
21. Rogoff, 2003, p. 139
22. Vygotsky, (n.d.)
23. Orr, 1992
24. Arenas, 2008
25. Vasquez, et. al, 1994
26. Jimenez, et. al, 1999, pp. 223-224
27. hooks, 1994, p. 41
28. Cattey, 1980
29. hooks, 1994, p. 41
30. Jimenez, et. al, 1999, p. 218

Chapter 15

1. Bob Keeshan, 1927-2004
2. Rogoff, 2003
3. Kaplan, 1995
4. Taylor, Kuo, & Sullivan, 2001
5. Kaplan, 1995
6. Taylor, Kuo & Sullivan, 2001, p.73
7. Borrie & Roggenbuck, 2001; Chawla, 2006; Dasha & Ziviani, 2007; Ewert, et. al, 2005; Foster-Riley, 1999; Frumkin, 2001; Gulwadi, 2006; Hartig, 1991; Kahn & Kellert, 2002; Larson, 2007; Lohr & Pearson-Mims, 2006; Mackenzie, 2008; Maller, et. al, 2006; Nash, 2001; Orr, 1992; Sheard & Golby, 2006; Taylor, et. al, 2001; Ulrich, et. al, 2003; Wells, 2000
8. Karsten, 2005; Louv, 2005, p. 115-122
9. Karsten, 2005
10. Karsten, 2005
11. Valentine & McKendrick, 1997
12. Pergams & Zaradic, 2006
13. Karsten, 2005
14. Louv, 2005, p. 123
15. Karsten, 2005
16. Orr, 1992, 2004; Louv, 2005
17. Karsten, 2005; Louv, 2005; Pergams & Zaradic, 2006; Tandy, 1999
18. Valentine & McKendrick, 1997
19. Clements, 2004; Hofferth & Sandberg, 2000; Karsten, 2005; Louv, 2005; Pergams & Zaradic, 2006; Tandy, 1999
20. Frumkin, 2001; Grant, 1998; Taylor, et. al, 2001; Wells, 2000
21. McCafferty, 2007
22. Cleaver, 2007
23. Delgado-Galitan, 1993; Mackenzie, 2008, field notes; Valdes, 1996
24. Gober, 2007; Louv, 2005
25. Puhl & Latner, 2007
26. Puhl & Latner, 2007
27. Gober, 2007
28. Puhl & Latner, 2007
29. Puhl & Latner, 2007
30. Puhl & Latner, 2007
31. Chawla, 2006
32. Louv, 2005
33. Vygotzky, (n.d.)
34. Kellert, 1993; Louv, 2005
35. Van Matre, 1990
36. Kellert & Wilson, 1993; Louv, 2005
37. Wells, 2000
38. Larson, 2007
39. Gardner, 2000
40. Pergams & Zaradic, 2006; Tandy, 1999
41. Pergams & Zaradic, 2006
42. Heft & Kytta, 2006
43. Chawla, 2006
44. Moll, et. al, 1992
45. Noddings, 2003
46. Artiles & Trent, 1992; Valencia, 2002
47. Sizer & Sizer, 1999
48. Louv, 2005, pp. 161-198
49. Louv, 2005, p. 59
50. Louv, 2005, p. 63
51. Casper, 1996; Saracho, 2007; Taylor, et. al., 2000
52. Middlemiss & McGuigan, 2005
53. Mackenzie, 2007
54. Karsten, 2005
55. Mackenzie, personal journal, November 2, 2008

56. Romero-Contreras, 2006
57. Chapman & Perreira, 2005; Hayes, 1992; Ogbu, 1990, 1992a
58. Romero-Contreras, 2006
59. Rogoff, 2003, p. 303
60. Kemper & Royce, 2002
61. Mackenzie, 2010
62. Childstats, 2009: National Survey of Infants, children and youth's Health, Poblano, et al., 2002
63. Mackenzie, 2010

Chapter 16

1. Bonetati, D., 1994

Index

About the Author

DR. JACQUELINE ZALESKI MACKENZIE is the first academic research-er to relocate permanently to a low-socioeconomic-status village in ru-ral Central Mexico. She is an expert in the education of Mexicans and management of nonprofit corporations. She was an Arizona-certified teacher with over 95% Mexican students and has taught in Mexico be-ginning May 2005. Her doctoral award from the University of Arizona included exceptional education, bilingual education and sociocultural studies, including four research projects in Mexico. Since 1986, she has continuously served as a nonprofit administrator, using skills acquired from her formal education in Business Systems Management and exper-tise acquired from over 40 years of business management work. She holds Master of Science and Bachelor of Science degrees from Florida Institute of Technology. Her faith, compassion, and passion for fairness also led her to earn a Bachelor of Arts in Divinity from Universal Brotherhood. Her spirit of adventure was nurtured in a military family, with father, uncle, and husband serving in the U.S. Air Force, and son serving in the U.S. Army. Her father served under General Curtis E. LeMay; he was once transferred 22 times in 22 months. Her playmates came from diverse cul-tures. Inspiration from family military history—which includes relatives serving in World War II, Korean War, and Vietnam—led her to become an FAA-certified flight instructor; she was the only pilot flying a round trip from Florida to Alaska and back to Florida. (In Alaska, she met fel-low trailblazer Astronaut Sally Ride and visited an Inuit village.) A femi-nist, she was the first female Teamster in Chicago (second in U.S.) and belonged to the initial group of women to pass the Illinois State Trooper's Exam. Her dedication to ecology began in high school; her residence for 12 years (1996–2008) was off the power grid on the Arizona/Sonora bor-der. Her imagination led her to study Art Education for six quarters at the

University of Illinois Circle Campus and for two years under the late artist/sculptor Robert Von Neumann. Her astrological birth chart shows that her sun, moon, and Mercury are placed within 2 degrees of each other in the sign of Aquarius: She is an idealist, a reformer, and a rebel with Virgo rising, which also makes her service-oriented. Her Myers-Briggs personality type is ENTJ, representative of an assertive, innovative, long-range thinker with an excellent ability to adapt theories and possibilities into concrete plans of action.

Dr. Mackenzie was awarded the Able Toastmaster Silver distinction. She is a charismatic and inspirational speaker. She won a Toastmasters Regional Award for her public speaking after completing 350 presentations in 24 months. As a professional student, she welcomes readers' feedback.

Contact her at: jzm@email.arizona.edu

or:

220 North Zapata Hwy, Suite 11
PMB 512-A
Laredo, TX 78043-4464

www.jacquelinemackenzie.com
www.spanishimmersioneducation.org

Book Order Form — Paperback Prices Only

Thank you for your interest in the book, *"Engaging the Soul of Spanish Speaking Students: Simple Questions—Complex Answers Relating to the Education of Mexicans."*

A section of the book is available for free and can be downloaded from our website at: http://www.jacquelinemackenzie.com.

Single or multiple copies can be ordered through our website for $29.95 per copy plus shipping. Print on Demand is available through Ingram Book Company. PayPal is the only method of payment accepted online.

BULK ORDERS 3–10 books are 33% off at $20.00 each, 11–100 books are 50% off at $15.00 each, 101–1,000 books are 65% off at $10.50 each, and 1,000 or more books are 70% off at $9.00 each. Bulk pricing is plus shipping.

If you are interested in placing an order through postal mail with a personal or business check please fill out the following form and send to Summerland, 220 North Zapata Hwy, Suite 11, PMB 512-A, Laredo, TX 78043-4464.

First Name: _____

Last Name: _____

Title: _____

Organization Name: _____

Mailing Address: _____

_____

City / State / Zip: _____

Telephone: _____

E-mail: _____

Number of Copies Requested: _____

Total with shipping: _____

Comments:

Printed in the United States of America using methods that are in line with our corporate goals of deep ecological commitments.

Our printer is in good standing with:

- Sustainable Forestry Initiative® (SFI®)
- Program for the Endorsement of Forest Certification™
- Forest Stweardship Council™ (FSC®) FSC® C084699

www.ingramcontent.com/pod-product-compliance
Lightning Source LLC
Chambersburg PA
CBHW061834260326
41914CB00005B/996